Debating Affirmative Action: Conceptual, Contextual, and Comparative Perspectives

Edited by

Aileen McHarg
and
Donald Nicolson

Blackwell
Publishing

© 2006 by Cardiff University Law School
except for editorial material and organization © 2006 Aileen McHarg and Donald
Nicolson

BLACKWELL PUBLISHING
9600 Garsington Road, Oxford OX4 2DQ, UK
350 Main Street, Malden, MA 02148-5018, USA
550 Swanston Street, Carlton, Victoria 3053, Australia

The right of Aileen McHarg and Donald Nicolson to be identified as the Authors
of the Editorial Material in this Work has been asserted in accordance with the
UK Copyright, Designs and Patents Act 1988.

First published 2006 by Blackwell Publishing Ltd as a special issue of *Journal of
Law and Society*

Library of Congress Cataloging-in-Publication Data
A catalogue record for this title has been applied for.

A catalogue record for this title is available from the British Library.

ISBN: 140514839X
ISBN13: 9781405148399

Set in the United Kingdom
by Godiva Publishing Services Limited
Printed in Singapore by Fabulous Printers Pte Ltd

The publisher's policy is to use permanent paper from mills that operate a
sustainable forestry policy, and which has been manufactured from pulp processed
using acid-free and elementary chlorine-free practices. Furthermore, the publisher
ensures that the text paper and cover board used have met acceptable
environmental accreditation standards.

For further information on
Blackwell Publishing visit our website:
www.blackwellpublishing.com

Contents

JOURNAL OF LAW AND SOCIETY
VOLUME 33, NUMBER 1, MARCH 2006
ISSN: 0263-323X, pp. 1–23

Justifying Affirmative Action: Perception and Reality

AILEEN MCHARG* AND DONALD NICOLSON**

This article surveys developments in United Kingdom law and policy which require, permit or are more accommodating towards, the use of affirmative action. It then considers the various justifications that can be used in support of affirmative action and their philosophical and political strengths and weaknesses. Finally, it advocates a strategic approach to the justification and use of affirmative action, taking account of relevant political, contextual, pragmatic, and practical considerations.

INTRODUCTION

Anti-discrimination laws and policies in the United Kingdom have clearly yet to realize fully their promise to end historic patterns of discrimination, exclusion and disadvantage. However, potentially significant changes appear to be under way. Having for years adopted a rigidly formal or symmetrical approach to the pursuit of equality, with only very limited exceptions, law and practice are now more accommodating towards the use of positive measures to improve the position of disadvantaged groups. Although change is still limited and piecemeal, the United Kingdom appears to be converging with many other jurisdictions, notably in North America and the European Union, where the limitations of a formal approach to equality have been officially recognized for some time. Special measures have therefore been permitted in order to increase the participation of previously excluded groups in important social activities, such as education, employment, the award of business contracts, politics, and public appointments.

Such measures go by various names depending on the context and their perceived acceptability. In this volume, the American term 'affirmative

* School of Law, University of Glasgow, Stair Building, 8 The Square, Glasgow G12 8QQ, Scotland
** Law School, University of Strathclyde, Stenhouse Building, Glasgow G4 0RJ, Scotland
a.mcharg@law.gla.ac.uk   donald.nicolson@strath.ac.uk

1

action' is generally used because, as we shall argue, it avoids some of the (intended or unintended) pejorative connotations associated with alternatives like 'positive discrimination', 'reverse discrimination', and 'preferential treatment', whereas the less pejorative term 'positive action', which is favoured in the EU context, is sometimes confined to what are otherwise called 'soft' or 'weak' forms of affirmative action. The latter usually involve either outreach programmes, designed to encourage members of under-represented groups to apply for positions, or training programmes, intended to enable them to compete on equal terms with more privileged candidates – though they might also be said to include accommodation strategies, which take account of physical or cultural characteristics which might otherwise reduce particular groups' ability to take advantage of opportunities. At the other extreme, 'hard' or 'strong' affirmative measures assist members of previously excluded or under-represented groups at the point of allocation either through 'decision-making preferences' in their favour or quotas which reserve a certain percentage of positions or business contracts for them. Situated somewhere on the continuum between weak and strong affirmative action is the setting of goals and timetables for increasing the representation of those from under-represented groups.[1]

The contributors to this volume examine a variety of contexts in which such measures are being or, in their view, should be introduced. Thus, Noreen Burrows and Muriel Robison discuss the legal possibilities for extending affirmative action to improve women's position in the labour market; Lois Bibbings, and Andrew Francis and Iain McDonald explore the case for special measures in university admissions and in the treatment of part-time law students; Donald Nicolson calls for hard forms of affirmative action in the legal profession; Kate Malleson challenges the idea that the merit principle stands in the way of increasing judicial diversity; Aileen McHarg defends the use of affirmative action in the selection of election candidates; and Robert Dunbar argues that measures to support minority languages are justified and should be extended. Compared to the experience in other jurisdictions, these and other developments are rather belated. However, as the contributions of Nicole Busby, Anke Stock, and Martin Sweet on various aspects of affirmative action practice in, respectively, Canada, Germany, and the United States of America show, this provides an opportunity for United Kingdom legislators and policymakers to learn from experience elsewhere.

This introductory essay surveys the nature of, and reasons for, change in United Kingdom law and policy as a whole. Conscious that affirmative action, particularly in its stronger forms, remains highly controversial here as elsewhere,[2] we then go on to consider the different ways in which it can be

---

1 They are soft in the sense of not requiring mandatory preferences, but can effectively act as quotas if backed by sufficient pressure; see, for example, n. 31 below.
2 See, for example, A. McColgan, *Discrimination Law: Text, Cases and Materials* (2005, 2nd edn.) 143.

2

justified. We do not seek to argue that one form of justification is superior to others in an absolute sense. As John Gardner points out, there are complex motivations for the social practice of affirmative action which defy categorization in terms of a single legitimating principle.[3] However, the intimate connection between the way in which affirmative action is justified and conceptualized, and even the terminology used to describe it, means that different justificatory strategies may have profound implications for what measures, if any, can be 'sold' politically and legally in different contexts. Thus, while it is important to challenge criticisms of affirmative action by pointing to the gap between perception and reality, at the same time, it must be acknowledged that these misconceptions have a real hold and rhetorical power. We therefore seek to advocate a strategic approach to affirmative action: one that is alive to the benefits of positive measures in advancing real equality, but which is sensitive to the political risks involved.

THE RISE OF AFFIRMATIVE ACTION IN THE UNITED KINGDOM

The main impetus behind the growing acceptability of affirmative action in the United Kingdom appears to be dissatisfaction with the equal treatment model embodied in current anti-discrimination law as a means of securing significant improvement in the position of disadvantaged groups. One set of problems relates to the comparative nature of this approach, and hence its requirement that members of disadvantaged groups be compar*able* to those in a more favourable position. Discrimination is defined as the failure to treat equally people who are similarly situated; where people are *not* similarly situated, the law cannot bite.

As Busby argues, one situation in which lack of comparability becomes problematic is where there is significant occupational segregation along gender, racial or other lines. Recognition of this limitation seems to explain the exceptions in the Sex Discrimination Act 1975 (SDA)[4] and the Race Relations Act 1976 (RRA)[5] allowing employers to encourage women/black people to apply for jobs hitherto dominated by men/white people, and to provide targeted training. In theory, these measures should bring excluded groups up to a comparable position, enabling them to compete on equal terms, or exposing discrimination if they continue to be excluded. However, as Burrows and Robison demonstrate in relation to the SDA, the provisions are very narrowly drawn and little used in practice.

Much more radical in their scope are the equivalent Northern Irish provisions – initially contained in the Fair Employment (Northern Ireland)

---

3 J. Gardner, 'Liberals and Unlawful Discrimination' (1989) 9 *Oxford J. of Legal Studies* 1, at 15–16.
4 ss. 47 and 48.
5 ss. 35, 37, and 38.

Act 1989, now the Fair Employment and Treatment Order 1998. Here, there is substantial occupational segregation along religious lines, reinforced by high levels of sectarian harassment and a 'chill' factor deterring potential applicants from applying to establishments known to be dominated by a different community.[6] This is thought to be a significant factor behind the higher levels of unemployment amongst Catholics compared with Protestants. Accordingly, not only does the legislation explicitly employ the terminology of affirmative action to ensure 'fair participation' in employment by both groups, but it goes further than the British provisions in a number of respects. Thus, in addition to encouragement and training, employers may adopt indirectly discriminatory redundancy selection procedures in order to protect the gains of affirmative action programmes, and may also restrict recruitment to the unemployed, which again is likely to have an indirectly discriminatory effect in favour of the Catholic community. Moreover, unlike the British legislation, the provisions are underpinned by mandatory monitoring of workplace composition, and, if a lack of 'fair participation' is revealed, the Equality Commission can require employers to undertake affirmative action, including setting goals and timetables.

In general, the Northern Irish legislation does not permit direct discrimination at the point of recruitment. However, in the only current example of a mandatory quota in United Kingdom law,[7] the Police (Northern Ireland) Act 2000, section 46, requires equal numbers of Catholics and others to be appointed to the Police Service of Northern Ireland from a pool of qualified applicants. Since more non-Catholics than Catholics may not be appointed even if it means that recruitment needs are not met,[8] this creates a powerful incentive to engage in serious outreach work and to address the institutional and cultural factors that deter Catholics from applying to join the police.

A slightly different comparability problem is addressed by the Disability Discrimination Act 1995 (DDA). Since disabled people, by definition, have different capacities to the able-bodied, insistence upon strict comparability would mean that less favourable treatment of the former would often be unchallengeable. Hence the 1995 Act departs from the model of earlier anti-discrimination legislation in two significant respects. First, it is *not* symmetrical in its operation; it outlaws discrimination on grounds of *dis*ability, not differential treatment of disabled and non-disabled persons. Secondly, subject to a justification defence, it requires employers, and providers of goods, services, and facilities to make 'reasonable adjustments' to accommodate the special needs of disabled persons. Thus affirmative

---

6 S. Fredman, *Discrimination Law* (2002) 145.
7 The Disabled Persons (Employment) Act 1944 imposed a 3 per cent quota for the employment of registered disabled persons. However, having been widely ignored in practice, it was repealed by the Disability Discrimination Act 1995.
8 Though the quota can be varied by ministerial order if it would result in a serious recruitment shortfall.

4

action in favour of disabled persons is not only permitted, but may actually be required.

A second set of problems with the equal treatment model relate to its individualistic focus: the need to find an individual victim of discrimination, and to ascribe fault to a specific perpetrator.[9] This is a particular weakness when it comes to addressing the deep institutional and structural causes of inequality. The concept of indirect discrimination, which attacks facially neutral, but substantively unequal, rules and practices, goes some way to addressing this problem. However, it still requires an individual challenger, who must establish at least a prima facie case of discrimination, which is attributable to a single source,[10] and it gives rise only to a remedy of individual compensation, rather than a requirement to adjust the offending rules or practices.

Affirmative action policies, by contrast, switch the focus from the individual victim to the disadvantaged group, and place the initiative on those in the best position to address institutional and structural barriers to equality, regardless of fault or individual responsibility.[11] Thus, for example, section 49 of the SDA, which allows trade unions, and employers' or professional associations to reserve seats for women on their elected executives, and the Sex Discrimination (Election Candidates) Act 2002 (SDECA), which exempts candidate selection from the scope of the SDA, allow strong affirmative action in circumstances where barriers to female participation seem particularly deeply entrenched.[12]

Of potentially broader significance, however, are the positive obligations recently imposed on certain public bodies under various enactments to advance equality of opportunity. Once again, the furthest reaching is the duty placed on Northern Irish public authorities by the Northern Ireland Act 1998 to promote equality of opportunity between men and women, people with and without a disability, people of different religious belief, political opinion, racial group, age, marital status or sexual orientation, and between people with and without dependants. The bodies in question must draw up equality schemes, in consultation with those affected, subject to the approval of, and enforceable by, the Equality Commission.[13] Following the Macpherson Report's finding of 'institutional racism' in the Metropolitan police,[14] the Race Relations (Amendment) Act 2000 imposed a similar duty on listed

---

9 Compare S. Fredman, 'Equality: a New Generation?' (2001) *Industrial Law J.* 145, at 163.

10 See, for example, *Lawrence* v. *Regent Office Care Ltd*, Case C320/00, [2002] ECR I-7325.

11 Freedman, op. cit., n. 9, p. 164.

12 See McHarg, in this volume, pp. 149–51.

13 s. 75 and sch. 9. The Welsh Assembly and the Greater London Authority are under similar duties, though not subject to external scrutiny – Government of Wales Act 1998, s. 120; Greater London Authority Act 1999, s. 33.

14 *The Stephen Lawrence Inquiry* (1999; Cm. 4262; Chair, Sir W. Macpherson).

5

public authorities in carrying out their functions to 'have due regard to the need to eliminate unlawful discrimination and to promote equality of opportunity and good race relations between persons of different racial groups', also requiring them to draw up equality schemes, enforceable by the Commission for Racial Equality.[15] The Disability Discrimination Act 2005 imposes an equivalent duty in respect of disabled people,[16] and the Equality Bill, before Parliament at the time of writing, will do the same in respect of gender. The significance of these duties is that they require public authorities to eliminate the causes of discrimination, irrespective of individual complaints, and may also require them to engage in affirmative action, where such action would be lawful.

This trend towards relaxation of the equal treatment principle has been reinforced by EC and international human rights law. As regards the former, recent directives have changed the definition of indirect discrimination[17] in a way which allows greater scope for justifying differentially impacting policies where these have been adopted to benefit disadvantaged groups.[18] More importantly, in order to accommodate affirmative action practised in other European countries (see, for example, Stock in relation to Germany), EC law also now permits member states to introduce (proportionate) positive measures should they choose to do so.[19] So far, the United Kingdom has not acted upon this invitation; the religion and belief, and sexual orientation regulations,[20] enacted in partial implementation of the Framework Directive,[21] go only slightly further than the SDA and RRA in authorizing affirmative action.[22] However, as Burrows and Robison demonstrate, this

15 ss. 71–71E RRA.
16 s. 21B DDA 1995.
17 Employment Equality (Religion or Belief) Regulations 2003, S.I. 1660, Employment Equality (Sexual Orientation) Regulations 2003, S.I. 1661, implementing Directive 2000/78/EC, OJ L 303/16, 2 December 2000; s. 1(1A) RRA, implementing Directive 2000/43/EC, OJ L 180/22, 19 July 2000; Employment Equality (Sex Discrimination) Regulations 2005, S.I. 2467, implementing Directive 2002/73/EC, OJ L269/15, 5 December 2002.
18 Previously, these could only be justified if they related to the employer's specific needs, not by reference to wider social issues – *Greater Manchester Police Authority* v. *Lea* [1990] IRLR 372. Now, they must simply be a proportionate means of achieving a legitimate aim.
19 See Directive 2002/73/EC, and Art. 141 EC regarding gender; Directive 2000/43/EC, regarding race; and Directive 2000/78/EC, regarding religious belief, sexual orientation, discrimination and age, all at n. 17 above.
20 id.
21 Directive 2000/78/EC, id.
22 See Burrows and Robison, in this volume, pp. 39–40. But the regulations implementing the age discrimination provisions of Directive 2000/78/EC, id, will allow direct discrimination to be justified. This may include, for example, fixing a minimum age to qualify for certain employment-related advantages in order to recruit or retain older people – DTI, *Equality and Diversity: Coming of Age: Consultation on the Draft Employment Equality (Age) Regulations 2006* (2005) para. 4.1.7.

6

creates an opportunity which can be exploited by those seeking further reform to bring the United Kingdom into line with other member states.

The European Convention on Human Rights, similarly, permits some affirmative action to secure substantive rather than merely formal equality. This is important in undercutting potential objections that affirmative measures violate the rights of dominant group members. For example, the Northern Irish High Court rejected a challenge to the police recruitment quota based on violation of article 14 of the Convention (non-discrimination), read with article 9 (freedom of religion), holding that the measure pursued a legitimate aim and was not disproportionate in its effect.[23] Moreover, as Bibbings and Dunbar argue, the Convention and other international instruments may require positive measures in certain circumstances, and the former also extends the grounds of unlawful discrimination beyond those protected by domestic or EC law, most significantly to include socio-economic status.

Another general theme underpinning recent developments is concern about the lack of representativeness of many United Kingdom institutions. Having successfully used affirmative action whilst in Opposition to increase significantly the number of female Labour MPs elected in 1997, the Labour government has subsequently attempted to secure similar improvements in diversity not only in elected institutions, but also in areas such as higher education, judicial and other public appointments, and policing.[24] Although partly motivated by a desire to avoid discrimination, a diversity approach goes beyond simply ensuring equal treatment, in terms of assimilating excluded groups to the dominant culture.[25] Thus, the government seems to recognize the positive value of diversity to the legitimacy of public institutions, or at least the threat to their legitimacy posed by lack of diversity. Stress has also been placed on the 'business case' for diversity in relation to public bodies, drawing on research showing that heterogeneous groups are more effective and creative than homogeneous ones.[26] These arguments about legitimacy and effectiveness have been made particularly strongly in relation to policing, especially in Northern Ireland where the recruitment quota effectively acknowledges that normal policing is impossible in a situation in which a large minority of the population in a divided society views the police force as representing the majority.[27]

The business case for diversity is increasingly being made in the private sector as well, both in terms of improving productivity and quality of service,

---

23 *In the Matter of an Application by Mark Parsons for Judicial Review* [2002] NIQB 46. The Court of Appeal later also rejected the argument that the provision breached Art. 9 – [2003] NICA 20.

24 See, generally, McColgan, op. cit., n. 2, pp. 151–7; see, also, L. Barmes, 'Public Appointments and Representativeness' [2002] *Public Law* 606.

25 L. Barmes with S. Ashtiany, 'The Diversity Approach to Achieving Equality: Potential and Pitfalls' (2003) 32 *Industrial Law J.* 274, at 276–7.

26 Barmes, op. cit., n. 24, p. 611.

27 McColgan, op. cit., n. 2, p. 153.

7

and in securing contracts, particularly from the public sector.[28] This may partly reflect the influence of United States business culture, where affirmative action in pursuit of diversity has been absorbed into management practice, despite its questionable legality.[29] Contract compliance has also been used in Northern Ireland for some time as a means of securing fair participation in employment. Although prohibited in the rest of Britain by the Local Government Act 1988, this has been relaxed somewhat under the 'best value' regime,[30] and this is now an important way in which public authorities may seek to discharge their positive equality duties.

Nevertheless, for the most part, these initiatives involve only soft forms of affirmative action – at most setting goals and timetables. With the exception of election candidacies and police recruitment in Northern Ireland, the government has ruled out quotas or other strong measures, with business leaders similarly opposed.[31] These, therefore, largely remain unlawful. However, there have been calls for the adoption of harder measures by, for example, the Metropolitan police,[32] and, as Aileen McColgan points out, without more general legal change, there is a danger that even soft diversity policies could give aggrieved white males material from which to infer (unlawful) direct discrimination.[33] Anti-discrimination law and policy in the United Kingdom is therefore at a crossroads. Although, as McHarg argues in relation to election candidacies, SDECA and the Police (Northern Ireland) Act could be regarded as precedents paving the way for further reform, there is a risk that they simply remain limited and temporary[34] aberrations: another false dawn.[35] Which direction we take therefore depends upon how persuasively the case for (particularly hard forms of) affirmative action can be stated.

28 See D. Nicolson, 'Demography, Discrimination and Diversity: A New Dawn for the British Legal Profession' (2005) 12 *International J. of the Legal Profession* 201; Barmes with Ashtiany, op. cit., n. 25; and see Francis and McDonald, in this volume, p. 101.
29 C.L. Bacchi, *The Politics of Affirmative Action* (1996) 23.
30 Local Government Best Value (Exclusion of Non-commercial Considerations) Order 2001, S.I. 909.
31 However, in the civil service, diversity targets have recently been strengthened by linking them to performance bonuses, a practice also employed by some companies – 'Too Few Black and Asian Faces at the Top' *Guardian*, 17 November 2005.
32 McColgan, op. cit., n. 2, p. 155.
33 id., p. 171, referring to *Acas* v. *Taylor*, Appl No EAT/788/97, unreported, 11 February 1998. In limited circumstances, direct discrimination in order to ensure a diverse workforce may be justified as a 'genuine occupational qualification' – S. Fredman, 'Reversing Discrimination' (1997) 113 *Law Q. Rev.* 575, at 583; and see n. 22 above, regarding age discrimination.
34 The former expires in 2015; the latter must be renewed on a triennial basis. It currently runs until March 2007 – Police (Northern Ireland) Act (Renewal of Temporary Provisions) Order 2004, S.I. 114.
35 Compare C. McCrudden, 'Rethinking Positive Action' (1986) 15 *Industrial Law J.* 219, at 219.

8

A major obstacle facing proponents of affirmative action is the way in which it seems to be permanently hostage to the rhetoric and counter-arguments of its opponents. There seems to be a (deliberate or unconscious) popular association of affirmative action with 'reverse discrimination', 'positive discrimination' or 'preferential treatment', and a knee-jerk assumption that it creates 'innocent victims' and 'undeserving beneficiaries', and contravenes the merit principle, thereby lowering standards and stigmatizing its targets as inferior.[36] In reality, however, affirmative action can be conceptualized in a number of different ways depending upon the particular route taken to its justification, and different justificatory strategies may be able to avoid some or all of its alleged negative consequences.

1. *Reverse discrimination and compensatory justice*

Clearly, the most pejorative synonym for affirmative action is 'reverse discrimination'. Unlike 'positive discrimination', which can be interpreted neutrally as involving justified differentiation, the term suggests a tit-for-tat – 'you have discriminated against us so we will discriminate against you' – motive. But, even accepting this pejorative conceptualization, it does not necessarily follow that affirmative action is illegitimate. In fact, this is not too far removed from the earliest justification for affirmative action in the United States. Relying on compensatory (or corrective or restorative) justice, it was initially conceived as providing reparations to African-Americans for the suffering caused by slavery, segregation, and discrimination.

Viewed in this light, the idea of society repaying the harm it has caused or condoned has considerable emotional appeal and moral resonance.[37] It reflects the uncontroversial idea, embedded in private law and currently motivating campaigns for reparations and collective apologies for historical atrocities, that those who cause harm must compensate their victims.[38] Significantly, if victims of discrimination do have rights to reparation, it is irrelevant if this leads to contravention of the merit principle or any other alleged negative consequence. Admittedly, the United Kingdom has not witnessed

---

36 See, for example, 'Women: Putting Women in their Place' *Guardian*, 3 December 1991; 'Comment' *Independent*, 28 July 1995; 'Equality in Education RIP' *Daily Mail*, 7 October 2002; 'Admissions Bias Alarms Heads' *Times Educational Supplement*, 26 September 2003, 19.

37 Compare R. Delgado, 'The Imperial Scholar: Reflections on a Review of Civil Rights Literature' (1984) 132 *University of Pennsylvania Law Rev.* 561, at 570–1; M.J. Radin, 'Affirmative Action Rhetoric' (1991) 8 *Social Philosophy and Policy* 130, at 136; G. Ezorsky, *Racism and Justice: The Case for Affirmative Action* (1991).

38 The idea of society repaying its debts to particular groups also underlies uncontroversial preference schemes for war veterans: compare Stock, in this volume, p. 69.

9

discrimination on a scale approaching that suffered by African-Americans. However, group compensation could perhaps be regarded as justified by historical episodes such as the exclusion of women from the franchise, public office, and the professions, systematic discrimination against Northern Irish Catholics, and the suppression of indigenous minority languages.

Nevertheless, even if these analogies are regarded as sufficiently strong to justify some form of affirmative action,[39] the compensatory justice rationale is beset with problems. At a technical level, it is unclear what form compensatory measures should take and how long they should last. Strictly speaking, restorative justice requires, for instance, the total exclusion of male MPs and professionals for the same period that women were excluded from Parliament and the professions, but this is politically unrealistic to say the least. In the United States, it is often said that victims should receive the opportunities that would have materialized without discrimination, but this is impossible to calculate accurately[40] and allows for far less extensive compensation.

Even more problematic is the group-based nature of affirmative action reparations. In an individualistic society, there is widespread suspicion of group rights and remedies,[41] and many reject the idea that one part of society should compensate for discrimination or disadvantage in another.[42] However, the most familiar objection to the compensatory justice rationale, often backed up by concrete examples,[43] is that those who are required to 'pay', for instance, by losing out in the allocation of positions or contracts, are generally not responsible for the past discrimination, whereas the beneficiaries may themselves have escaped significant discrimination. This focus on the visible face of the 'innocent victims' of affirmative action ignores the faceless victims of past discrimination, as well as those who currently or will in future suffer its lingering effects if affirmative action is

---

39 But compare Bacchi, op. cit., n. 29, p. 43; M. Levin, 'The Free Market and Feminism' in *Ethics in Practice: An Anthology*, ed. H. LaFollette (2002, 2nd edn.), in relation to women.

40 See, for example, M. Levin, 'Reverse Discrimination, Shackled Runner, and Personal Identity' (1980) 37 *Philosophical Studies* 139; J. Edwards, *When Race Counts: The Morality of Racial Preference in Britain and America* (1995) 174–6, in relation to distributive justice schemes which use the same calculation.

41 As Justice Scalia put it in *Adarand* v. *Pena* 515 United States 200 (1995), at 241, there can be no such a thing as a debtor or creditor race. For a persuasive response, see W. Sadurski, 'The Morality of Preferential Treatment (The Competing Jurisprudential and Moral Arguments)' (1983–4) 14 *Melbourne University Law Rev.* 572, at 587–95.

42 T. Nagel, 'Equal Treatment and Compensatory Discrimination' (1973) 2 *Philosophy and Public Affairs* 348, at 358; *Hopwood* v. *Texas* 78 F 3d 932 (1996), where the state-funded University of Texas's affirmative action programme, designed to compensate for discrimination in Texan state schools, was invalidated.

43 See, for example, T. Eastland, *Ending Affirmative Action: The Case for Colorblind Justice* (1996).

rejected.[44] Moreover, the very language of compensation, with its legal connotations of fault and causation, encourages those threatened by affirmative action to feel righteous anger at being unjustifiably punished rather than moral guilt at being unjustly enriched.[45]

Perhaps if unjust enrichment rather than delict were seen as the appropriate analogy, the compensatory justice rationale would be more persuasive. Nevertheless, the strong perception that this involves 'undeserving beneficiaries' and 'innocent victims' paying for the 'sins of their forefathers' is still likely to lead either to outright rejection of affirmative action or its narrow confinement along delictual lines to specific remedies[46] for culpable acts of discrimination against identified victims.[47] Maybe for that reason, the compensatory justification has been raised only rarely in the United Kingdom[48] and specifically rejected in the EU context.[49]

2. Non-discrimination and distributive justice

A far more popular strategy for justifying affirmative action outside the United States has been to appeal to distributive rather than corrective justice. Accordingly, it is argued that in order to treat people equally it is sometimes necessary to treat them differently. Clearly, this involves a different conception of equality than the simple symmetrical model outlined above. For example, Burrows and Robison show how EC law has moved beyond equal

44 Compare H. Jones, 'Fairness, Meritocracy, and Reverse Discrimination' (1977) 4 *Social Theory and Practice* 211, at 212–13; T. Mullen, 'Affirmative Action' in *The Legal Relevance of Gender: Some Aspects of Sex-based Discrimination*, eds. S. McLean and N. Burrows (1988) 247-50. But see, also, P. Brest, 'The Supreme Court, 1976 Term – Foreword: In Defense of the Anti-Discrimination Principle' (1976) 90 *Harvard Law Rev.* 1, at 42, who argues that the compensatory justice case becomes less pressing and more vulnerable to the competing claims of other victims of social injustice the further that wrongs recede into the past; Edwards, op. cit., n. 40, pp. 191 ff., who distinguishes between enduring *wrongs*, which justify compensation, and lingering *harms*, which do not.
45 Compare C.R. Lawrence III, 'The Id, The Ego, and Equal Protection: Reckoning With Unconscious Racism' (1987) *Stanford Law Rev.* 317, at 325, fn. 31.
46 For example, in *Franks* v. *Bowman Transportation Co* 96 S Ct 1251 (1976), the defendant was ordered to give priority consideration in future vacancies and back-dated seniority benefits to those against whom it had discriminated.
47 For example, A. Goldman, *Justice And Reverse Discrimination* (1979). Indeed J.H. Verkerke, 'Compensating Victims of Preferential Employment Discrimination Remedies' (1989) 98 *Yale Law J.* 1479, goes further to suggest that affirmative action remedies should be replaced by monetary compensation.
48 But see R.B. Parekh, 'A Case for Positive Discrimination' in *Discrimination: The Limits of the Law*, eds. B. Hepple and E.M. Szyszczak (1992) who sees the healing of the wounds of discrimination victims through affirmative action as not simply a matter of backward-looking restitutive justice, but as necessary to create a better society.
49 See the Advocate-General's opinion in *Kalanke* v. *Freie Hansestadt Bremen* Case C-450/93, [1995] IRLR 660, 664.

11

treatment to embrace equality of opportunity and even to some extent equality of results. Nevertheless, the key point is that, on this approach, it is possible to conceptualize affirmative action as simply an extension of a non-discrimination strategy. Thus, for example, as Busby explains, Canadian policy-makers deliberately adopted the terminology of 'employment equity' in preference to affirmative action in the hope of avoiding the negative associations of that term in the United States. Similarly, Bibbings argues that 'widening participation' policies in higher education do not involve discrimination in favour of disadvantaged applicants, but rather an attempt to avoid discriminating against them. Hence, applications are 'contextual-ized' so as to ensure that indicators of academic potential other than examination results are not overlooked, whilst outreach activities are merely another aspect of normal recruitment activities.

The rhetorical and tactical appeal of this non-discrimination strategy is obvious: after all, no-one wants to be seen as being 'against equality'. More-over, it can be presented as a natural extension of current anti-discrimination law. Whereas the prohibition of direct discrimination follows the logic of corrective justice, indirect discrimination, Gardner argues, already embodies a principle of distributive justice.[50] It is also clear that the aims of anti-discrimination law cannot be reduced to equal treatment, since the latter is prohibited if it results in unjustifiable indirect discrimination.[51] Thus it may be argued that it is illogical to require decision-makers to alter their own practices where these produce disparate impacts, but not to permit them to take account of the underlying social differences which give rise to the disparate impact in the first place.[52]

This approach to justifying affirmative action has most obvious appli-cation in relation to groups whose needs are visibly different from those of the majority. For example, Stock shows how in Germany quotas guarantee-ing employment to disabled persons have been much less controversial than weaker decision-making preferences in favour of women. However, the argument is in principle applicable in a wide range of situations. Thus, Francis and McDonald invoke the accommodation strategy in the DDA to argue that requiring universities and the legal profession to take account of the special needs of part-time law students, so as to 'add value' to their degrees, does not amount to preferential treatment. Similarly, Dunbar argues that 'difference aware' equality in respect of linguistic minorities may

---

50 Gardner, op. cit., n. 3, pp. 4–5. But, for a cautionary view, A.J. Morris, 'On the Normative Foundations of Indirect Discrimination Law: Understanding the Competing Models of Discrimination Law as Aristotelian Forms of Justice' (1995) 15 *Oxford J. of Legal Studies* 199.

51 H. Collins, 'Discrimination, Equality and Social Inclusion' (2003) 66 *Modern Law Rev.* 16, at 16.

52 Compare McColgan, op. cit., n. 2, pp. 141–2. In fact, policies which aim to remove direct or indirect discrimination can be regarded as forms of affirmative action – see, for example, McCrudden, op. cit., n. 35, p. 223.

require special provision for education and access to public services in their mother tongues so that they can participate fully in society without sacrificing an important aspect of their identity. The question remains, though, how convincing such arguments are likely to be in practice.

One problem is that there is always a risk of differential treatment being portrayed as preferential treatment. For example, if a 'contextualized' university admissions policy means that some applicants are admitted with lower grades than others, or affirmative action for aspiring female politicians means that some seats are reserved for all-woman shortlists, then some disappointed candidates will inevitably feel aggrieved irrespective of arguments about the need to level the playing field. In addition, since any policy which involves group-based criteria is bound to involve an element of rough justice – and no practical policy can ever be perfectly individualized when dealing with complex, and possibly overlapping, forms of discrimination and disadvantage – they may sometimes have a genuine grievance.

As Hugh Collins points out, the flaw in any attempt to justify departures from the equal treatment principle by reference to a more substantive version of equality is that the two conceptions always remain in tension.[53] This is typically sought to be resolved by reference to the principle of proportionality (or, in the United States, 'strict scrutiny').[54] In other words, affirmative measures in favour of particular groups are allowed, so long as they do not impose an excessive burden on members of other groups. However, this solution gives rise to a number of further problems.

The first is that judgements about proportionality are inherently contestable. Hence '[w]herever the line is drawn [between formal and substantive equality] a decision can always be criticised as displaying either a slavish adherence to the equal treatment principle or a dangerous sacrifice of the principle.'[55] A good illustration is the European Court of Justice's decision in *Marschall* v. *Land Nordrhein-Westfalen*[56] that policies giving women tie-break preferences are permissible so long as they allow exceptions to be made in particular cases in favour of male candidates. In practice, these so-called 'savings clauses' seem likely to be mere formalities – insisted on by the Court simply as an excuse to depart from its earlier decision in *Kalanke*.[57] If not, though, they deny women any preference at all, as they must effectively show that they are *more* deserving of the position than any competing male candidate.

A second problem is that a proportionality test focuses attention on what forms of affirmative action are permitted, rather than on what factors are responsible for the continued exclusion of under-represented groups.[58] Thus,

---

53 Collins, op. cit., n. 51, p. 17.
54 id., p. 18; see, also, Fredman, op. cit., n. 6, pp. 147–50.
55 Collins, id.
56 Case C-409/95, [1997] ECR I-6363.
57 *Kalanke*, op. cit., n. 49.
58 Compare Bacchi, op. cit., n. 29, p. 34.

13

there may be a tendency to permit weaker forms of affirmative action because they are associated with relatively modest departures from the equal treatment principle, but to prohibit stronger forms as representing too radical a conceptual shift, and therefore as imposing too great a cost on others. In fact, though, different affirmative action strategies are merely tools which can be employed in the service of a range of ends. For example, quotas may seek equality of outcome on the ground that in an ideal non-discriminatory world all social groups would be involved in all social activities in proportion to their social distribution, or at least their distribution in the pool of applicants.[59] However, as the Northern Ireland police recruitment quota illustrates, they may simply represent an expanded outreach policy designed to achieve equality of opportunity. Similarly, decision-making preferences may reflect a notion of equality of consideration – taking account of the fact that candidates from some groups have had to overcome greater obstacles in order to reach the same position as those from more privileged groups – or may simply seek to advance equality of opportunity by providing role models.

The final difficulty is that, to the extent that proportionality arguments tend to rule out quotas or strong decision-making preferences, the non-discrimination approach appears to concede that hard affirmative action is incompatible with merit-based allocation. In fact, though, as Nicolson and Malleson argue, even if we accept that merit is correctly regarded as dispositive of particular selection decisions, its alleged incompatibility with affirmative action is overstated. Typically, supporters of affirmative action are not arguing for the abandonment of merit, but for different means of identifying merit or different criteria of what constitutes merit. As Malleson demonstrates, merit is not an immutable concept: for instance, what is regarded as desirable in candidates for judicial office has altered signifi-cantly over the years as the nature of the candidate pool has itself changed. Indeed, a key aim of affirmative action programmes may be to change conceptions of merit from within.

Nevertheless, we should not be surprised if such arguments sometimes fail to persuade. For one thing, this is clearly a disturbing discourse, likely to provoke resistance not only from those with vested interests in upholding conventional ideas of merit, but also from the intended beneficiaries of affirmative action programmes themselves. For instance, Francis and McDonald show how both institutions and students cling to the assumption of equivalence between full-time and part-time degrees; the former because it excuses them from having to make extra provision for part-time students; the latter, understandably, because they fear being seen as inferior to full-timers and in need of special assistance. In addition, it is not enough to point to the biased nature of existing merit criteria. These must be convincingly displaced by new norms; otherwise existing criteria may remain in play. For

---

59 R.J. Fiscus, *The Constitutional Logic of Affirmative Action: Making the Case for Quotas* (1992).

14

instance, a contextualized university admissions policy does not ignore examination results altogether, and these have the benefit of apparent objectivity which other measures of academic potential may lack. Moreover, unless new criteria can be justified independently of any advantages they offer to previously excluded groups, it may again be difficult to avoid the charge that affirmative action does indeed amount to preferential treatment, or even reverse discrimination.

3. *Preferential treatment and social utility*

If affirmative action is always vulnerable to being portrayed as preferential treatment, a final approach to justification is to embrace this conceptualization. After all, even the mildest forms of affirmative action, which create no 'innocent victims', involve an opportunity cost in terms of devoting resources to assist particular groups which could have been used elsewhere. Viewed from this perspective, however, it is clear that many other policies also involve (whether directly or indirectly) preferential treatment of some sort, but do not attract the same opprobrium as affirmative action because they are regarded as contributing to some overarching social or organizational goal. Examples include provisions relating to pregnancy and maternity leave, subsidized childcare, or even the minimum wage, which has disproportionately benefited low-paid black and female workers. Accordingly, if affirmative action policies can similarly be said to contribute to wider goals, then they too ought to be regarded as justified.

Unlike the compensatory and distributive justice rationales, social utility focuses more on disadvantage and exclusion than on discrimination as such. In fact, affirmative action can be presented as analogous to the mechanisms conventionally used to address class-based disadvantage, which (no doubt partly because of definitional difficulties) has not traditionally been regarded as a prohibited ground of discrimination. This is not inappropriate because socio-economic and other forms of disadvantage clearly overlap, and social exclusion is not attributable to poverty alone.[60] Indeed, Collins argues that social inclusion, rather than equality, should be regarded as the goal of anti-discrimination legislation, claiming that this better explains both the targeted nature of discrimination prohibitions,[61] and why it is sometimes necessary to depart from the equal treatment principle.[62] From this perspective, far from

---

60 See, for example, Collins, op. cit., n. 51, pp. 21–6.
61 That is, only certain, socially significant grounds of discrimination are prohibited, and in respect only of certain, socially significant goods.
62 Collins, op. cit., n. 51, pp. 26 ff. For similar critiques of the relationship between anti-discrimination, equality, and substantive goals see, also, P. Westen, 'The Empty Idea of Equality' (1982) 95 *Harvard Law Rev.* 537; Gardner, op. cit., n. 3, pp. 17–22; N. Bamforth, 'Conceptions of Anti-Discrimination Law' (2004) 24 *Oxford J. of Legal Studies* 693, 703–15; E. Holmes 'Anti-Discrimination Rights Without Equality' (2005) 68 *Modern Law Rev.* 175.

15

preferential treatment being problematic, it is normally a ground for criticism if social policies do not target benefits on those who are most in need.

However, other substantive goals might also be invoked to justify affirmative action, such as the need to defuse social tension – a consideration which clearly underpins the pursuit of 'fair participation' in Northern Ireland[63] – or, as we have already seen, the benefits that flow from increased diversity in particular organizational settings. These kinds of justifications break the link with need altogether. For example, Dunbar argues that the most convincing rationale for legislative support for Gaelic and Welsh is the promotion of cultural diversity, since Gaelic and Welsh speakers do not suffer from significant discrimination or disadvantage. For that reason, he argues that these measures should not in fact be regarded as a form of affirmative action, though he is critical of the failure to extend similar support to speakers of other minority languages who do face more pressing material disadvantage. The advantage of these kinds of justification is that they may avoid stigmatizing affirmative action beneficiaries; preferential treatment is being given because of what they can offer society, not because they need special assistance.

Breaking out of the individualistic paradigm of the compensatory and distributive justice rationales carries other potential benefits as well. For one thing, it provides an alternative response to the objection that affirmative action compromises merit. Since merit-based allocation is itself justified on utilitarian grounds,[64] it can clearly be overridden by considerations of greater social utility. In addition, to locate affirmative action on a continuum with other forms of social policy has the benefit of making clear that it represents a social choice, to be used whenever it provides the best means of addressing particular social problems, and not, as compensatory and distributive justice arguments may seem to suggest, a matter of right, to be employed irrespective of the consequences and only when the difficult task of establishing that right has been completed. This, in turn, highlights the importance of seeing affirmative action as part of a broader strategy of social transformation, rather than merely a matter of equalizing opportunities to become unequal.[65]

Nevertheless, admitting that affirmative action involves preferential treatment inevitably carries risks. In fact, it opens up a whole new area of potential political controversy around the goals which affirmative action claims to promote. Of course, some might object that any form of state-sponsored preferential treatment for particular groups is illegitimate because it is paternalistic and breaches the principle of state neutrality.[66] This general objection is easily met; by not intervening to redistribute social goods, the

---

63 See B. Hepple, 'Discrimination and Equality of Opportunity – Northern Irish Lessons' (1990) 10 *Oxford J. of Legal Studies* 408.
64 See Nicolson, in this volume, p. 117.
65 Compare Bamforth, op. cit., n. 62, p. 710.
66 See, for example, Justice Thomas in *Adarand* v. *Pena*, op. cit., n. 41, at pp. 240–1.

16

state is implicitly endorsing existing distributions and thereby also favouring particular groups.[67] However, it remains the case that, as matters of social utility rather than deontological principle, particular substantive goals are likely to be more contentious than those of making reparation for past wrongs or promoting equality. Diversity arguments seem particularly problematic in this respect. For instance, McHarg points out that, even for democratic institutions, the claim that their members should be reflective of society is highly controversial. Hence it is likely to be even harder to make a persuasive case for social diversity in relation to an institution like the judiciary, where the dominant constitutional understanding is that decisions should based on law and not on personal or public opinion.[68]

Further, even if the validity of a particular goal is accepted, unlike arguments from justice, this kind of utilitarian argument always requires calculation of whether the benefits of pursuing the goal outweigh any ensuing costs. It is always therefore vulnerable to the possibility that others might weight the costs and benefits differently. For example, Fredman argues that unless diversity programmes also serve a remedial purpose, their value in, say, enriching the educational experience does not justify the exclusion of highly qualified applicants from socially privileged groups.[69] Moreover, without a remedial element, there is no way of determining which characteristics are to count as contributing towards diversity.[70]

However, this focus on goals does at least appear to have the advantage of deflecting attention from questions about the legitimacy of affirmative action as a *means* of achieving social benefits. If preferential treatment is necessary in order to achieve a compelling social goal, then to that extent it can be regarded as justified. But this opens up another set of issues around the effectiveness of affirmative measures. For instance, Bibbings suggests that widening participation policies may not be the best long-term solution to educational disadvantage. From this perspective, it is also crucial to consider the possibility of backlash. Whilst social-utility based justifications may be less stigmatizing for the beneficiaries of preferential treatment, they may conversely be more disturbing for others who may feel that their contribution is being devalued.[71] For this and other reasons, it may be implausible to argue that affirmative action is an appropriate way of seeking to defuse social tension (indeed it may have the opposite effect). Ironically, it may be the case that affirmative action is more effective in achieving narrower organizational goals – such as the business benefits of diversity – than

---

67 See, for example, Fredman, op. cit., n. 6, p. 129.
68 But see L. Barnes, 'Adjudication and Public Opinion' (2002) 118 *Law Q. Rev.* 600.
69 Fredman, op. cit., n. 33, p. 596.
70 Compare McHarg, in this volume, pp. 154–6; Barnes with Ashtiany, op. cit., n. 25, pp. 290–1.
71 Compare Barnes with Ashtiany, id., pp. 291–2.

17

broader social goals. But these are the kinds of goals which are unlikely to be regarded as justifying significant sacrifices on the part of those who lose out because of affirmative action programmes.

In any case, questions about the legitimacy of affirmative action cannot be regarded as wholly subsumed by questions about goals and effectiveness. It might still be objected that it is illegitimate to use gender, race or other classifications, regardless of the consequences. An alternative reading of the purposes of anti-discrimination law is that it is not about promoting equality or some form of social utility, but merely aims to prohibit certain decision-making criteria which are regarded as particularly invidious.[72] If this is true, we might expect preferential treatment on grounds of class or language, which are not prohibited forms of discrimination, to be regarded as much less problematic than gender- or race-based preferences, with more recently prohibited grounds such as disability, sexual orientation, religious belief or age somewhere in between.

The obvious response is that it is simply wrong to regard all racial, gender or other group classifications as equally suspect irrespective of the purpose for which they are made. The real social evils are prejudice towards women, black people, and so on, not gender, race or similar discrimination in itself. As Gardner puts it, if we shift focus away from the harm associated with prejudice to the mere unfairness associated with suspect classifications:

> we risk identifying the wrongness of sexual subjugation or slavery with the failure of those invidious and enduring historical traditions to be perfectly meritocratic, and we start . . . to treat all non-meritocratic preferences as being on all fours with slavery.[73]

Prohibiting discrimination is thus simply a means by which we attempt to combat prejudice, and should not therefore be allowed to stand in the way if there is a better way of achieving that goal.[74]

Nevertheless, the use of group classifications, even for benign purposes, does carry with it dangers of perpetuating stereotypes and reifying differences. For example, a troubling aspect of the Northern Irish police quota is that applicants who do not, for what may be good reasons, self-identify as belonging to any religious community, must nevertheless be so classified, and on the basis of, among other things, such ostensibly secular criteria as their leisure activities. Because of these difficulties, it may be easier in practice to justify indirect forms of affirmative action, which do not expressly rely on prohibited group classifications, and which also have the

---

72 See, for example, M. Cavanagh, *Against Equality of Opportunity* (2002); Holmes, op. cit., n. 62, p. 194.

73 Gardner, op. cit., n. 3, p. 8.

74 In fact, it might be argued that there is no discrimination at all where group classifications are made for benign purposes. For example, white people who fail to benefit from affirmative action programmes are not 'like' their black counterparts because treating them differently would not cause them to be stigmatized as racially inferior – Westen, op. cit., n. 62, pp. 582–3.

18

advantage of resolving so-called 'diagonal discrimination' issues[75] – that is, where members of the dominant group nevertheless suffer the same disadvantage as those in the minority, such as male single parents, or unemployed Protestants. However, by focusing on the symptoms of prejudice rather than the underlying causes, this again risks blunting the potential radicalism of affirmative action as a policy tool.

A STRATEGIC APPROACH TO AFFIRMATIVE ACTION

A number of general implications can be drawn from this overview of the various approaches to justifying affirmative action. The first relates to terminology. Whilst it is important to counter the negative connotations of terms like 'reverse discrimination' or 'preferential treatment', the campaign to gain acceptance for affirmative action cannot be won on this battleground alone. In particular, attempts to sidestep the controversy surrounding affirmative action by definitional fiat are doomed to failure, not least because there is no essential meaning to that term. What we perceive as included in or excluded from the scope of affirmative action is very much a matter of perspective. As Busby's description of the fate of Canada's 'employment equity' legislation demonstrates, the desire to avoid the charge that this was merely affirmative action in disguise led policy-makers to limit it to soft measures only. Yet the policy continued to be portrayed as involving 'unfair' quotas and reverse discrimination, and, having declined to use the terminology of affirmative action, this may have reinforced – or at least done nothing to counter – the popular perception that it was illegitimate. Equally, as we have seen, acceptance of the terminology of 'reverse discrimination' or 'preferential treatment' no more guarantees that opposition can be overcome. Each of the various justificatory strategies contains in-built problems which tend to limit the type of or extent to which affirmative action measures can be justified in practice.

In fact, the debate over affirmative action is often seen as involving set-piece exchanges between supporters and opponents,[76] giving the impression that any conclusions reached simply reflect pre-existing value judgments. However, our discussion reveals that this is true only if the various justificatory strategies for and the objections to affirmative action are discussed in the abstract; in specific contexts particular justifications may appear far more, and particular objections far less, plausible.

75 See G. Davies, 'Should Diagonal Discrimination Claims be Allowed?' (2005) 25 *Legal Studies* 181.
76 Compare Bacchi, op. cit., n. 29, p. 25; D.A. Farber, 'The Outmoded Debate Over Affirmative Action' (1994) 82 *California Law Rev.* 893; D.B. Wilkins and G.M. Gulati, 'Why Are There So Few Black Lawyers in Corporate Law Firms? An Institutional Analysis' (1996) 84 *California Law Rev.* 496, at 513.

For instance, objections based on the merit principle are far more applicable to occupations such as the professions or the judiciary, where the alleged lowering of standards might conceivably harm the quality of services to the public, than they are to unskilled workers, and in any case do not have equal purchase against every rationale for affirmative action. Nevertheless, one cannot choose to rely on a particular justification solely because of the political benefits it offers in meeting potentially problematic objections. Certain justifications are simply inapplicable, implausible or political non-starters in particular contexts, or in relation to particular groups. For example, if the compensatory justice rationale can ever be 'sold' in the United Kingdom, it is far less applicable to recent immigrants than to social groups, such as women, which have suffered substantial and long-standing discrimination. On this basis, the working class seems to be the group which actually has the best claim to compensation. Realistically, though, the disadvantages faced by its members are likely to be regarded as either due to their lack of ambition or effort, or the inevitable consequences of a generally beneficial economic system.

Conversely, affirmative measures which are questionable in theory might, for pragmatic reasons, be regarded as acceptable in practice. For example, although quotas and decision-making preferences are likely to be both over- and under-inclusive if the aim is to ensure substantive equality, this might be regarded as a price worth paying for the sake of administrative convenience and because the results are fairer overall than maintaining formal equality.

All this suggests the need to be strategic in one's approach to justifying affirmative action, choosing a route to justification in the light of the relevant political, contextual, and pragmatic considerations. However, as part of that strategic approach, it is also necessary to consider whether, in any particular instance, affirmative action is itself the most appropriate strategy for achieving the goals one wishes to pursue. In other words, a crucially important consideration which is often overlooked is the question of whether it is actually effective. Here, Sweet's empirical research, which shows that contractual set-asides for minority business enterprises in the United States do not bring about increased minority employment, may give pause for thought. On the other hand, Busby reports that Canadian employment targets have achieved moderate success for women, though not other targeted groups, while research on affirmative action in Northern Ireland tentatively concludes that it has led to increased employment in Catholic communities and greater integration within firms.[77] We may conclude from this that the effectiveness of affirmative action cannot be judged in the abstract, but again depends on contextual factors, including how well particular programmes are designed, the resources devoted to them, and the commitment of those

---

77 C. McCrudden et al., 'Legal Regulation of Affirmative Action in Northern Ireland: An Empirical Assessment' (2004) 24 *Oxford J. of Legal Studies* 363. See, more generally: Edwards, op. cit., n. 40, chs. 4 and 5; Farber, id., p. 913.

20

charged with implementation.[78] Of course, the question of empirical support is also relevant to the objections to affirmative action. For instance, research in the United States shows that it has not only greatly improved the chances of African-Americans gaining a university education but has not given rise to the claimed stigmatizing effect.[79]

Finally, a number of important practical questions must also be addressed. These include the questions of which groups require assistance;[80] how long affirmative measures should subsist;[81] how to treat individuals who face multiple disadvantages[82] or who benefit from countervailing advantages, such as a wealthy background; whether affirmative action should apply to promotion and to redundancy, as well as initial selection, decisions;[83] and whether to base targets and quotas on the proportion of the members of targeted group in society as a whole, in particular localities or the pool of relevant applicants,[84] or on some lower or higher figure reached independently of these proportions.[85] Given the centrality of the merit principle to the debate, perhaps the most important practical issues relate to whether quotas and targets can apply to those who only minimally qualified or whether some higher qualifications are required,[86] and whether decision-making preferences are justified even if their targets' qualifications and perceived abilities approximate to but do not equal those of their competitors.[87] Some of these problems are seized upon as defeating the case for affirmative action altogether.[88] However, as Nicolson demonstrates in

---

78 Compare Bacchi, op. cit., n. 29, ch. 8.
79 W.G. Bowen and D. Bok, *The Shape of the River: Long-Term Consequences of Considering Race in College and University Admissions* (1998).
80 For useful guidelines, see R.H. Fallon and P.C. Weiler, 'Firefighters v. Stotts: Conflicting Models of Racial Justice' [1984] *Supreme Court Rev.* 1, 47.
81 See McHarg, in this volume, pp. 157–9, for discussion of the appropriateness of the sunset clause in SDECA.
82 Providing them with only one preference or quota place might underestimate the obstacles they faced, but awarding a preference for every additional form of disadvantage might ignore overlapping causes of disadvantage: J. Kaplan, 'Equal Justice in an Unequal World: Equality for the Negro – The Problem of Special Treatment' (1966-7) 61 *Northwestern University Law Rev.* 363, at 371.
83 Compare n. 6 above and accompanying text regarding Northern Ireland; Fiscus, op. cit., n. 59, pp. 92 ff.; Fallon and Weiler, op. cit., n. 80, pp. 54 ff. See, also, Malleson, this volume, p. 132, who argues that affirmative action becomes increasingly untenable the longer applicants have invested in existing markers of merit.
84 Compare Edwards, op. cit., n. 40, pp. 31–3; Fiscus, id., pp. 85–92.
85 See Kaplan, op. cit., n. 82, p. 370 on the differing problems with either strategy.
86 Compare Bacchi's distinction between 'moderate' and 'radical' quotas: op. cit., n. 29, p. 148.
87 Compare Nicolson's distinction, in this volume, between 'ball-park' and 'tie-break' preferences, p. 110.
88 See, for example, W. Van Alstyne, 'Rites of Passage: Race, the Supreme Court and the Constitution' (1978-9) 46 *University of Chicago Law Rev.* 755, at 805, regarding the question of which groups deserve assistance; and in response, O.M. Fiss, 'Groups and the Equal Protection Clause' (1976) 5 *Philosophy and Public Affairs* 107.

21

relation to the legal profession,[89] they are, in fact, merely difficult rather than insurmountable if the general case for affirmative action is accepted.

CONCLUSION

Hopefully this collection has gone some way to ensuring that this case is accepted. At the very least, the contributions show a distinct lack of the defensiveness which usually marks arguments for affirmative action.[90] To this extent, the tide does seem to be turning and we may now be approaching the point where opponents of affirmative action are forced to justify *their* position. Are they arguing that discrimination and disadvantage is a thing of the past? Or that they constitute ineradicable features of current social arrangements? Or can they be addressed without resort to affirmative action, and, if so, how? In many cases, one suspects that antagonism towards affirmative action stems, at best, from an unwillingness to pay the necessary price to ensure that discrimination and disadvantage are eradicated.

For some, however, the objection to affirmative action is that it stops short of, and may even undermine, more effective means of redressing the problems that it is designed to address.[91] The very language of assistance, preference, and special measures, it is argued, smacks of charity, conveying the impression that the problem lies with affirmative action targets themselves rather than social norms and structures which are designed by and for the powerful and privileged, and which condemn them to social exclusion. Moreover, affirmative action can be said to divide groups that should be campaigning together for social reform rather than clashing over the justifiability of affirmative action[92] or competing for the limited assistance it provides. In fact, though, it might be argued that it is precisely because such fundamental social reform seems further away than ever that more limited strategies such as affirmative action have risen to prominence. If social structures are to remain inherently unequal, ensuring fair distribution of

---

89 See, also, G. Liu, 'Affirmative Action in Higher Education: The Diversity Rationale and the Compelling Interest Test' (1998) 33 *Harvard Civil Rights–Civil Liberties Law Rev.* 381, at 427–8, regarding the argument that affirmative action has no logical stopping point.

90 C. Bacchi, 'Policy and Discourse: Challenging the Construction of Affirmative Action as Preferential Treatment' (2004) 11 *J. of European Public Policy* 128, at 142.

91 See, for example, Bacchi, op. cit., n. 29 and id; D.A. Bell Jr., '*Bakke*, Minority Admissions, and the Usual Price of Racial Remedies' (1979) 67 *California Law Rev.* 3; R. Delgado, 'Affirmative Action as a Majoritarian Device: Or, Do You Really Want to be a Role Model?' (1991) 89 *Michigan Law Rev.* 1222; S. Sturm and L. Guinier, 'The Future of Affirmative Action: Reclaiming the Innovative Ideal' (1996) 84 *California Law Rev.* 953.

92 For example, Richard Nixon allegedly supported affirmative action in the hope that it would divide the Democratic vote: Eastland, op. cit., n. 43, p. 51.

22

existing social advantages becomes all the more pressing – though equally this raises the stakes for those who are likely to lose out from affirmative action.

In any event, although acknowledging the need for more far-reaching measures, many of the contributors to this volume remain convinced that affirmative action has a significant role to play.[93] This is either because of the positive psychological and emotional benefits experienced by its targets or more fundamentally because, having taken their rightful places in important social institutions, they might bring about internal reform or even, in some cases, wider social reform. In this way, affirmative action may have a potentially significant contribution to make in eradicating discrimination and disadvantage from 'the inside out'.[94]

---

93 Bibbings; Francis and McDonald; Nicolson. Compare, also, Fredman, op. cit., n. 6, p. 160; L.C. Harris and U. Narayan, 'Affirmative Action as Equalizing Opportunity: Challenging the Myth of "Preferential Treatment"' in LaFollette, op. cit., n. 39, 450–1.
94 Busby, in this volume, p. 45.

JOURNAL OF LAW AND SOCIETY
VOLUME 33, NUMBER 1, MARCH 2006
ISSN: 0263-323X, pp. 24–41

Positive Action for Women in Employment: Time to Align with Europe?

NOREEN BURROWS* AND MURIEL ROBISON**

In recent years positive action to improve women's position in the labour market has risen up the political agenda, with measures ranging from quotas to special training. The legal framework has been slower to change. Initially seeking to eliminate all forms of discrimination, it now reflects a more sophisticated approach, attempting to achieve substantive equality. This may encompass measures which appear to disadvantage men but are aimed at rectifying women's structural, economic or historical disadvantage. We investigate the limits imposed on EU member states' ability to take positive action under Community law, and examine the much narrower provisions of the Sex Discrimination Act. We argue that the time is now ripe, with the ongoing review of equality law, to reappraise domestic law and to use the freedom provided under Community law to expand the scope of positive action under the Sex Discrimination Act.

INTRODUCTION

In this article we explore some of the ways to conceptualize positive action measures in relation to sex discrimination in the context of the law of the European Community (EC) and of Great Britain.[1] We explore the existing provisions, and attempt to conceptualize them in an equality framework and

* School of Law, University of Glasgow, Stair Building, 5–8 The Square, Glasgow G12 8QQ
** Equal Opportunities Commission Scotland, St Stephen's House, 279 Bath St, Glasgow, Scotland
n.burrows@law.gla.ac.uk   muriel.robison@eoc.org.uk

The views expressed in this article are those of the authors. They do not represent the position of the EOC.

1 Because of the considerable differences, we do not discuss discrimination law as it applies in Northern Ireland.

24

make proposals for extending British law to align it with European developments. These two legal orders are inextricably linked in this area since British law must not go beyond what is permissible in terms of EC law. At the same time the United Kingdom, as a member state of the European Union, is obliged to implement EC law and has recently legislated to introduce positive action measures in the area of religion and belief and sexual orientation.[2]

It has been argued that the approach of EC law in relation to sex discrimination in employment and related matters is not as rigidly symmetrical as the provisions of the Sex Discrimination Act (SDA).[3] A symmetrical, or formal, approach is one that seeks to eliminate discrimination on the grounds of sex rather than to eliminate discrimination against women and is defined in legal terms as equal treatment of men and women.[4] With some limited exceptions,[5] the SDA seeks to eliminate discrimination against both men and women even though it is widely accepted that women suffer greater disadvantages than men in the labour market. By contrast, the Equal Treatment Directive (ETD), whilst acknowledging the central importance of the equal treatment principle, recognizes the need for measures that will achieve substantive equality.[6] More recent European legislation, in the form of the amended Treaty provision in Article 141(4)EC and the General Framework Directive, goes further towards substantive equality and is more permissive in the freedom accorded to member states to use positive action measures.[7] Thus there is currently a divergence in British law, both between the British and the European approaches to positive action, and between the provisions of the SDA (and the Race Relations Act (RRA)) and the more recently introduced Regulations on Sexual Orientation and Religion and Belief, which reflect more closely current European approaches. We argue that the Discrimination Law Review, set up by the government to consider the opportunities for creating a clearer and more streamlined legislative framework, provides an opportunity to reconsider the law in this area and to

---

2 The Employment Equality (Religion or Belief) Regulations, S.I. 2003 No. 1660; the Employment Equality (Sexual Orientation) Regulations, S.I. 2003 No. 1661.

3 A. McColgan, *Discrimination Law: Text, Cases and Materials* (2005, 2nd edn.).

4 Both terms convey a sense of equality before the law irrespective of the context in which discrimination law operates.

5 See below, p. 34.

6 Council Directive 76/207/EC of 9 February 1976 on the implementation of the principle of equal treatment for men and women as regards access to employment, vocational training and promotion, and working conditions, OJ/9 February 1976/L39/40.

7 Article 141(4) TEC and Council Directive 2000/78 of 27 November 2000 establishing a general framework for equal treatment in employment and occupation, OJ/27 November 2000/L303/16. Article 7 of the Directive states that 'with a view to ensuring full equality in practice, the principle of equal treatment shall not prevent any Member State from maintaining or adopting specific measures to prevent or compensate for disadvantages linked to any of the grounds' referred to in the Directive.

25

introduce some consistency of approach.[8] In particular we argue that EC law provides insights into possible legislative reform.

Because European law in the field of sex discrimination was exclusively focused on employment matters until very recently, the focus in this article will be on employment law. We also concentrate on 'hard-law' measures – the Treaty provisions and the secondary legislation. We argue that British legislation could be amended quite radically and still remain within the boundaries of EC law, and that it is desirable to do so.

CONCEPTS OF EQUALITY AND POSITIVE ACTION

Any such amendments are likely to be contentious and therefore it is important to have clearly defined underlying principles to explain any legislative changes. Clear guiding principles also make it easier for employers to understand their own freedom of action and for the courts to adjudicate in difficult cases.

Borrowing from McCrudden's analysis of types of positive action, we can distinguish three types of measures that might be utilized in the context of a revision of employment legislation.[9] The first type, defined as 'purposefully inclusionary policies', are those which are apparently neutral but which would benefit women more than men and which otherwise might be construed as indirect discrimination against men if it were not that they were targeted at disadvantage and therefore justifiable. An example might be the provision of parental leave. The second are outreach measures which include encouragement to apply for particular jobs or special training to bring the under-represented sex into a particular sector or category of employment.[10] The third category is preferential treatment which might cover a broad range of flexible or inflexible quotas, targets, tie-break rules or other forms of preferences accorded to one sex. EC law allows for extensive preferential measures whereas the SDA renders illegal most forms of preferential treatment. This is because EC law and British law are grounded in different concepts of equality.

Three concepts of equality offer themselves as potential frameworks for sex discrimination law. The first model is based on the equal treatment principle, which requires that there shall be no discrimination whatsoever on the grounds of sex. As Fredman, for example, has stated, the principle of equal treatment is an expression of formal equality based on the assumption that the law should be gender neutral. It is based on an individualistic conception which ignores the cumulative disadvantages of the group in which the individual is situated.[11] Because of the symmetrical nature of the

8 See <http://www.e-government.cabinet-office.gov.uk/about/>.
9 C. McCrudden, quoted in McColgan, op. cit., n. 3, p. 131.
10 See, further, below, pp. 30, 34.
11 S. Fredman, *Discrimination Law* (2002) 126.

26

equal treatment principle, measures such as preferential treatment in favour of the out-group are deemed to be direct discrimination and are therefore excluded.

The second model is based on the principle of equal opportunity which moves beyond the principle of equal treatment but still remains within the formal equality paradigm:

> Equality of opportunity recognises the historical and structural disadvantages faced by women in the employment sphere and seeks to move towards equal starting points.[12]

Measures which would otherwise infringe the principle of equal treatment can be approved provided that they are designed to remove barriers 'which disproportionately disadvantage the out-group'.[13] This is equality of opportunity in a substantive sense. This conception accepts that measures which remove barriers to participation do not offend against the principle of equality because such barriers are a genuine impediment to women, but not men, participating in the labour market. Outreach measures which bring men and women to the same starting point in selection for employment, promotion, education or other benefit are not considered to offend the principle of equality. Neither are measures which encourage women to apply for posts or promotion in a gender-segregated market since they do not affect the chances of male applicants. Similarly, gender-neutral 'but purposefully inclusionary policies' are seen as legitimate.[14] However, the principle of equal opportunities can only have limited success in achieving equality. As Fredman argues, the removal of barriers to participation does not necessarily equip individuals to move forward. She cites the example of removing word-of-mouth recruitment (a gender-neutral but purposefully inclusionary measure for many top jobs) to open up opportunities and argues:

> But this does not guarantee that more members of the disadvantaged group will in fact be in a position to benefit from those opportunities, they may lack the relevant qualifications or may be constrained by other social factors such as child care obligations.[15]

The third model is based on a concept of substantive rather than formal equality. Substantive equality requires the law to address the disadvantages faced by women. Therefore it is also equated with equality of outcomes/results. Substantive equality looks to the law to provide full equality in practice and to target disadvantaged groups rather than advantaged ones. Equality of results focuses on the disadvantages faced by members of out-

---

12 T. Hervey, 'EC Law on Justifications for Sex Discrimination in Working Life' in *Collective Bargaining, Discrimination, Social Security and European Integration*, ed. R. Blanpain (2003) 104.
13 S. Fredman, *The Future of Equality in Britain* (2002) 6.
14 The term is McCrudden's, op. cit., n. 9.
15 Fredman, op. cit., n. 13, p. 6.

groups, then seeks to remedy the disadvantage. This may be by imposing a disadvantage on advantaged individuals, such as exclusion from a shortlist for a post, or it might be by advantaging disadvantaged individuals over others in recognition of past discrimination. All forms of positive action, including preferential measures, are legitimate if the disadvantages faced by an out-group are sufficiently serious. Legal provisions which provide advantages for women in the labour market would not be deemed to breach the principle of equality provided they aim to redress discriminatory advantages enjoyed by men. Measures might also be designed to compensate for past disadvantages. This approach underlines what Fredman describes as the remedial purpose of equality laws and it arises out of the positive duty to achieve equality. To explain this position, she cites the Canadian Supreme Court which stated:

> the equality principle is not breached where a measure has an ameliorative purpose, even if it excludes more advantaged individuals, provided that the exclusion corresponds to the greater need or different circumstances experienced by the disadvantaged group being targeted by the legislation.[16]

The positive duty to achieve equality takes remedial measures outside the ambit of the equal treatment principle. Remedial measures are not discriminatory because individuals are not similarly situated. Positive action measures designed to achieve equality of results should not therefore be seen as exceptions to the principle of equal treatment but as an alternative mechanism to achieve the principle of equality. Provided that they target disadvantage and are suitably designed, such measures serve the equality principle. It is undoubtedly the case that the more radical the positive action measure, the more important it is to have a justification for it. A measure that might appear as direct discrimination, provided that it is a remedial measure, should not therefore be analysed in terms of the equal treatment principle but in the broader terms of the principle of equality. There is no question therefore of providing a justification for an apparently directly discriminatory provision.[17]

In the next section, we argue that EC law is developing a more expansive interpretation of the equality principle as it applies to sex discrimination. We would not go so far as to agree with Sargeant that Article 141(4) 'now incorporates the principle of positive discrimination',[18] but we do argue that it involves a different approach to positive action designed as a means to target disadvantage and to allow for a greater use of measures having a remedial quality.

---

16 id., p. 12.
17 Unlike, for example, in relation to election candidacies: see A. McHarg, 'Quotas for Women! The Sex Discrimination (Election Candidates) Act 2002', in this issue, pp. 145–7.
18 M. Sargeant (ed.), *Discrimination Law* (2004) 39.

1. *The Equal Treatment Directive*

The Equal Treatment Directive is a classic example of legislation framed in terms of the equal treatment principle, but which recognizes the existence of barriers to women's participation in the labour market and the need for measures to remove such barriers. Article 1(1), which states that the purpose of the directive is to put into effect the principle of equal treatment of men and women, is balanced by Article 2(4) which states that the directive 'shall be without prejudice to measures to promote equal opportunity for men and women, in particular by removing existing inequalities which affect women's opportunities'.

The European Court of Justice has interpreted this balance between Article 1(1) and Article 2(4) six times in the last decade.[19] At first the Court in *Kalanke* appeared reluctant to interpret Article 2(4) in anything but a restrictive sense. Rather than a balance, the Court saw Article 2(4) as an exception to the principle of equal treatment. Thus the Court stressed that Article 2(4) could not authorize positive action measures leading to equality of results as it was designed specifically to 'allow measures which, although discriminatory in appearance, are in fact intended to eliminate or reduce actual instances of inequality which exist in the realities of social life'.[20] A rule which gives absolute and unconditional priority to women, according to the Court, goes beyond promoting equal opportunities and 'substitutes equality of opportunity with equality of results'. However, in *Marschall*, the Court held that Article 2(4) authorizes 'national measures which give a specific advantage to women with a view to improving their ability to compete on the labour market and to pursue a career on an equal footing with men'. The Court recognized that men tended to be promoted more frequently than women and that this could be the result of prejudice and stereotyping. The Court held that 'the mere fact that a male candidate and a female candidate are equally qualified does not mean that they have the same chances'. A rule which gives preference to women could fall within Article 2(4) if the rule counteracts the adverse effects of prejudice on female candidates. However, because Article 2(4) is a derogation from a fundamental right, such a rule cannot give unconditional and absolute priority to women. In subsequent cases, the Court has tended to seek an appropriate balance between Articles 1 and 2 of the directive.

---

19 Case C-450/93, *Kalanke* v. *Freie Hansestadt Bremen* [1995] ECR 1-3051; Case C-409/95, *Marschall* v. *Land Nordrhein-Westfalen* [1997] ECR I-6363; Case C-158/97, *Badeck* v. *Hessischer Ministerprasident* [2000] ECR I-1875; Case C-407/98, *Abrahamsson and Anderson* v. *Fogelqvist* [2000] ECR I-5539; Case C-476/99, *Lommers* v. *Minister van Landbouw, Natuurbeheer en Visserij* [2002] ECR I-2891, Case C-319/03, *Briheche* v. *Ministre de l'Intérieur, Ministre de l'Education and Ministre de la Justice*, not yet reported in ECR.
20 *Kalanke*, id., para. 18.

Using the typology of positive action measures suggested by McCrudden, it is possible to analyse the case-law of the Court to date and to specify with some degree of certainty the range of measures that are currently permitted by EC law.

(a) Purposefully inclusionary policies:
(i)   A requirement in selection and promotion decisions to take into consideration experience in looking after children and to discount seniority, age and the date of the last promotion unless these were important in assessing the suitability, capability and performance of the applicant (*Badeck*);
(ii) A requirement to discount family status or income of a partner in making decisions on selection (*Badeck*);
(iii) A provision prohibiting part-time status or delay in completing training because of domestic care having a negative assessment in assessment of service (*Badeck*);
(iv) A scheme under which nursery places made available to staff are reserved to female employees and, in exceptional circumstances to, male staff (*Lommers*).

(b) Outreach measures:
(i)   A requirement for public services to produce a two-year advancement plan setting out binding targets for the proportion of women in appointments and promotions where women are under-represented and the methods to achieve this. Where targets are not met, a prohibition on appointment or promotion of males without approval (*Badeck*);
(ii) A pro-rata quota providing a minimum percentage of women in academic posts at least equal to the percentage of women among graduates, holders of higher degrees, and students in each discipline (*Badeck*);
(iii) A recommendation that half the places on employees' representative bodies and administrative and support bodies be reserved to women (*Badeck*).

(c) Preferential treatment:
(i)   A tie-break rule giving preference to women where men and women are equally qualified, provided that an equally qualified male had the opportunity to demonstrate that a reason specific to his case could tilt the balance in his favour (*Marschall*);
(ii) A reservation of public sector training places for women, where they are under-represented in particular grades for which the training is designed, provided that men have access to alternative forms of training, for example, in the private sector (*Badeck*);
(iii) A requirement to interview as many women as men or all the women applicants for a post or grade where women are under-represented (*Badeck*);

30

(iv) A selection process which gives priority to women, where men and women are equally qualified, but which guarantees that all candidates are subject to an objective assessment taking account of their specific personal situations. (*Badeck*).

On the other hand the following forms of preferential treatment are prohibited:
(i)   A tie-break rule giving automatic preference to women where they were under-represented in a particular promoted grade (*Kalanke*);
(ii) A system of promotion, in place for one year, of women to professorial posts where they had sufficient qualifications but were less qualified than a male as long as the difference in qualifications was not so great as to give rise to a breach of the principle of objectivity (*Abrahamsson*);
(iii) A scheme which allowed the age limit of 45 for applicants to the civil service to be lifted in the case of widows who have not remarried and are obliged to work but cannot be lifted for widowers in the same position (*Briheche*).

From this it can be seen, that the Court has opposed schemes for appointment or promotion which provide for women to be automatically preferred to men and hence where selection is entirely based on sex and there is no opportunity to assess the merit of male candidates. In these cases, the Court focuses on the individual who is disadvantaged by the rule in question without examining the disadvantages faced by the out-group. However, whereas in *Kalanke* the Court stated that Article 2(4), as an exception to the principle of equal treatment, must be interpreted narrowly, in *Briheche*, the Court, relying on its interpretation of positive action measures in *Lommers*, introduced a proportionality test to determine the scope of any derogation from the principle of equal treatment. The proportionality principle requires:

> that derogations must remain within the limits of what is appropriate and necessary in order to achieve the aim in view and that the principle of equal treatment be reconciled as far as possible with the requirements of the aim thus pursued.[21]

Measures which give specific advantages to women to compete in the labour market and to pursue a career on an equal footing with men, which are proportionate to these aims are compatible with Article 2(4).

Conversely, cases in which the Court has approved measures that member states have introduced are those where no automatic preference is given to women. In *Marschall*, for example, a tie-break rule almost identical to that in *Kalanke* was saved because of the provision that allowed for the individual circumstances of a male applicant for promotion to be assessed. In *Badeck*, a comprehensive and wide-ranging scheme for advancement of women had

---

21 *Briheche*, op. cit., n. 19, para. 24.

31

been devised. The Court approved the totality of the measures which it defined as a 'flexible results quota' where in any particular decision the sex of the individual did not determine the outcome of a decision-making process. The Court held that the system intended to lead to substantive rather than formal equality. Even the pro rata quota, which reserved certain academic posts to women in proportion to the number of graduates in that discipline, was approved by the Court on the basis that no absolute ceiling was being set and there was a quantitative criterion being used to determine the quota. Men could have access to posts in proportion to their representation amongst the graduates. Similarly, men were not excluded from training just because some places were reserved for women. In *Lommers*, the Court approached the question of a restriction on access to nursery places as one of an equality opportunity measure, designed to allow women to pursue their careers on an equal footing with men.

2. *Positive action and equal pay*

The ETD does not cover employment matters in so far as they relate to pay. Instead, Article 141(4)EC governs positive action measures in equal pay cases. The Court has only twice interpreted this provision. In *Abdoulaye*,[22] the employer made a lump sum payment to female workers on maternity leave which was designed to compensate them for disadvantages such as their inability to access promotion or training opportunities whilst on maternity leave. In *Griesmar*, the French government credited additional pension service credits to female civil servants with children.[23] In both cases the Court stated that the principle of equal pay presupposes, with regard to a particular payment, that male and female workers are in a comparable situation. Where they are not in comparable situations it is not contrary to the principle of equal pay to provide an advantage to certain members of one sex, provided that the advantage is designed to offset specific occupational disadvantages. In *Abdoulaye*, the Court accepted that there are several occupational disadvantages inherent in taking maternity leave. Members of the advantaged group were not in need of the ameliorative effects of the payment and therefore to deny them the payment did not breach the equality principle. By contrast, in *Griesmar*, the Court rejected the argument of the French government that the payment was intended to offset the occupational disadvantages of women who bring up children because these women faced generalized disadvantages throughout their careers and the payments were not designed to offset particular disadvantages. The Court was particularly concerned that men with

22 Case C-218/98, *Abdoulaye* v. *Régie Nationale des Usines Renault SA* [1999] ECR I-5723.
23 Case C-366/99, *Griesmar* v. *Ministre de l'Economie, des Finances et de l'Industrie* [2001] ECR I-9383.

32

responsibility for bringing up children, who were similarly situated, did not have access to the additional pension credits.

3. *The future of positive action in EC law*

The discussion so far suggests that the Court of Justice is still in a process of refining its approach to the concept of positive action. In interpreting Article 2(4) of the ETD, it has established that a range of positive action measures can be accommodated provided that they meet the proportionality test. They must aim to improve the ability of women to compete on the labour market and to pursue a career on an equal footing with men, and they must be appropriate and necessary to achieve that aim. In addition, the measures must be reconciled as far as possible with the principle of equal treatment.

However, since the ETD was adopted in 1976 there have been two substantial developments in the law relating to positive action. The first is the amendment to the Treaty in 1997, which introduced Article 141(4) EC and the second is the adoption of a directive amending the ETD (the ETAD).[24] The effect of both of these is to reaffirm the member states' commitment to taking measures which will ensure full equality in practice between men and women.

Article 141(4)EC was inserted into the Treaty by the Treaty of Amsterdam. Previously, there had been no Treaty provision devoted to positive action. Its very existence in the Treaty demonstrates the concern of the member states that they may be constrained in their own positive action policies by the case law of the Court. The insertion of a Treaty provision which allows them wide scope for action is designed to keep the Court at arm's length. Article 141(4) provides that:

> With a view to ensuring full equality in practice between men and women in working life, the principle of equal treatment shall not prevent any Member State from maintaining or adopting measures providing for specific advantages in order to make it easier for the under-represented sex to pursue a vocational activity or to prevent or compensate for disadvantages in professional careers.

As is clear from *Briheche*, however, Article 141(4) does not give *carte blanche* to member states to adopt any measures they see fit. Such measures must be proportionate to the aim to be pursued and member states must still therefore be in a position to justify any positive action legislation.

The ETAD incorporates the Treaty provision. It states that:

---

24 Directive 2002/73/EC of the European Parliament and of the Council of 23 September 2002 amending Council Directive 76/207/EEC on the implementation of the principle of equal treatment for men and women as regards access to employment, vocational training and promotion, and working conditions, OJ/5 December 2002/L 269/15.

Member States may maintain or adopt measures within the meaning of Article 141(4) of the Treaty with a view to ensuring full equality in practice between men and women.

The ETAD entered into force in October 2002, and member states must implement its provisions by October 2005. Article 2(4) only permitted measures to promote equal opportunity between men and women: hence the reluctance of the Court to approve measures designed to achieve equality of results. In ETAD, the reference to equal opportunity has been replaced with the more open-ended formulation of 'measures providing for specific advantages'. Neither Article 141(4) nor the ETAD, of course, requires the member states to take any measures at all, but the reformulation of the Community legal framework gives them a much wider margin of appreciation in the area of positive action, provided always that any measures meet the proportionality test. In this context, the assessment of whether or not measures are proportionate will involve evidence of the extent to which women continue to be disadvantaged, for example, in a particular sector, at a particular level of the organization, or in relation to child-care responsibilities.

THE CURRENT BRITISH POSITION

Britain has had laws permitting positive action initiatives for combating historical disadvantage suffered by women in the workplace since the mid-1970s. These are contained in sections 47 and 48 of the SDA,[25] which constitute an exception to its general symmetrical or formal approach to equality.[26] These provisions permit employers and training providers to provide single-sex training or specific encouragement to one sex to seek appointment or promotion in sectors where that sex is under-represented and therefore disadvantaged. They, therefore, permit outreach measures to ensure equality of opportunity by equalizing the starting point when it comes to selecting candidates for posts. There is also a specific provision for persons returning to work after discharging domestic responsibilities, which could be categorized as a purposefully inclusionary measure.

1. Positive action – encouragement

Sections 47(1)(b) and 48(1)(b), respectively, authorize training providers and employers to take steps to address gender imbalance by 'encouraging' women only to take advantage of opportunities for doing particular work. Positive action 'encouragement' can take the form of directing recruitment

---

25 The equivalent provisions of the RRA are ss. 37 and 38.
26 The only other exceptions are s. 49 relating to trades unions' elective bodies and the recent changes made by the Sex Discrimination (Election Candidates) Act: see McHarg, op. cit., n. 17.

initiatives towards areas where women are under-represented, publishing adverts for vacancies and promoted posts which specifically encourage applications from women, or providing 'taster' days for women.[27]

Such outreach measures will be permitted only where the initiative relates to 'particular work' in which women are under-represented. The training provider or employer must make a judgement that it 'reasonably appears' to them that there are no women doing that work, or that the numbers are 'comparatively small'. This phrase is not defined, and there have been no cases determined under these provisions which can give guidance regarding the extent of underrepresentation. However, the notes on clauses compiled while the SDA was making its way through Parliament suggest that 'it is intended to cover a proportion which may not be negligible but which falls well short of half'.[28] Further, any statistics consulted to justify the introduction of outreach measures should indicate that this is the position within the preceding twelve month period, either for Britain as a whole, or, to address local skills shortages, 'for an area of Great Britain'.[29]

These provisions allow for an equality of opportunity approach only to a very limited extent: they recognize that in areas where women are severely under-represented they may need particular encouragement to apply for jobs, but they do not exclude men from applying. Nor do they recognize that women may not be able, because of lack of skills and experience, to compete on the same terms for these jobs, and hence do not target those women who are not in a position, because of past disadvantage, to benefit from these opportunities.

2. Positive action – training

The SDA does, however, allow for equality of opportunity in a more substantive sense, by recognizing that the reason that women cannot compete equally with men is because they lack skills as a consequence of past disadvantage. In order to equip women with the skills necessary for them to compete for jobs where men dominate, training providers and employers are permitted to run single-sex training courses.[30] The training course must relate to 'particular work' where women are severely under-represented. Again, the training provider must make a judgement about the extent to which women are under-represented in a particular sector. 'Particular work' is not defined, but arguably this refers not only to a specific skilled job, but also to a job function, such as supervisory or management skills. The content

---

27 See <http://.eoc.org.uk/EOCeng/EOCcs/Advice/managing_successful_postive_action.asp>.
28 Sex Discrimination Bill Notes on Clauses, Clause 41, Standing Committee, Sixth Sitting, 8 May 1975.
29 ss. 47(2)(b) and 48(2)(b).
30 ss. 47(1)(a) and 48(1)(a), respectively.

35

of any training course must however bear a relation to the particular work in question. For instance, a course concerning basic-level computing could not be restricted to one sex since it is not linked to particular work, even though women may well be under-represented in the information technology sector more generally, whereas training in computer programming may pass the test. Other permissible initiatives include job sampling, work experience, 'taster' days or work-shadowing experience.

Thus these provisions seek to allow women to obtain the skills necessary to compete equally with men for jobs in male-dominated areas. The equality of opportunity approach allows women the same opportunities as men to compete for the jobs by enhancing their skills to the level of their male competitors. These outreach measures are permitted by the equality of opportunity approach because they are designed to remove barriers which disproportionately disadvantage women. This is a substantive sense of equality of opportunity which, although excluding men from the training courses, recognizes that men are in the advantaged group who through training or on-the-job experience have been in a position to gain the necessary skills for the job. However, the scope for such positive action is very limited, focusing on those areas where there are no women at all doing particular work or where their numbers are severely restricted. Only a relatively narrow range of courses and initiatives will in fact fall within the definition.

3. *Positive action for those who have discharged domestic responsibilities*

The SDA also recognizes that one of the ways in which women are disadvantaged in the job market is by taking time out to bring up children. Thus, section 47(3) allows training for people who have been out of full-time employment due to discharging domestic responsibilities to help fit them for employment more generally. Here, there is no need to show that one sex is under-represented.[31] All that is required is that the delegates on the course are in 'special need' of training because they have been out of the labour market due to caring responsibilities.

But for section 47(3), the provision of training for returners only (open to both sexes) might be an unlawful form of indirect discrimination, excluding more men who are less likely to take parental leave or a career break than women, requiring justification. Some concern has been expressed, however, about whether this section of the Act would allow the restriction of training to women returners rather than returners of either sex since, rather unusually for the SDA, section 47(3) mentions 'persons' instead of 'women' or 'men'. Section 47(3) also indicates that the discrimination referred to may result *either* from confining the training to those who have discharged domestic responsibilities, *or* from the way persons are selected for training, *or* both.

31 s. 47(3).

This must mean that the discrimination contemplated is more than simply a condition that the person had been discharging domestic responsibilities, otherwise there would be no need for this additional paragraph. Courses can therefore be confined to women only if the provider reasonably considers that women are in special need of such training. This view is supported by Parliamentary debates, where Lord Jacques spoke of this provision principally as benefiting women.[32] It was clearly contemplated therefore that section 47(3) would make a course restricted to women returning to the labour market lawful.

Section 47(3) apparently does not allow selection solely on the ground of sex since it is doubtful whether a person could reasonably consider that all women, irrespective of other criteria, are in special need of training because of having discharged domestic or family responsibilities. For example, this would be very unlikely to apply to young women. Some criterion other than simply sex must also be applied. For example, section 47(3) may allow discrimination by restricting access to training to women over a certain age limit, if the person giving the access to training reasonably considers that members of this group are most likely to be in special need of training because of their age and the length during which they have been out of the labour market. As more women remain in the workforce for part or all of their child-rearing years, criteria which do not at least include a specific requirement that they have been out of the workforce for such domestic reasons must become less likely to satisfy the reasonableness test.

Thus section 47(3) contemplates purposefully inclusionary measures going beyond the narrower circumstances when employers and training providers can provide encouragement and training to the under-represented sex, but it is also an underutilized provision, which may well be explained by its complexity and lack of clarity.[33]

4. *The limits of the equality of opportunity approach*

While these provisions allow employers and training providers, through training and other methods, to assist women to develop the skills and knowledge and perhaps confidence needed to compete with other applicants, they draw the line at the point of recruitment. Hence no advantage may be given to the under-represented sex at the recruitment and selection stage,[34] nor in relation to promotion. In *Jones* v. *Chief Constable of Northamptonshire Police*,[35] the employment tribunal held that section 48 provided no

32 Lord Jacques, 362 *H.L. Debs.*, col. 1214 (15 July 1975).
33 Equal Opportunities Commission, *Advancing Women in the Workplace: Statistical Analysis*, working paper no. 12 and *Advancing Women in the Workplace: Case Studies*, working paper no. 13 (both 2004).
34 s. 47(4).
35 ET case no. 1201171/98 (EOR DCLD 41).

defence to a claim of sex discrimination from a male officer whose application was refused in an attempt to address the under-representation of women in the special branch. Further, the Employment Appeal Tribunal in *ACAS* v. *Taylor*[36] held that a tribunal was entitled to draw the inference that the employers had operated a policy of unlawful positive discrimination in favour of women where a sifting panel selected all the female candidates but only a few of the male candidates from a particular category for further assessment for promotion. Hence, while employers can set 'targets' to get more women into particular jobs, encourage them to apply for those jobs, and help them to compete when they do apply, they would not be able to set 'quotas' whereby a representative of an under-represented sex could be selected over a candidate who was apparently better qualified for the job or introduce a tie-break rule giving preference to a woman where candidates were equally qualified.

5. *The use of the positive action provisions*

These provisions of the SDA are little known and little understood. The whole question of positive action is controversial and it would appear that organizations prefer to steer clear of the debate rather than seek to justify lawful positive action initiatives. The fact that the provisions are narrowly drawn and complex must surely be a disincentive to employers and training providers concerned not to fall foul of the law.

Where employers and training providers, including colleges and universities, do run positive action training courses, this is usually because of the existence of funding through European Social Fund (ESF) programmes. Those accessing funding have tended to assume that where the funding is granted, this gives them the endorsement of legality. However, there appears to be a lack of understanding around the need for such courses to pass not only the test for attracting European funding but also to fall within the positive action exceptions in the SDA. It is assumed that an ESF grant must comply with European law, and if the course passes the European test, then it is considered axiomatic that it passes the British test, because British law requires to comply with European law. However, since European law in this area is permissive only, the fact that a positive action measure is compatible with European law will not provide a defence for an employer or training provider if their actions breach domestic law.

The ESF programme organizers are now alert to this issue, and require those applying for funding to 'self-certify' that a particular course meets the tests laid down in the SDA (or RRA equivalent) before they will approve the application. The most common problem with these courses comes when a complainer, usually male, alleges that he has been excluded from a particular

---

36 EAT/788/97.

course because of his sex. Upon investigation it then becomes obvious that the course organizers have not properly applied the tests laid down by the SDA, and that the issue of under-representation is not at all clear cut. On a number of occasions, training providers have run courses on subjects which will equip delegates for work in jobs where women in fact quite clearly dominate, such as basic financial services or basic information technology.[37]

For those sectors where there is a real desire to redress gender imbalance in the workforce, and in the higher levels of the hierarchy, such as the uniformed services, there is a concern that the SDA does not allow them to go far enough in their efforts to recruit and retain women members. Clearly, for those employers who are genuinely committed to addressing the under-representation problem, who recognize that the situation is the result of past disadvantage, a more liberal positive action exception which looks to equality of results, is necessary.

REFORMING THE POSITIVE ACTION PROVISIONS

It is clear that the equal treatment and equality of opportunity approaches are not delivering equality for women in the labour market.[38] We need to focus on equality of results and to introduce measures which allow for preferential treatment if further advances are going to be made. This involves a very different conceptual framework from the current approach of the SDA. Any amendment to British law must of course be compatible with European law. However, provided that such measures are proportionate, European law allows a wide margin of appreciation to member states who wish to use positive action measures to provide specific advantages to women in order to assist them in pursuing a vocational activity or to prevent or compensate women for disadvantages in their professional careers. Even within its previous formulation, limited as it was to measures designed to achieve equality of opportunity, European law would not have prevented the amendment of the SDA to allow greater freedom to employers to introduce measures to improve the situation of women in the workplace. Since the amendment of the Treaty and the adoption of the ETAD, the range of permissible measures has expanded to the extent that measures to achieve equality of results may now be adopted.

One possible model for reform would be to replicate the positive action provisions in the regulations relating to discrimination on the grounds of religion or belief or sexual orientation, which are based on the positive action

---

37 *Samuel Hardie* v. *James Watt College*, ET case no. S/101550/98.
38 COM(2005) 44, final report from the Commission to the Council, the European Parliament, the European Economic and Social Committee, and the Committee of the Regions on Equality Between men and Women. DTI, Women and Equality Unit, *Key Indicators of Women's Position in Britain* (2002).

provisions laid down by the Framework Directive. However, these regulations are limited to training or other encouragement measures:

> where it reasonably appears to [the training provider] that it prevents or compensates for disadvantages linked to sexual orientation/religion or belief suffered by persons of that sexual orientation/religion or belief doing that work or likely to take up that work.[39]

These positive action provisions are clearly not so narrowly drawn as those under the SDA which involve pointing to statistics to show that there are very small numbers of women engaged in 'particular work'. Under the regulations, by contrast, there is no requirement to focus on numbers or proportions at all, but simply, on a reasonable view, on whether or not the training or encouragement will 'prevent or compensate for disadvantages'. The SDA could be amended to allow training providers greater freedom in relation to the single-sex courses which they run, as there would be less need to focus on statistics. The provision would certainly be broad enough to encompass both training courses for women returners on the basis that this will 'compensate' them for the disadvantage suffered as a result of time out of the labour market, and guaranteed places for women on training courses relating to areas where they are under-represented, but not necessarily to the extent required by the current definition.

However, additional training is not going to address the structural inequalities faced by women in the labour market. A second model is one that requires or empowers employers to set goals and timetables to achieve equality in representation of women in the workforce and in promoted posts as part of a positive duty to promote equality.[40] Such an approach is similar to that approved in *Badeck*, although that scheme was limited to the public sector. Part of that scheme, namely, guaranteed interviews for all women who satisfy the conditions of particular posts where they are under-represented, is already a feature of the 'double tick scheme' used by many British employers committed to improving the rates of recruitment of persons with a disability.[41]

A third model would be to allow employers to devise specific schemes designed to allow parents to reconcile competing work and family priorities. Whilst such schemes run the risk of reinforcing gender stereotypes, they would nevertheless target a well-documented problem faced by many women. Examples might include: the provision of subsidized nursery places; the right of employees with caring responsibilities to work part-time at crucial periods in their careers;[42] and the requirement to consider skills

---

39 See n. 2 above.
40 Discussed in McColgan, op. cit., n. 3, pp. 151–7.
41 The Disability Symbol, double tick, was developed by Jobcentre Plus. See <http://www.jobcentreplus.gov.uk/cms.asp?Page=/Home/Customers/HelpForDisabledPeople/DisabilitySymbol>.
42 As is currently the case in Germany: *Equal Opportunities Review*, April 2001.

acquired in the family setting as part of promotions procedures where skills such as negotiation or multi-tasking are relevant to the post.

We would argue that a simple amendment of the SDA would not suffice to achieve such a fundamental revision of the approach taken by British equality laws. The structure of the legislation and its underlying concepts need to be revisited. Whilst accepting that the law should not advantage one sex over another where all things are equal, we would argue that the current law ignores the substantial disadvantages faced by women in the labour market. Always accepting that law is only one tool, and a limited tool at that, to achieve equality in the work place, the law needs to be amended to recognize that men and women are not equally situated and that positive measures need to be put in place to rectify past disadvantage and current discrimination.

41

JOURNAL OF LAW AND SOCIETY
VOLUME 33, NUMBER 1, MARCH 2006
ISSN: 0263-323X, pp. 42–58

Affirmative Action in Women's Employment: Lessons from Canada

Nicole Busby*

The use of affirmative action to increase women's representation in employment is recognized under European Community law. The European Court of Justice has identified affirmative action permissible under EC law and what constitutes reverse discrimination, deemed incompatible with the equal treatment principle. Despite these developments, gendered occupational segregation – vertical and horizontal – persists in all member states as evidenced by enduring pay gaps. It is widely argued that we now need national measures which take advantage of the appropriate framework and requisite political will which exists at the European level. Faced with a similar challenge, the Canadian government passed the Employment Equity Act 1986 which places an obligation on federal employers to implement employment equity (affirmative action) by proactive means. Although subject to some criticism, there have been some improvements in women's representation since its introduction. This article assesses what lessons might be learned from Canada's experience.

INTRODUCTION

It has long been recognized that the mere legal prohibition of discrimination will not lead to significant changes in the socio-economic position of historically disadvantaged groups. In the employment context, this is illustrated by the persistence of gendered pay gaps[1] despite the existence of

* Department of Accounting, Finance and Law, University of Stirling, Stirling FK9 4LA, Scotland
n.e.busby@stir.ac.uk

This paper is dedicated to the memories of Tom Busby, a proud Canadian, who encouraged me to look at the jurisdiction of his birth, and Doug Vick who helped me to get started.

1 In Great Britain, full-time female workers earn 18 per cent less than their male counterparts; this rises to 40 per cent for part-time workers – Equal Opportunities Commission, *Facts about Men and Women in Great Britain* (2005).

specific legislation targeted at eliminating inequalities in pay and associated terms and conditions.[2] Differences in aggregate pay levels between the sexes are not only attributable to the discriminatory acts of employers, but also arise due to the complex interrelationship between supply and demand factors. These lead to high levels of labour market segregation so that women generally work in different occupations from men and at different levels within occupational hierarchies. The reasons why individual members of particular groups work in particular jobs are manifold and it is beyond the scope of this article to provide any meaningful analysis of this issue. However, it is widely accepted that many women experience a lack of free choice and control over their career development due to barriers to both employment and promotion.[3] In the United Kingdom, current anti-discrimination measures are at their most effective in dealing with the less favourable treatment of one sex compared with the other.[4] However, where access to employment or career progression is thwarted by covert institutional factors, it can often go undetected and untouched by the law. Even in circumstances where the law might usefully be employed, many women are effectively excluded from its provisions because they do not have a suitable male comparator on whom to base a case. What is needed to ensure a more effective operation of current equality law is the redistribution of men and women across sectors of employment and occupations so that both sexes work alongside each other.

The federal government of Canada has introduced legislation[5] intended to assist the members of specific groups to overcome barriers to equality in employment. The legislation is targeted at improving the distribution of members of the designated groups across employment sectors, with the ultimate aim:

> To achieve equality in the workplace so that no person shall be denied employment opportunities or benefits for reasons unrelated to their ability and ... to correct the conditions of disadvantage in employment experienced by [members of the designated groups] by giving effect to the principle that employment equity means more than treating persons in the same way but also requires special measures and the accommodation of differences.[6]

The 'designated' groups are women, aboriginal peoples, persons with disabilities, and members of visible minorities. The legislation applies mandatory affirmative action measures to employers in the federal jurisdiction. The purpose of this article is to assess the effectiveness of those measures in

---

2 Such as the United Kingdom's Equal Pay Act 1975 and Sex Discrimination Act 1976 (SDA).
3 Based on factors such as access to education, training, and affordable childcare, restrictive working practices, and employers' assumptions about female workers.
4 For example, the prohibition of direct discrimination by s. 1(1)(a) SDA.
5 Employment Equity Acts of 1986 and 1995 (EEA).
6 EEA 1995, id., s. 2.

43

order to identify what broader lessons can be drawn from Canada's experience that might be of use to other jurisdictions, with particular emphasis on the United Kingdom. Rather than an alternative approach, Canada provides an example of supplementary legal intervention based on the same conceptualization of equality which could therefore be transplanted without the need to dismantle the current legal framework. However, the idea of affirmative action more generally *does* encompass measures that could theoretically challenge the very foundations of that framework, and these stronger measures could address some of the shortcomings of the current approach.

The Canadian legislation employs terminology that varies, in some respects, from that used elsewhere. The term 'affirmative action' itself is not present in the legislation but is replaced by 'employment equity'. This consists of a combination of 'positive policies and practices'[7] and 'reasonable accommodations' which should be made to ensure that members of the designated groups:

> achieve a degree of representation in each occupational group in the employer's workforce that reflects their representation in (i) the Canadian workforce, or (ii) those segments of the Canadian workforce that are identifiable by qualification, eligibility or geography and from which the employer may reasonably be expected to draw employees.[8]

Although emphasis is placed on setting and meeting targets, the use of quotas is prohibited.[9] Hence employment equity does not amount to reverse discrimination but is rather a form of positive action aimed at assisting members of the designated groups to reach their full potential. Although the Canadian legislation is targeted at members of the four designated groups, the focus of this article is on women's employment. It is recognized that individual women may belong to two or more of the designated groups and thus experience multiple discrimination – indeed, as discussed later, the impact of the legislation varies with respect to different groups of women. However, for reasons of simplification, gender will be considered in isolation wherever possible.

THE CONCEPTUALIZATION OF AFFIRMATIVE ACTION IN EMPLOYMENT

The attainment of equal representation of women and men in employment has long been viewed as a desirable goal, be it across sectors of employment, occupations within those sectors or within occupational hierarchies. Its achievement is desirable for reasons of social justice and because the causes

7 id., s. 5.
8 id., Part 1.
9 id., s. 6.

44

of institutional sex discrimination can best be attacked and ultimately eradicated from the inside out. Identification of the most suitable measure for achieving this goal has, thus far, eluded policy-makers, although affirmative action measures have been used with some success in related circumstances.[10] Such measures may take the form of radical policies based on sex-conscious criteria such as selecting a less well qualified female over a better qualified male for employment or promotion in order to reach a prescribed quota – so-called 'reverse discrimination'. This type of activity, although effective in improving representation and arguably morally defensible due to the deep-rooted discrimination faced by generations of women, is unlawful in most jurisdictions. This is because legal intervention is generally based on the equal opportunities approach which requires that, to show discrimination, the complainant must prove that he or she has received less favourable treatment than a member of the opposite sex.[11] This symmetrical application gives equal rights to men and women, thus preventing different treatment of either sex. However, where historical factors have been the cause of inequalities between social groups, institutional or systemic discrimination may be so deeply entrenched in the practices and processes of organizations that the provision of equality of opportunity is illusory. Furthermore, if one group has a weaker starting point, the attainment of equality is unlikely without some intervention aimed at overcoming barriers that are insurmountable by the individual members of that group.

Positive action comprises alternative forms of affirmative action which are diverse in their methods but which commonly recognize such historical inequalities and are aimed at providing assistance to the discriminated group by levelling the playing field. The targeted provision of training to increase the promotional prospects of the members of a particular group might be one such activity. Arguably, the provision of maternity rights in recognition of the relationship between women's labour market participation and family formation is another form of affirmative action.[12] Such measures must walk a political tightrope between promoting women's representation whilst avoiding legal challenge.

Canada's legislation provides an example of a mandatory positive action programme. The federal government's recognition of the need to legislate is in stark contrast to the United Kingdom's lack of activity in relation to the

---

10 For example, in the United States of America in the context of race and under Northern Ireland's fair employment legislation aimed at countering religious sectarianism.

11 See, for example, the SDA in the United Kingdom and the European Community provisions of the Equal Treatment Directive 76/207/EC. Classifications of anti-discrimination legislation generally distinguish between three approaches: formal, substantive, and equal opportunities – see S. Fredman, *Discrimination Law* (2002) 7–15.

12 Under EC law, motherhood constitutes a special case requiring different treatment for a specified 'protected period' – see Case C-394/96, *Brown* v. *Rentokil* [1998] ECR I-4185.

45

problems associated with segregated labour markets, exemplified by its benign reliance on the negative rights provided by fault-based legislation. What sets the Canadian legislation apart from its United Kingdom counterpart is its target-based approach, which requires employers to achieve prescribed outcomes or to identify and justify their failure to do so. This apparently proactive stance is worthy of consideration as a possible exemplar of what governments can do given the requisite political will. The legislation and its operation have not been without their critics and due consideration will be given to the approach of the federal government described as 'a world leader in developing equity legislation – if not in enforcing it, extending its coverage and getting results.'[13]

The Canadian legal system provides a useful comparator for United Kingdom purposes due to certain similarities between the two jurisdictions, particularly if the United Kingdom is placed within the broader context of its position as a EU member state. The top-down method of federal law making with the co-existence of provincial measures has obvious similarities with the legal competence of EU institutions and the implementation of resulting legislation within the member states. The similarities between Canada's legal and political systems and those of the United Kingdom provide further scope for comparison.[14]

The European Court of Justice has ruled that any national measure that departs from the equal treatment approach will be prohibited.[15] Similarly, although seemingly progressive, the Canadian legislation is in reality a somewhat conservative form of affirmative action at the opposite end of the spectrum from the more radical, results-based reverse discrimination. The effectiveness of such an approach is questionable, but the importance of what the public will accept in this regard should not be underestimated. The Canadian example shows how, at the very least, the under-representation of historically disadvantaged social groups can be placed on the public policy agenda.

THE DEVELOPMENT OF AFFIRMATIVE ACTION IN CANADA

The Canadian Constitution provides rights on the grounds of sex, national or ethnic origin, colour, religion, age, and mental and physical disability. The Canadian Charter of Rights and Freedoms[16] compels courts to invalidate any

---

13 C. Agócs, 'On the Need for Effective Employment Equity and Pay Equity in a Global Labour Market' in *Globalization and the Canadian Economy: The Implications for Labour Markets, Society and the State*, ed. R. Chaykowski (2001) 147.
14 The federal system of law-making is similar to that of the bicameral United Kingdom parliament and, with the exception of Quebec whose civil law is based on the Napoleonic code, the dominant model for provincial and federal law in Canada is the Anglo-Irish system.
15 Case C-450/93, *Kalanke* v. *Freie Hansestadt Bremen* [1995] ECR I-3051.
16 Inserted into the Constitution in 1982 by Schedule B of the Constitution Act 1982.

legislation introduced by the federal or provincial governments which is found to be in conflict with its provisions.[17] At the federal level, issues surrounding employment equity became prominent in public policy debates during the late 1970s. In 1978, the government launched a voluntary affirmative action programme aimed at private industry. In the same year, the Canadian Human Rights Act came into force with a mandate to reduce barriers to equality in employment. The Act permitted the use of special programmes to eliminate or reduce disadvantage. As a result of this, and a 1987 Supreme Court decision,[18] the Human Rights Tribunal was able to order affirmative action programmes to rectify systemic discrimination.[19]

In 1983, the Royal Commission on Equality in Employment[20] was established under the leadership of Judge Rosalie Silberman Abella to investigate the causes and effects of inequality in employment. The Commission engaged in extensive national research, concluding that members of the designated groups had been historically disadvantaged. Reliance on equality of opportunity alone to address such disadvantage was rejected due to the recognition that the attainment of equality sometimes involves treating people the same, despite their differences, and sometimes accommodating their differences in order to overcome barriers. To ignore or refuse to accommodate differences would be to deny equity, which will not necessarily result from the same treatment for all.[21]

In its report,[22] the Commission noted that systemic discrimination[23] created employment barriers, which could only be dismantled through specific legislation:

> It is not that individuals in the designated groups are inherently unable to achieve equality on their own, it is that the obstacles in their way are so formidable and self-perpetuating that they cannot be overcome without intervention. It is both intolerable and insensitive if we simply wait and hope that the barriers will disappear with time. Equality in employment will not happen unless we make it happen.[24]

---

17 Subject to the 'notwithstanding clause' provided by s. 33, which provides legislators with a possible 5-year exclusion. This is overridden by s. 28 which provides that the rights and freedoms are 'guaranteed equally to male and female persons'.
18 *CNR* v. *Canada (Human Rights Commission)* [1987] 1 SCR 1114.
19 This power was subsequently withdrawn.
20 Known as the Abella Commission.
21 This is an extension of the classic Aristotelian view of distributive justice that like cases should be treated alike and different cases differently. For a fuller discussion of the two prevailing approaches to the elimination of discrimination, see R.A. Lee, 'The Evolution of Affirmative Action' (1999) 28 *Public Personnel Management* 393.
22 R. Abella, *Equality in Employment: A Royal Commission Report* (1984) (the Abella report).
23 Defined as the 'unintentional consequence of employment practices and policies that have a differential effect on specific groups': H.G. Krahn and G.S. Lowe, *Work, Industry and Canadian Society* (1993).
24 Abella report, op. cit., n. 22, p. 214.

47

Their recommendations focused on three areas for policy implementation: education, childcare, and the removal of systemic barriers. The first two have received little attention over the ensuing years, with the third providing the rationale for the introduction of federal employment equity legislation.

Fear of political backlash has had a marked effect on the legislation, which has been largely shaped by the threat of public rejection.[25] Anticipation of rejection has sometimes lead to the moderation of terminology and dilution of proposed measures. However, as the Ontario experience demonstrates, it is also grounded in real experience. In Ontario, employment equity was the subject of a controversial public debate resulting in the repeal of what would have been the most progressive provincial legislation[26] and a failed challenge to the validity of this action under the Canadian Charter of Rights and Freedoms.[27] The short-lived legislation was introduced by the Ontario New Democratic Party in 1994 and required all relevant employers to take part in a planning, monitoring, and reporting process with sanctions for non-compliance, including prosecution and fines of up to $50,000. The legislation was repealed before its enactment[28] by the incoming Progressive Conservative government, which regarded it as too radical. All directives referring to employment equity were reversed and all monitoring information collected under the Act destroyed. Although the Ontario experience is based on opposition to provincial rather than federal legislation, the knee-jerk reaction demonstrates the depth of dissent that apparently radical policy in this area is likely to attract.

This is further illustrated by the terminology adopted in the drafting of the federal Acts. The phrase 'affirmative action' had been used widely since the 1970s and was given due consideration.[29] However, 'the Commission was told again and again that the phrase was ambiguous and confusing.' This led to the proposal that a new term, 'employment equity', be adopted. In attempting to provide assurances that the change in terminology did not signify a change in conception, the report states that '[n]o great principle is sacrificed in exchanging phrases of disputed definition for new ones that may be more accurate and less destructive to reasonable debate.'[30] However, there was concern that the apparent bow to political pressure might also

25 See M. Cohen, 'Employment Equity is not Affirmative Action' (1984) 6 *Cdn. Woman Studies* 23.
26 An Act to Provide for Employment Equity for Aboriginal People, People with Disabilities, Members of Racial Minorities and Women 1994.
27 *Ferrel et al.* v. *Attorney General of Ontario* [1998] 42 OR (3d) 97. See, further, Alliance for Employment Equity, 'Charter Challenge – The Case for Equity' (Spring 1998), update at <http://www.web.net/~allforee/>.
28 By the provocatively named Act to Repeal Job Quotas and Restore Merit-based Employment Practices in Ontario 1995. The repeal process was completed in just eight weeks.
29 See the Abella report, op. cit., n. 22, pp. 6–7.
30 id., p. 7.

influence the drafting and operation of the legislation itself, thus compromising its original objectives. The reasons why 'affirmative action' had such negative associations lie in the United States' experience of such programmes, predominantly in the context of race, which had caused such controversy that the term itself was deemed too strong for public acceptance.[31] Affirmative action was suffering a backlash with related practices deemed too expensive by United States employers[32] and the past use of quotas widely perceived as being unfair to white, able-bodied males.[33]

Commissioner Abella's attempts to retain the principles and overall objectives of affirmative action, albeit with the use of more palatable terminology, appear to have been lost in the detail. Very few of the Commission's 117 recommendations made it into the statute, and those that did were substantially watered down. It is difficult to assess the extent to which the divergence between the Commission's vision and the resulting legislation was attributable to the change in terminology, but it does reflect the political climate at the time which was less than welcoming to the new approach.

THE EMPLOYMENT EQUITY ACTS 1986 AND 1995

The first Employment Equity Act (EEA) was enacted on 13 August 1986. The Act had three major premises: first, no one should be denied employment opportunities and benefits for reasons unrelated to ability; second, special measures would be necessary to improve the employment situation of members of the designated groups; and third, the duty to make a 'reasonable accommodation' would require employers to recognize legitimate differences between groups and to take steps to accommodate them.[34] Its scope was restricted to those employed by federally regulated companies[35] with 100 or more employees, covering 350 employers in total. The federal public service was excluded from its scope and, instead, required to participate in an employment equity programme requiring employers to prepare statistical

---

31 See L. Chavez, *The Color Blind: California's Battle to End Affirmative Action* (1998).
32 See Cohen, op. cit., n. 25.
33 For the Canadian take on the 'business case' against affirmative action legislation, see T. Wilson, *Diversity at Work: the Business Case for Equity* (1996). For an analysis of the effects of male backlash on the organizational climate, see J.A. Gilbert and J.M. Ivancevich, 'Organizational Diplomacy: The Bridge for Managing Diversity' (1999) 22 *Human Resource Planning* 29. A further study found that the backlash had not subsided following the introduction of the legislation with resultant negative effects on employers' attitudes: J.A. Gilbert et al., 'Diversity Management: A New Organizational Paradigm' (1999) 21 *J. of Business Ethics* 61.
34 *Ontario Human Rights Commission and O'Malley* v. *Simpson Sears Ltd* [1985] 2 SCR 536.
35 So-called 'Crown corporations'.

data on their workforce to identify under-representation of the designated groups and to endeavour to meet predetermined numerical targets.[36]

Although the legislation was welcomed as an agenda-setting initiative,[37] criticism was levelled on a number of grounds including its restricted scope.[38] The legislation's focus on *reporting* rather than *achieving* was seen as a major weakness: failure to report was subject to a maximum fine of $50,000, but discrimination against the designated groups attracted no penalty. Furthermore, the continuation of discriminatory practices and/or the identification of retrograde positioning of the designated groups were not formally sanctioned. The lack of clear enforcement mechanisms was identified as particularly problematic. The Minister for Employment and Immigration's response that the public disclosure of reports required under the Act would mean that those in breach of their obligations would 'have to answer to the people of Canada if they fail to achieve equality in employment'[39] was received with derision.

Following a parliamentary review, a revised Act came into force in 1996. More comprehensive than its predecessor, the new Act extended coverage to the federal public service, mandated the Human Rights Commission to conduct on-site compliance reviews, and provided for the Act's enforcement by an Employment Equity Review Tribunal which has the power to hear disputes and issue orders. Employers' obligations were also extended and the monitoring, consultation, and reporting functions required under the Act were improved. Part 1 sets out the obligations placed on employers to identify and eliminate employment barriers against those in the designated groups. The focus is on achieving levels of representation in accordance with those in the wider population wherever possible. Section 6 provides that employers will not be required to take any particular measure 'where the taking of that measure would cause undue hardship to that employer'. Furthermore, employers are prevented from hiring or promoting unqualified persons or from creating new positions in the workforce. These provisions prohibit the use of quotas[40] so that employment equity does not amount to reverse discrimination but, rather, to positive action achieved through the setting of 'flexible, rational targets that employers can use, like all business goals, as planning and evaluation tools.'[41]

---

36 Minister of Supply and Services, *Employment Equity in the Public Service, Annual Report 1992–1993* (1994).
37 The literature does record some minor improvements following the Act's introduction: see H.C. Jain and R.D. Hackett, 'Measuring Effectiveness of Employment Equity Programs in Canada: Public Policy and a Survey' (1989) XV *Cnd. Public Policy* 189; J.D. Leck and D.M. Saunders, 'Canada's Employment Equity Act: Effects on Employee Selection' (1992) 11 *Population Research and Policy Rev.* 21.
38 See Cohen, op. cit., n. 25, p. 24.
39 Press release to accompany the Employment Equity Bill C-62 (1985).
40 See Department of Human Resources and Skills Development, *Employment Equity: Myths and Realities* (2003).
41 id., p. 7.

50

Section 9 requires employers to collect and analyse information to determine the degree of representation of the designated groups in each occupational sector and to review all employment systems, policies, and practices to identify barriers. Only those who self-identify as members of the designated groups will be monitored, with all information classified as confidential and used only to satisfy the employer's obligations under the Act. The employment equity plan must specify the 'positive policies and practices' instituted by the employer in the short term[42] in relation to hiring, training, promotion, and retention of persons in the designated groups and for the making of reasonable accommodations to correct any under-representation. The long-[43] and short-term goals for increasing representation should be specified along with the measures to be taken to eliminate identified barriers. A timetable for implementation must be established. Under section 11, employers should ensure that the plan would constitute 'reasonable progress' toward implementing employment equity. The workforce must be informed of the contents of the plan and of any progress made.[44] Employee representatives shall be consulted on the plan's contents and their views sought on how they might assist the employer to implement employment equity.[45]

The record-keeping requirements of the Act are provided for under sections 17–21. Annual reports must be filed with the appropriate governmental body. For private sector employers, this is Human Resources Development Canada (HRDC) and, for public sector employers, the Treasury Board.[46] The relevant Ministers table annual consolidated reports in Parliament on the state of employment equity in the private and public sectors. A copy of every employer's report is filed with the Canadian Human Rights Commission (CHRC), which is responsible for ensuring compliance with the Act[47] and is authorized to conduct an audit of every employer governed by the Act. In cases of non-compliance, an officer will negotiate a written undertaking from the employer to take specific remedial steps. If such an undertaking cannot be obtained, the Commission has the power to issue a direction to take specific action.[48] If an employer fails to act on such direction, the matter can be referred to the Employment Equity Review Tribunal for an order,[49] which will not be subject to appeal, except for judicial review under the Federal Court Act. No order can be made that would cause an employer undue hardship or require the hiring or promotion

---

42 Defined, under s. 10 (3), as a period of not less than 1 year and not more than 3 years.
43 Defined, under s. 10(3), as a period of more than 3 years
44 s. 14.
45 s. 15.
46 Public Service Human Resources Management Agency of Canada, *The Employment Equity Act (1996) from a Public Service Perspective* (2002).
47 s. 22.
48 s. 24.
49 s. 29.

of unqualified persons, creation of new positions or the imposition of quotas.[50] The CHRC makes a consolidated report on the employment equity audits in its Annual Report.

MEASURING SUCCESS

Although the Act places clear record-keeping obligations on employers and the CHRC, a lack of available resources has caused a delay in the national audit process and restrictions in the type of information included. At the time of writing, the most recent year for which these statistics are available is 2001.[51] Women's representation in the private sector has risen from 40.9 per cent in 1987 to 44.8 per cent in 2001. The current figure represents 96.6 per cent of their labour market availability of 46.4 per cent. In the federal public service, women's representation has increased from 42.4 per cent in 1987 to 51.5 per cent in 2001. The distribution of women's employment has continued to be highly concentrated in clerical-related occupations, although significant progress has been made in management and professional occupations since the Act's introduction.[52]

Given the Act's focus on employers within the federal jurisdiction, it is perhaps not surprising that levels of women's representation vary significantly between provinces.[53] Within the federal framework, the provincial governments have responsibility for the development, implementation, and administration of local legislation and policy.[54] At the time of writing, only one of the ten provinces (British Columbia) has employment equity legislation in place. In their study of provincial approaches to employment equity policy, Bakan and Kobayashi found such wide variations that 'even the development of a series of common criteria risks obscuring the nuances'.[55] They concluded that the existence of provincial policy does make a difference to the employment experiences of individuals with marked improvements in female representation occurring in those provinces with more advanced and better resourced policies.[56]

---

50 s. 33.
51 Canadian Human Rights Commission <http://www.chrc-ccdp.ca/publications/page4-en.asp>.
52 J.D. Leck, 'Making Employment Equity Programs Work for Women' (2002) XXVIII *Cnd. Public Policy Supplement* 85, 89.
53 The highest representation of women in the workforce was found in New Brunswick (51.8 per cent) and the lowest in Manitoba (37.4 per cent).
54 On the various provincial policy initiatives, see H. Antecol and P. Kuhn, 'Employment Equity Programs and the Job Search Outcomes of Unemployed Men and Women' (1999) 25 *Cnd. Public Policy* 28.
55 A. Bakan and A. Kobayashi, *Employment Equity Policy in Canada: An Interprovincial Comparison* (2000) 8.
56 id., p. 65. The authors make a distinction between representation and distribution, noting that the distribution of women across occupations had not significantly

In the federal public service, numerical progress towards achieving representation of the designated groups has been modest but steady over the last decade. Out of the four designated groups, women have fared best, closing the representation gap most quickly, by about 1 per cent per year. This has occurred during a period of major downsizing within the Canadian labour market[57] so that, although the actual number of women in the public sector declined by about 10 per cent during the 1990s, their proportional representation increased from 46.1 per cent in 1993 to 50.5 per cent in 1998.

It is impossible conclusively to attribute such increases wholly or even partially to the effects of the legislation; however the indications are that employment equity has been moderately successful in improving women's representation[58] despite unfavourable economic conditions. Even so, the data and their interpretation must be viewed with extreme caution. The three other designated groups have not experienced the same level of improvement in representation and a lack of cross-referencing information makes it difficult to identify the effects on women who are members of one or more of the other designated groups. Furthermore, the indicators show little sign that distribution has improved or that systemic barriers, which hinder women's movement across sectors and up occupational hierarchies, have been removed.[59] The increase in women's representation signals a starting point in the process of change rather than a happy ending. As Bakan and Kobayashi have observed:

> Equity is like an onion, consisting of many layers and no core; without numerical representation, the other layers – including redistribution, removal of systemic barriers and changing workplace culture – cannot be supported.[60]

improved. Furthermore, despite the advances made by 'women' as a designated group, women in the other three groups had not experienced any improvements in representation or distribution.

57 The total public service declined by 16.2 per cent between 1994 and 1997: Public Service Commission of Canada, *Diversity Management Directorate, Employment Systems Review: A Guide for the Federal Public Service* (1998).

58 The literature appears to support this, see Antecol and Kuhn, op. cit., n. 54. The same survey also found negative perceptions of employment equity among respondents with women unable to identify or acknowledge increases in re-employment rates and men believing themselves (erroneously) to be the victims of reverse discrimination.

59 See J. Leck and D. Saunders, 'Hiring Women: The Effects of Canada's Employment Equity Act' (1992) 18 *Cnd. Public Policy* 203; C. Edwards and O. Robinson, 'Lost Opportunities? Organisational Restructuring and Women Managers' (1999) 9 *Human Resource Management J.* 55.

60 Bakan and Kobayashi, op. cit., n. 55, p. 17.

Having surveyed the Canadian experience, consideration will now be given to how it might be used to inform the future development of affirmative action policies in other jurisdictions, particularly in the United Kingdom. First, the provisions of the Canadian legislation will be examined to identify areas of weakness. Secondly, the conceptualization of equality on which the legislation is based will be considered.

One of the main criticisms levelled at the Canadian Acts has been their restrictive scope. This arises, at least in part, due to the introduction of the legislation at federal level. The Acts' provisions now extend to 1,400 federally regulated private and public sector organizations with a minimum of 100 employees each, representing approximately 2 million workers or 12 per cent of Canada's labour force.[61] Conversely, 88 per cent of Canada's labour force falls under provincial jurisdiction. As noted above, not all of Canada's provinces have employment equity policies in place and there is evidence of widespread diversity in levels of awareness and understanding of common terms and approaches.[62] This indicates the importance of well-resourced educational programmes as a means of supplementing and supporting affirmative action legislation, particularly when used as a top-down policy instrument. Education *was* identified as an essential component in Abella's vision of effective employment equity legislation[63] and perhaps more attention should have been paid to this recommendation, particularly in light of the nature of Canada's legal system and the geographical and socio-economic diversity between the provinces.

Weaknesses in the current Canadian enforcement mechanisms are also attributable to a lack of investment in the necessary resources. The focus on monitoring requires a substantial and sustained investment in the audit process if the resulting data is to be used in any meaningful way. A comprehensive system of record-keeping is only as good as the quality and usefulness of the information collected. This should facilitate deeper analyses of the root causes of disadvantage by such methods as cross-referencing to identify multiple discriminations.

In addition, the bodies charged with upholding and developing the law must have defined functions and duties, preferably enshrined in the legislation itself. In Canada, the CHRC has called for a clearer mandate in

---

61 Communications, Energy and Paperworkers Union of Canada (CEP), 'Submission to the Canadian Human Rights Commission concerning the Federal Employment Equity Act' (2002), at <http://www.cep.ca.human_rights/equity/brief/>.

62 Bakan and Kobayashi, op. cit., n. 55.

63 On the importance of education, employee involvement, and training in improving understanding and acceptance of employment equity programmes at the organizational level, see Leck, op. cit., n. 52.

respect of its role,[64] arguing that the statutory requirements for employer compliance need to be more clearly articulated to aid enforcement and avoid confusion at the workplace level. Furthermore, the standards used by the Commission are not explicit within the legislation, giving rise to legal challenges by employers resulting in delays in enforcement and the diversion of valuable resources. If such difficulties are to be avoided in other jurisdictions, it is imperative that adequate resources are made available to relevant statutory bodies, which must be equipped with clearly defined and effective powers of enforcement.

All of these aspects indicate that affirmative action legislation cannot be viewed as a quick fix, but requires serious and on-going commitment on the part of government as part of a broader policy framework. This factor has resonance in the United Kingdom context, particularly in light of any future legislative initiatives that might arise due to its position as an EU member state. Given the EU institutions' recent focus on the coordination of employment policy in favour of the harmonization of social standards through legislation,[65] the emergence of new initiatives via this route seems unlikely in the foreseeable future. However, should affirmative action ever find its way onto the Commission's legislative programme, the need to ensure the widest possible scope, well-resourced educational and monitoring provisions, statutory enforcement at national level, and constant review might make progress under the European system of law-making difficult to achieve.

As well as such operational difficulties, there is a more fundamental barrier to the success of Canada's employment equity. Its central flaw is its dependence on the pre-existing legal framework and corresponding conceptualization of equality. As noted in the Introduction, the equal opportunities approach to remedying historical disadvantage is severely limited due to its acceptance of the very foundations of such disadvantage. Although the Canadian approach may appear to offer a more proactive means of confronting inequalities, it is not in fact that different from existing United Kingdom legislation. This point can be illustrated with reference to what is generally accepted as the major contributory factor to women's continuing economic inequality: gendered work patterns and resultant occupational segregation.

Canada's employment equity has been designed to provide equality within standard work arrangements based on the full-time, permanent model.

---

64 Canadian Human Rights Commission, *Legislative Review of the Employment Equity Act, Report and Recommendations to the House of Commons Standing Committee on Human Resources and Development and the Status of Persons with Disabilities* (2002).

65 Under the European Employment Strategy, see D. Ashiagbor, 'EMU and the Shift in the Labour Law Agenda: from "Social Policy" to "Employment Policy" ' (2001) 7 *European Law J.* 311.

However, the labour markets of most industrialized economies are increasingly moving towards non-standard arrangements with high proportions of the workforce currently engaged in so-called 'atypical' employment.[66] With many of the new working arrangements operating at the lower-paid, more 'flexible' end of the market, newly created jobs are predominantly filled by women.[67] Conversely, the work arrangement used as a standard against which other employment types are judged to be 'atypical' is a male standard and has little in common with the career experiences of most low-paid female workers. Despite its claims to be proactive, the Canadian legislation is the same as that already in use in the United Kingdom, in that it does not question the comparative nature of the equal opportunities conceptualization of anti-discrimination law, but actually reinforces the dominance of the male norm.

The problems associated with occupational segregation will never be eradicated until labour market policies which single out non-standard working patterns as somehow deviant are adequately challenged. The retrospective monitoring required under the EEA does nothing to assist in this respect, but rather tells us where and how the designated groups are employed. This is a useful starting point but requires clear provisions aimed at changing such persistent patterns of labour market behaviour if equal representation is to be achieved. The stumbling block here is that, under the current legal regime, such measures are likely to be interpreted as preferential treatment, thereby crossing the line between the legally acceptable realms of positive action and reverse discrimination prohibited by law. For example, the EEA's focus on targets rather than quotas appears, at first glance, to be a results-based means of addressing under-representation. However, the legal framework with which employers must comply is highly restrictive and actually serves to reproduce inequalities present in the wider Canadian economy.

Targets must correspond to the proportion of suitably qualified and eligible members of the designated groups available for employment within the relevant segment of the Canadian labour market.[68] Rather than challenging the reasons why high numbers of designated group members are unable to comply with the necessary criteria, the EEA serves to justify employers' decision-making on the basis of such criteria. Of course, employers cannot be compelled to employ applicants incapable of carrying out the job merely to achieve representational targets, but how deeply does

---

66 One-third of Canada's workforce is currently engaged in such arrangements: see J. Fudge and L. Vosko, 'Gender, Segmentation and the Standard Employment Relationship in Canadian Law and Policy' (2001) 22 *Economic and Industrial Democracy* 271; C. Cranford et al., 'Precarious Employment in the Canadian Labour Market: A Statistical Portrait' (Fall 2003) 3 *Just Labour* 6.

67 S. Fredman, 'Women at Work: The Broken Promise of Flexicurity' (2004) 33 *Industrial Law J.* 299.

68 EEA 1995, s.5.

the legislation require scrutiny of the selection criteria for employment or promotion? What steps are taken to ensure that such criteria are valid and not merely part of an arbitrary value system based on exclusionary factors? Even if the criteria *are* valid, what measures are in place to determine why designated group members are not making the grade? To address such issues effectively, the 'accommodation of difference' must form a cornerstone of legislative activity requiring reconsideration of what is commonly perceived as 'preferential treatment',[69] yet the Canadian prohibition of reverse discrimination prevents this. The differences between women and men's attachment to the labour market are both biological (childbirth, breast-feeding) and socially constructed by defined gender roles (division of labour within families). To truly accommodate such differences would require a wide range of measures aimed at redressing the current imbalances that typify the experiences of women in the public sphere and those of men in the private.[70] Anything less than this would merely amount to tinkering around the edges. Quotas are part of the solution, although not in isolation; their achievement depends on other measures such as legal protection for those engaged in 'non-standard' working arrangements[71] and a re-evaluation of the more subjective criteria on which employers' decisions are based.[72] As the Canadian experience has shown, numerical targets alone are unlikely to prove an effective means of eradicating existing inequalities.[73]

CONCLUSION

The central lesson to be learned from Canada is that employment equity simply does not go far enough. It may be affirmative action, but it has not achieved what it set out to do. Although, in theory, the Canadian legislation

69 For a compelling critique of the conceptualization of affirmative action in policy-making, see C. Bacchi, 'Policy and Discourse: Challenging the Construction of Affirmative Action as Preferential Treatment' (2004) 11 *J. of European Public Policy* 128.
70 C. Echevarria and M. Huq, 'Redesigning Employment Equity in Canada: The Need to Include Men' (2001) XXVIII *Cnd. Public Policy* 53 suggest that the next logical step is to increase male employment in female-dominated occupations. This would have the dual benefits of reducing the occupational segregation that ghettoizes 'women's work' and producing an effective response to the male backlash which arises where programmes are focused on increasing women's representation.
71 This would necessitate provisions far beyond the United Kingdom's current 'right to request' a flexible working arrangement provided by s. 104(c) of the Employment Rights Act 1996.
72 For example, to take account of experience other than that based on length of service for promotion purposes.
73 Incidentally, although not specifically provided for in the United Kingdom's legislative framework, the use of targets is already legally acceptable and is actually encouraged under European provisions.

provides a model, its reliance on inputs and processes rather than results means that it is too weak and its progress too slow to amount to a success story. The only way to achieve equality of outcomes is through the imposition of measures which are prohibited under the current legal framework, at least until all designated groups achieve true representation within all sectors and at all levels within employment structures.[74] The need for public acceptance in the adoption of new policy make it easy to see why Canada chose the direction that it took at that time in its history. The Canadian legislation *does* refer to 'special measures'[75] and 'positive policies and practices' and it is reasonable to question, therefore, whether there is any potential scope for the development of these provisions in the future. Likewise, experience in the United Kingdom has steered policy makers away from this approach, but would a re-evaluation of the conception of equality really constitute an unacceptable departure from current thinking? Without it, Abella's vision of affirmative action will never be realized, in Canada or beyond.

74 See Ronald Dworkin's argument that an individual's right to 'equal treatment' can be set aside if justified by a policy goal which aims to provide 'treatment as an equal' to all members of society: R. Dworkin, *Taking Rights Seriously* (1978) 223–39.
75 ss. 2 and 10(1)(a) EEA 1995. The CHRC has called for improved articulation of these terms, which have, until now, been interpreted in accordance with a perceived prohibition of quotas and related measures.

JOURNAL OF LAW AND SOCIETY
VOLUME 33, NUMBER 1, MARCH 2006
ISSN: 0263-323X, pp. 59–73

Affirmative Action: A German Perspective on the Promotion of Women's Rights with Regard to Employment

ANKE J. STOCK*

This paper discusses affirmative action policies in Germany. After German reunification, women from both east and west had hoped for a new codification of their rights, including positive obligations on the state to promote gender equality. However, the amendments to the Basic Law in November 1994 did not clearly endorse this approach. Opinions still differ as to whether Articles 3(2) and 3(3) of the Constitution allow for affirmative action with regard to women's employment. In 2001 quotas for the public employment sector were finally introduced, but the use of quotas for private sector employment still faces serious opposition. Nevertheless, the concept of affirmative action is not new to the German legal system: since the eighteenth century, quota schemes have been used to ensure the employment of (war-)disabled persons. This article examines the different approaches to employment quotas for women and disabled persons, and critically evaluates the reasons for divergence.

INTRODUCTION

The social integration of groups that have been discriminated against is determined by, among other things, their labour force participation rate, which is a clear indication of the power structure within a social group.[1] This observation is all the more valid in circumstances of high unemployment, such as pertain in Germany today.[2]

* *Women in Europe for a Common Future, Blumenstrasse 28, 80331 Munich, Germany*
anke.stock@web.de

1 J.H. Sidanius and R.C. Veniegas, 'Gender and Race Discrimination: The Interactive Nature of Disadvantage' in *Reducing Prejudice and Discrimination*, ed. S. Oskamp (2000) 47 ff.
2 In 2005, c. 9.5 per cent, <http://www.destatis.de/indicators/d/arb430ad.htm>.

One means of promoting labour force participation is through the use of affirmative action. Special measures are currently used within the public sector in Germany to promote women's employment, and, since 2001, these have included binding quotas. However, the legality and appropriateness of affirmative action for women remains controversial, and this has so far prevented any extension of mandatory quotas to the private employment sector. Yet, the introduction of quotas was not the legal novelty that it might have appeared. Quotas have, in fact, been used to ensure employment for disabled persons since the eighteenth century. Moreover, these have never been restricted to the public sector.

It is not the aim of this article to assess the effectiveness or desirability of a quota system for women's employment in the private sector. Rather, the aim is to challenge the distinction between quotas for women and for disabled persons. The argument is that this distinction is not due to any difference in the social position of these two groups, nor in the constitutional protection afforded to them. Rather, the difference is merely in the social and political acceptability of providing special assistance to them. Accordingly, it is argued that the acceptance of quotas for disabled persons means that there can be no objection in principle to the adoption of quotas for women.

DISCRIMINATION AGAINST WOMEN AND DISABLED PERSONS

The Federal Republic of Germany has a population of some 82 million people. Women account for the majority of the population (51.2 per cent). In 2001, women made up 43.6 per cent of the workforce in the former federal territory and 45.5 per cent in the new federal states and East Berlin.[3] The labour force participation rate of women is around 65 per cent compared to 79 per cent of men.[4] The average gross monthly earnings of female employees in manufacturing, wholesale and retail trade was still €1,000 less than that of male employees in 2001.[5]

In May 2003, 8.4 million people were living with a disability, around 10 per cent of the German population.[6] The labour force participation rate of younger disabled persons is around 72 per cent, compared to 88 per cent of

---

3 United Nations, Convention on the Elimination of All Forms of Discrimination against Women, *5th Periodic Report of States Parties* (5 February 2003) Appendix 1, CEDAW/C/DEU/5 at <http://daccessdds.un.org/doc/UNDOC/GEN/N03/250/50/ PDF/ N0325050.pdf?OpenElement>.
4 Statistisches Bundesamt Deutschland, employment statistics (2004) at <http:// www.destatis.de/ basis/d/erwerb/erwerbtab1.php>.
5 UN, op. cit., n. 3, Appendix 1.
6 Statistisches Bundesamt Deutschland, *Living Conditions of Disabled Persons* (2004) at <http://www. destatis.de/presse/deutsch/pm2004/p5140085.htm>.

non-disabled persons.[7] Disabled persons also earn less on average than non-disabled persons.[8]

These figures show that there are still huge discrepancies in the position of men and women in Germany, as well as between disabled and non-disabled persons. Neither group holds a dominant position in German society. So far, for example, only three women, and no disabled people, have held high-ranking positions in the German state bureaucracy.[9] In the constitutional court (*Bundesverfassungsgericht*), similarly, only three out of sixteen judges are women and none is disabled.[10] No exact statistics are available for management positions in the private sector, but the percentages of women and disabled persons are again very low.

Accordingly, although women constitute a far larger proportion of the population than disabled people, both may be said to constitute minority groups. There is no generally acknowledged definition of a minority, but one main criterion that is used to distinguish a minority from the majority is the group's position of power in society.[11] As minorities, it may thus be argued that both women and disabled persons are in need of, and entitled to, special protection that is not accorded to the majority. Nevertheless, the two groups are distinguished from the majority group by different criteria. As we shall see, the law treats, and it appears that society perceives, the criterion 'disability' differently from the criterion 'sex'.

AFFIRMATIVE ACTION FOR WOMEN: THE DEVELOPMENT OF THE LAW

1. *Academic arguments*

Prior to the amendment of the Basic Law of the Federal Republic of Germany (*Grundgesetz*) in 1994, women's rights were guaranteed in one Article of the Constitution – Article 3. The first sentence of Article 3(2) – the 'equal rights Article' – read: 'Men and women are equal'. Article 3(3) set out a general ban on discrimination on specific grounds such as sex, parentage, language, homeland and origin, faith, religious and political opinions.

---

7 id.
8 id.
9 Annemarie Renger was the Bundestag's presiding officer from 1972 to 1976 and Rita Süssmuth held the same office between 1988 and 1998. In November 2005, Angela Merkel became Germany's first female chancellor.
10 See the website of the Bundesverfassungsgericht <http://www.bundesverfassungs gericht.de/cgi-bin/link.pl?richter>.
11 D. Eglin, *Demokratie und Minderheiten* (1998) 180; D. Murswieck, 'Schutz der Minderheiten in Deutschland' in *Handbuch des Staatsrechts der Bundesrepublik Deutschland Band 8*, eds. J. Isensee et al. (1995).

Nothing within these two paragraphs of Article 3, which came into force in 1949, hinted at the possibility of affirmative measures. The prevailing interpretation was that both paragraphs contained a simple prohibition of discrimination and that only biological differences could justify differentiation between the sexes.

However, in the 1970s a number of academics argued that the equal rights principle in fact imposed a 'positive obligation' on the state to promote equal rights wherever there are inequalities in the social position of men and women.[12] This idea, it was claimed, was embedded within the 'welfare state principle' of Articles 20(1) and 28(1) of the Basic Law. This latter principle, which has constitutional status, counterbalances the individualistic regulatory principles of the basic rights. It serves to protect weaker members of society and commits the state to ensuring that such people enjoy, like everyone else, freedom from want, human dignity, and an adequate share in general prosperity. Its broader aim is to guarantee a just and balanced organization of social conditions. The definition of the welfare state principle is not exclusionary; its scope of application includes, for example, the entire field of social security and state social security benefits.

Nevertheless, there were different opinions about the precise nature of this positive obligation. Some saw the equal rights principle of Article 3(2) of the Basic Law (old version) as a guiding principle (*Richtlinienfunktion*) to be taken into account when developing law and policy;[13] others, more as a binding obligation (*Verfassungsauftrag*)[14] on the state to work towards the advancement of women's rights.

More progressive academics[15] put forward an interpretation of the equal rights Article as a collective right in comparison to the individual rights approach of Article 3(3). They argued that the existence of systemic and structural discrimination against women should give women *as a group* the right to equality of treatment through affirmative action. This interpretation was based on the plural wording of Article 3(1) ('Men and women are equal'), in contrast to the singular wording of the prohibition of discrimination principle of Article 3(3). Furthermore, this argument was underpinned by the idea that Article 3(2) constituted a *lex specialis* to Article 3(3); in other words, being more specific, it prevails over the general rule set out in Article 3(3).

12 K.H. Friauf, *Gleichberechtigung der Frau als Verfassungsauftrag* (1981).
13 W. Schmitt Glaeser, *Abbau des tatsächlichen Gleichberechtigungsdefizits der Frauen durch gesetzliche Quotenregelungen* (1982) 32.
14 For example, A. Dix, *Gleichberechtigung durch Gesetz* (1984) 374; H.M. Pfarr, *Quoten und Grundgesetz* (1988) 55 ff., 73.
15 V. Slupik, *Die Entscheidung des Grundgesetzes für Parität im Geschlechterverhältnis* (1988) 98; S. Raasch, *Frauenquoten und Männerrechte* (1991) 77 ff.; U. Sacksofsky, *Das Grundrecht auf Gleichberechtigung* (1996) 312 ff.

2. The Federal Constitutional Court

Until 1987, the Federal Constitutional Court (*Bundesverfassungsgericht*) endorsed the view that Articles 3(2) and 3(3) of the Basic Law (old version) contained a simple prohibition of discrimination, and hence that any differentiation between men and women except '. . . objective biological and functional differentiations . . .' was unconstitutional.[16]

However, this interpretation began to change in 1987. In a judgment on retirement age (*Rentenalterentscheidung*),[17] the Court for the first time allowed differential treatment *not* based upon biological difference if this served to compensate for disadvantages, relying on the welfare state principle to justify its decision. This made it possible to justify a younger retirement age for women as compensation for their disadvantages deriving from the double burden of family and work.

In 1992, the Court expanded this new formula and held, in its now-famous judgment on night work (*Nachtarbeitsurteil*),[18] that provisions that differentiate may be acceptable '. . . if they are essential to solve problems that by nature either apply to men or to women . . .'. Moreover, the Court held that '. . . factual disadvantages which are typically borne by women can be compensated through promotional actions . . .'. Thus, a strict test had been developed, requiring that any unequal treatment be proportional to the aim of securing *de facto* equality between men and women.

Henceforth, the Court endorsed the view that Article 3(2) of the Basic Law (old version) included more than the equal rights principle; it also included an obligation (or a constitutional guarantee) on the state to endorse the equal rights principle in social life. Article 3(2) was no longer seen as a provision that bans discrimination; it became a provision demanding equal participation of men and women in society. Nevertheless, the Court avoided specifying the precise extent to which this imposed a binding obligation on the state and it therefore remained open to further interpretation.

3. The 1994 amendment of the Basic Law

Although these academic and judicial developments had put the idea of promoting women's rights through positive state measures on the political and legal agenda, affirmative action, especially in the form of quotas, nevertheless remained unrealizable under the old Basic Law.

After the reunification of Germany, women from both the former German Democratic Republic and from the old western part of Germany had hoped for a new codification of their rights within a new Constitution, as was

---

16 See H.D. Jarass, 'Artikel 3' in H.D. Jarass and B. Pieroth, *Grundgesetz für die Bundesrepublik Deutschland* (2000) 81.

17 Decision of the Federal Constitutional Court, BVerfGE 74, 163 ff., 28 January 1987.

18 Decision of the Federal Constitutional Court, BVerfGE 85, 191 ff., 28 January 1992.

63

provided for in Article 146 Basic Law (old version) in this eventuality. In the end, however, the political majority opted simply for the accession of the German Democratic Republic to the Federal Republic of Germany according to Article 23 Basic Law (old version) and thus the perpetuation of the Basic Law, rather than drafting a wholly new Constitution. As regards women's rights, though, long discussions and over two years of work finally led to the following compromise within the existing Basic Law, adding what is commonly referred to as the 'compensation clause' to Article 3(2):

> Article 3 [Equality before the law]
> (1) All humans are equal before the law.
> (2) Men and women are equal. The state supports the effective realization of the equality of women and men and works towards abolishing present disadvantages.

Nevertheless, the anti-discrimination regulation of Article 3(3) remained unchanged in relation to sex discrimination, although another sentence was added reflecting the needs of disabled persons to codify their rights in the Constitution. It now reads:

> (3) No one may be disadvantaged or favoured because of his sex, parentage, race, language, homeland and origin, his faith or his religious or political opinions. No one may be disadvantaged because of his handicap.

Once again, therefore, it was not entirely clear from the wording of the new Article 3 whether affirmative action, in particular quota systems, would be lawful or not. In general it was understood that the new version of Article 3(2) should include a 'constitutional guarantee' (*Staatsziel*) of the equal rights principle,[19] but there was no agreement that it should constitute an individually justiciable right or be enforceable against third parties. However, the provision also seemed to endorse the Federal Constitutional Court's decision in its 1992 judgment on night work that '... factual disadvantages which are typically borne by women can be compensated through affirmative action.'[20] The question thus arose as to what kind of affirmative action would be constitutionally acceptable. Several Federal states, the so-called Länder, tested the principle by enacting progressive laws for the public sphere that stipulated affirmative action in the form of performance-linked quotas, that is, quotas that give women preference as long as they have the same qualifications as their male competitors. These laws provoked legal challenges, which finally came before the European Court of Justice (ECJ).

---

19 L. Osterloh. 'Artikel 3' in *Grundgesetz*, eds. M. Sachs et al. (1999) 262; R Scholz, 'Artikel 3 II' in *Grundgesetz I*, ed. G. Dürig (2001) 60.
20 Decision of the Federal Constitutional Court, BVerfGE 85, 191 ff. (207), 28 January 1992.

4. The impact of the European Court of Justice

In these cases, the European Court of Justice (ECJ) was able to provide the German legal system with assistance regarding the permissible scope of affirmative action, in particular, quotas. However, the first significant judgment of the ECJ, *Eckhard Kalanke* v. *Freie Hansestadt Bremen*,[21] came as a shock to German women's rights campaigners. The Court held that paragraph 4 of the Bremen Law on Equal Treatment for Men and Women in the Public Service, which automatically foresaw the preference of a woman over a man in a promotion procedure where both were equally qualified, was *not* compatible with Article 2(4) of the Equal Treatment Directive (ETD).[22] Article 2(4) reads:

> This Directive shall be without prejudice to measures to promote equal opportunity for men and women, in particular by removing existing inequalities which affect women's opportunities in the areas referred to in Article 1(1).[23]

The prevailing opinion[24] is that this has a wider reach than the new compensation clause in the Basic Law in relation to the extent of compensation of disadvantages permitted. Hence, women's rights campaigners feared that a measure that was not deemed lawful under the ETD would also fall outside the scope of Article 3(2) of the Basic Law.

However, it soon became clear that the ECJ had not intended to rule out any form of quotas to address the issue of equal opportunity. In another German case, *Hellmut Marschall* v. *Land Nordrhein-Westfalen*,[25] the Court held that an affirmative measure which allowed the preferential employment of a woman over a man provided that both are equally qualified *was* consistent with Community law as long as any disproportionate disadvantages to male competitors were balanced by a saving clause. Rules that give priority to women in employment or promotion procedures are thus in accordance with Community law if:

> ... in each individual case the rule provides for male candidates [...] a guarantee that the candidatures will be the subject of an objective assessment which take account of all criteria specific to the individual candidates and will override the priority accorded to female candidates where one or more of those criteria tilts the balance in favour of the male candidate ...[26]

---

21 Case C-450/93, *Eckhard Kalanke* v. *Freie Hansestadt Bremen* [1995] ECR I-3051.
22 Council Directive 76/207/EEC of 9 February 1976 on the Implementation of the Principle of Equal Treatment for Men and Women as Regards Access to Employment, Vocational Training and Promotion, and Working Conditions. (OJ/14 February 1976/L/039/pp. 40–42).
23 Article 1(1) includes access to employment, including promotion.
24 See, for example, K. Schweizer, *Der Gleichberechtigungssatz – neue Form, alter Inhalt?* (1998).
25 Case C-409/95, *Hellmut Marschall* v. *Land Nordrhein-Westfalen* [1997] ECR I-6363.
26 id., para. 35.

A further judgment in the case of *Badeck and Others*[27] confirmed this principle. The ECJ held that quotas do comply with Article 2(4) of the ETD[28] as long as the provisions include some kind of saving clause, since the legislative intention had not been to restrict the introduction of affirmative action measures by member states. The view seemed to prevail that a broad interpretation of Article 2(4) was appropriate, particularly in the light of the insertion of Article 141(4) into the Treaty by the Treaty of Amsterdam, which allows member states to adopt specific advantageous measures in order to promote equal opportunities in the employment sector.

Accordingly, despite the lack of clarity as to the constitutionality of affirmative action in the Basic Law itself, the ECJ's jurisprudence on Article 2(4) of the ETD gave helpful indications to the *Bundesgesetzgeber* (federal legislator) as to what was feasible at a national level under Community law and hence under the new compensation clause in Article 3(2) of the constitution.

5. The quota system

(a) Public sector

It took nearly seven years and the reassurance from Luxembourg for the Bundestag to react to the new compensation clause and to start implementing the 'effective realization of the equality of women and men'.[29] On 5 December 2001, a new Federal Act on Equal Opportunities between Women and Men in the Federal Administration and in the Courts of the Federation[30] came into force. It introduced a number of affirmative action measures in order to promote equal opportunities. The legislator hoped that this new law would fulfil its obligations under Article 3(2), second sentence, of the Basic Law, as well as those arising from European Community law[31] (Articles 2,[32] 3(2)[33] and 141(4) EC) and other international conventions, such as the

---

27 Case C-158/97, *Badeck* v. *Hessischer Ministerprasident* [2000] ECR I-1875.
28 Directive 76/207/EEC, op. cit., n. 22.
29 In fact, a Federal Act on the Promotion of Women had been enacted in 1994. However, this did not impose binding obligations and amounted merely to window dressing.
30 Gesetz zur Gleichstellung von Frauen und Männern in der Bundesverwaltung und in den Gerichten des Bundes (Bundesgleichstellungsgesetz) (Article 3 of the Gleichstellungsdurchsetzungsgesetz of 30 November 2001, Bundesgesetzblatt I, 3234 ff).
31 id.
32 'The Community shall have as its task, by establishing a common market and an economic and monetary union and by implementing common policies or activities referred to in Articles 3 and 4, to promote throughout the Community a harmonious, balanced and sustainable development of economic activities, a high level of employment and of social protection, equality between men and women . . .'.
33 'In all the activities referred to in this Article, the Community shall aim to eliminate inequalities, and to promote equality, between men and women.'

66

Convention on the Elimination of All Forms of Discrimination against Women.[34]

The Act provides for gender mainstreaming,[35] regulates the rights and duties of equality commissioners, and defines and prohibits indirect discrimination during selection procedures. However, its most important effect is to introduce performance-linked quotas, which take into account the specific situation of each individual. Article 8, which applies to access to employment, including promotion and vocational guidance, gives preference to women with the same aptitude, qualifications, and professional achievements as men if they are under-represented in the relevant field, exempting disproportionate disadvantages to male competitors with a saving clause. This provision marks a new departure in German federal law to address the promotion of women's rights, taking due account of the ECJ's jurisprudence and other constitutional principles, such as the merit system within the public service (*Leistungsprinzip*) contained in Article 33(2) of the Basic Law.[36]

However, the defect in this Act, which has led to criticism from the women's movement, relates to its area of application. It only applies to the federal administration, the courts of the federation, and federally-owned corporations, all of which are governed by public law. The whole of the private sector, where most women are employed, is exempt from the Act's provisions, even though the government had originally intended that it should be included.

(b) Private sector

The Bundestag's failure to impose binding obligations on the private sector to take affirmative action to improve the position of women corresponds to the rather disappointing Directive 2002/73 of September 2002 amending the ETD,[37] which similarly fails to require member states to implement affirmative action. The European Parliament was not able to secure amendments, such as a statutory definition of affirmative action within Article 2 of the new Directive, which would have forced member states to implement affirmative action in the private sector.[38]

---

34 1249 UNTS 13 (1979) Art. 11.
35 This is aimed at the integration of a gender perspective into all general policies and measures.
36 'Every German shall be equally eligible for any public office according to his aptitude, qualifications and professional achievements'.
37 Directive 2002/73/EC of 23 September 2002 amending Council Directive on the Implementation of the Principle of Equal Treatment for Men and Women as Regards Access to Employment, Vocational Training and Promotion, and Working Conditions (OJ/5 October 2002/L/269/pp. 15–20). See, also, the proposal aiming at clarifying the principle of equal treatment by bringing together five existing directives in a single text (Proposal for a Directive of the European Parliament and of the Council on the Implementation of the Principle of Equal Opportunities and Equal Treatment of Men and Women in Matters of Employment and Occupation (2004/0084/COD)).
38 Further ideas regard Article 2(4) and Article 8(b) (see COM/2001/689).

In 1999, the newly-elected Social Democrat and Green coalition announced a new 'Women and Work' programme which included, among other things, a proposed Equal Opportunities Act for the private sector. The first draft suggested, as an initial step, the introduction of voluntary agreements to set minimum requirements regarding affirmative measures. Their implementation would be secured by linking public procurement to corporate policy regarding the implementation of equal opportunities for women. In addition, the policy was to be audited. The idea was to use public procurement and the favourable publicity garnered by a positive audit as incentives to encourage companies to work towards a feasible equal opportunities policy. At a second stage, binding rules would be applied to force private businesses to implement affirmative action.[39] However, sections of the government, responding to the concerns expressed by private employers, would not agree to such a Bill.

This led to a rather weak agreement between government and industry, the so-called 'Agreement to Promote the Equal Opportunities of Women and Men in Private Industry',[40] which was signed in July 2001 by the government and business associations, such as the Federal Employers' Association (*Bundesvereinigung der Deutschen Arbeitgeberverbände*) and the Federal Association of German Industry (*Bundesverband der Deutschen Industrie*). Under this agreement, employers committed themselves to implementing various best-practice measures in regard to the realization of equal opportunities, such as entrenching equal opportunity and family-friendliness as part of corporate philosophy or increasing the proportion of women in management positions. The agreement appeals to the goodwill of businesses without setting up a comprehensive system of sanctions. The government's side of the agreement was to reform the German educational system and not to initiate further Bills to promote equal opportunity for men and women in the private sector. In December 2003, the government and industry carried out an initial assessment of the progress made so far.[41] The report read like an advertorial, but it did not provide specific data on the achievements of industry: hence it was not substantial and of not much use.

It is clear that the failure to extend compulsory affirmative action for women in the form of quotas from the public sector to the private sector is not the result of legal restrictions, either from Community law or constitutional law. Rather, it is simply due to a lack of political will. There

---

39 H.M. Pfarr and E. Kocher, 'Kollektivverfahren im Arbeitsrecht' (1999) *Neue Zeitschrift für Arbeits- und Sozialrecht* 358.
40 Vereinbarung zwischen der Bundesregierung und den Spitzenverbänden der deutschen Wirtschaft zur Förderung der Chancengleichheit von Frauen und Männern in der Privatwirtschaft, 2 July 2001.
41 Bundesministerium für Familie, Senioren, Frauen und Jugend, *Bilanz 2003 Vereinbarung zwischen der Bundesregierung und den Spitzenverbänden der deutschen Wirtschaft zur Förderung der Chancengleichheit von Frauen und Männern in der Privatwirtschaft* (2003).

is no majority support for the use of quotas for women's employment in the private sector. However, German law does impose quotas on private sector employers for the benefit of disabled persons. Accordingly, we need discuss why these quotas were introduced and why they are regarded as being acceptable when quotas for women are not.

QUOTAS FOR DISABLED PERSONS

1. *Public sector*

As far back as the eighteenth century, quota schemes were used to ensure the employment of war-disabled persons in the Prussian public service.[42] Later the remit of the law broadened and became applicable to anyone who became disabled through an occupational accident.[43] However, it was only in 1974 that the law was extended by the Disability Act[44] to include all disabled people, whatever the cause of their disability.

The 1974 Act stipulated that 6 per cent of all jobs had to be filled by disabled people. This broadly corresponded to the proportion of the population at that time officially recognized as having a disability. The quota was *not* performance-linked and failure to comply with the Act entailed a penalty payment, initially set at 100 DM (about €50) per employee, though increased in 1986 to 200 DM (about €100).[45]

Notwithstanding the legislation, the unemployment rate for disabled people rose dramatically in the 1990s.[46] In fact, a key criticism of the Act was that employers were able to avoid their obligations simply by paying the penalties. Accordingly, in 1999, the Social Democrat/Green government introduced a programme with the aim of creating 50,000 jobs for disabled people. As a consequence, the Disability Act was amended in 2000 and the quota system was changed, the new Act being embedded in Book IX of the Social Code.[47] Despite the increase in the proportion of the population officially registered as disabled, the quota was reduced to 5 per cent. However, in combination with a new graded penalty system,[48] the intention

---

42 R. Grossmann and W. Schimanski, *Grosskommentar zum Schwerbehindertengesetz* (1999) Art. 5, n. 5 ff.
43 id.
44 Gesetz zur Sicherung der Eingliederung Schwerbehinderter in Arbeit, Beruf und Gesellschaft-Schwerbehindertengesetz (29 April 1974, Bundesgesetzblatt I, 1005 ff.).
45 Gesetz zur Sicherung der Eingliederung Schwerbehinderter in Arbeit, Beruf und Gesellschaft-Schwerbehindertengesetz (26 August 1986, Bundesgesetzblatt I, 1421 ff.).
46 In 1996, some 17.4 per cent were unemployed (see Bundesministerium für Arbeit und Sozialordnung, *Vierter Bericht der Bundesregierung über die Lage der Behinderten und die Entwicklung der Rehabilitation* (1998) 70).
47 Sozialgesetzbuch – Neuntes Buch – (SGB IX) Rehabilitation und Teilhabe behinderter Menschen (19 June 2001, Bundesgesetzblatt I, 1046 ff.).
48 id.

was to create a greater incentive for employers to abide by the law. The maximum penalty per job is now €260 if fewer than 2 per cent of positions are filled by disabled persons; if at least 3 per cent is reached, the penalty is reduced to €105.[49] Although these amounts are arguably still too low, the important point is that the appropriateness of the quota system itself has never been seriously questioned.

2. *Private sector*

The quota system in the 1974 Act applied across the public and private sectors without distinction. However, the amendments of the Social Code in 2000 reduced the burdens on private employers, since the scope of the law was restricted to businesses that employ more than twenty people, compared with only five under the 1974 Act. Small businesses that often struggled to fulfil their legal obligations have particularly benefited from this provision.

Nevertheless, there is no constitutional reason for differentiating between the public and private sectors. Even before the 1994 amendment of the Basic Law to extend the scope of the non-discrimination principle to disabled persons, the Federal Constitutional Court had held that the quota was constitutionally justified. In 1981, the Court[50] decided that the legislator was entitled to require employers to employ disabled persons and that this measure infringed no other constitutional right. In particular, the Court referred to the state's obligation based on the welfare state principle of Articles 20(1) and 28(1) of the Basic Law. At that time the scope of the ruling was limited to disabled persons since the issue of quotas for other groups had not yet been taken up for discussion.

WHY ARE WOMEN AND DISABLED PERSONS TREATED DIFFERENTLY?

It is clear from the above discussion that there is no objection in principle in the German legal system to the imposition of quotas on private sector employers. Nor is the different treatment of quotas for women and for disabled persons attributable to the slight difference in the wording of the two relevant sentences of Article 3 of the Basic Law regarding disabled persons and women. Rather, there seems to be a difference in the social and political acceptability of applying quota systems to different minority groups, and this is the reason why quotas for women's employment have not so far been extended to the private sector.

In Germany, groups promoting the rights of disabled persons were and still are extremely successful in networking and lobbying for their rights.

49 Article 77(2)(3) of the Social Code IX.
50 Decision of the Federal Constitutional Court, BVerfGE 57, 139ff. (159) 26 May 1981.

This is partly the result of the efforts after the Second World War to integrate war-disabled veterans into post-war society. The different groups and associations campaigning for disabled rights had an enormous impact on the constitutional assembly in 1993/1994 during the discussions about the amendment of the Basic Law.[51] The same happened during the drafting process of the Civil Anti-Discrimination Bill[52] which will eventually fulfil Germany's obligations under various anti-discrimination Directives.[53] At the start of the latter process, the intention was that only Directive 2000/43,[54] requiring equal treatment irrespective of racial or ethnic origin, would be implemented by a national Civil Anti-Discrimination law. However, thanks to a successful campaign by disability groups and associations,[55] it was soon accepted that the Bill should be extended to include discrimination on grounds of disability. The power of these groups derives, among other things, from their extensive public support, which in turn is attributable to a relatively broad public understanding of the problems faced by disabled persons and acceptance of the need to remedy them.

The question is why is it seen as acceptable to take special action to improve the position of disabled persons when women are not seen as deserving similar treatment? One possible explanation might be the difference in the numbers involved. As noted above, around 10 per cent of the German population are disabled, whereas around 51 per cent[56] are women. Accordingly, an allocation of 5 per cent of all jobs to this 10 per cent of the population may be supported more easily than an equal distribution between men and women. In other words, it is socially and politically acceptable to support disabled persons and to promote equal rights and opportunities for this relatively small minority group because this does not put the welfare of the majority group at risk. Similarly, because the number of people involved is small, quotas for disabled persons' employment are relatively cheap to

---

51 A. Stock, *Gleichstellung im Vergleich* (2003) 118 ff.
52 Deutscher Bundestag (15. Wahlperiode), Entwurf eines Gesetzes zur Umstezung europäischer Antidiskriminierungsrichtlinien, Drucksache 15/4538, 16 December 2004.
53 Council Directive 2000/43/EC of 29 June 2000 Implementing the Principle of Equal Treatment Between Persons Irrespective of Racial or Ethnic Origin (OJ L/180/22, 19 July 2000); Council Directive 2000/78/EC of 27 November 2000 Establishing a General Framework for Equal Treatment in Employment and Occupation (OJ L/303/16, 2 December 2000); Directive 2002/73/EC of 23 September 2002 amending Council Directive on the Implementation of the Principle of Equal Treatment for Men and Women as Regards Access to Employment, Vocational Training and Promotion, and Working Conditions (OJ L/269/15, 5 October 2002); Council Directive 2004/113/EC of 13 December 2004 Implementing the Principle of Equal Treatment Between Men and Women in the Access to and Supply of Goods and Service (OJ L/373/37, 21 December 2004).
54 Directive 2000/43/EC, id.
55 D. Schick, 'Umsetzung in nationales Recht und politische Entwicklung' (2004) 3 *Aktuelle Informationen des Deutschen Juristinnenbundes* 8, 10.
56 UN, op. cit., n. 3.

71

implement and impose a relatively limited burden on business, especially given the exemptions for small and medium-sized enterprises.

A judgment of the Federal Constitutional Court in 1997 (*Sonderschulurteil*)[57] reflects another view. It shows how a *visible* disability, such as a mobility impairment or mental disability, influences the readiness of society to grant affirmative action. The Court held that the new Article 3(2), second sentence of the Basic Law did not provide pupils with special needs with the right to attend a normal school and request remedial education as long as they had the possibility of attending a special needs schools. Nevertheless, the Court stated in relation to the special needs of disabled persons that '... even after the abolition of all prejudices against disabled persons, this group remains excluded from equal participation in social life without support from the rest of society ...'.[58] This indicates that society has a specific protective demeanour in favour of disabled persons who often visibly have special needs and have to rely on external support. However, except in the special circumstances of pregnancy and maternity leave, the same cannot be said of women.

CONCLUSION

This article has sought to demonstrate and account for the different treatment of quotas for the employment of women and disabled people within the German legal system. The argument has been that, since it is regarded as perfectly acceptable to require private businesses to employ a given percentage of disabled persons, there is no reason in principle why a similar quota system should not be put in place for women.

Although the effectiveness of quotas is controversial,[59] it is clear that the achievement of true equality of opportunity remains utopian without some measure of affirmative action. Moreover, quotas are the only measure that guarantees that minority groups are equally, or at least proportionately, represented in employment or any other social position. Before we can contemplate an ideal future in which prejudices have been abandoned we have to be aware of existing prejudices and try to fight them. This encompasses discrimination against both women and disabled persons, and it demands our commitment to true equal participation by affirmative action irrespective of the group for which it is used.

In order to move in this direction, a change in the social perception of discrimination is required. In Germany, there is some hope that the duty imposed on the state by European law to implement a range of anti-

---

57 Decision of the Federal Constitutional Court, BVerfGE 96, 288 ff. (302), 8 October 1997.
58 id., p. 302.
59 See the discussion in Stock, op. cit., n. 51, pp. 292 ff.

discrimination measures[60] will produce this result. As already noted, a Civil Anti-Discrimination Bill is being discussed at the time of writing, which will mainstream anti-discrimination principles throughout different areas of private law.[61] Once this has been successfully implemented, it may lead to a different social perception of the various minority groups to which it applies. Hopefully, this will mean that discrimination is no longer socially tolerated and will raise awareness of the necessity of affirmative action for all kinds of minority groups, in turn paving the way for quotas in favour of women in private sector employment.

---

60 op. cit., n. 53.
61 One main principle that is discussed is the protection against discrimination on the grounds of ethnicity, sex, religious belief, disability or sexual identity under private law.

JOURNAL OF LAW AND SOCIETY
VOLUME 33, NUMBER 1, MARCH 2006
ISSN: 0263-323X, pp. 74–91

Widening Participation and Higher Education

Lois S. Bibbings*

This article considers higher education 'widening participation' policy and practice, focusing upon attempts to widen access in relation to applicants from under-represented socio-economic groups and educational backgrounds. Some key United Kingdom approaches are described and discussed in the light of the concept of affirmative action. The article also examines the legal support for widening participation.

INTRODUCTION

Undergraduate admissions to higher education have been the subject of some controversy in recent years, with some (home) university applicants from independent schools, along with their parents and teachers, claiming that they have been unfairly treated because of 'positive discrimination' in favour of applicants from the state sector and that, as a consequence, institutions are 'dumbing down'.[1] The allegations relate to oversubscribed courses at prestigious universities and 'widening participation'[2] policies, which seek to

* School of Law, University of Bristol, Wills Memorial Building, Queens Road, Bristol BS8 1RJ, England
Lois.S.Bibbings@bristol.ac.uk

Papers on this subject have been given at a variety of conferences including events run by Universities UK, the Universities and Colleges Admissions Service, the Department for Constitutional Affairs, and the Socio-Legal Studies Association. I would like to thank those who attended for their comments along with the editors of this volume. In addition, thanks go to Luke Clements, Richard Huxtable, Wambui Mwangi, and Phil Thomas for their assistance with this research and to those involved with widening participation at Bristol – in particular, Lucy Collins, Antti Karjalainen, Jules Pickles, Pat Rayfield, Kate Tapper, and also Barry Taylor. Last, but by no means least, a big thank you to the pupils and students that I have worked with on summer schools and other events.

1 See, for example, 'These Insidious Social Engineers Destroying Merit and Aspiration' *Daily Mail*, 26 February 2003; 'March of the Social Engineers' *Daily Mail*, 1 October 2002.
2 There is some variation in relation to the terminology in this context, however, 'widening participation' has become the most commonly used term in policy-making.

increase the numbers of students from under-represented groups within higher education. Most notably, such concerns led to the announcement by the Girls' Schools Association and the Headmasters and Headmistresses Conference (representing the independent sector) of a 'boycott' of the University of Bristol because, allegedly, the institution had 'been very public about a policy which unfairly discriminates against applicants from good schools, whether independent or state.'[3] Subsequently, research has shown that the increases in participation by under-represented groups have been accompanied by increases in independent school applicants proceeding to higher education as a result of the overall expansions in student numbers. In addition, instead of standards falling, the average A level attainment of entrants to leading universities increased from 26.4 points in 1997/98 to 26.8 in 2002/03.[4] Moreover, a survey of independent school pupils' experiences of applying to university, conducted by the Independent Schools Council (and presumably seeking to prove discrimination), found that private school pupils tended to receive the same conditional offers as any other student and were no less likely to secure a place. The research concluded that there was 'no evidence of discrimination against independently schooled students' and, thus, 'rejections which may have seemed discriminatory to parents and schools have in fact, been due to a large rise in suitably qualified applicants'.[5] In light of such evidence it is unsurprising that complaints and accusations about widening participation are no longer at the fore; though there is no guarantee that such policies will not provoke further controversy.

This article focuses upon higher education widening participation policy (including admissions) in relation to teenage students from socio-economic groups under-represented in this sector, drawing upon widening participation policy, research, law, and practice. Although the policy extends to other groups, socio-economic disadvantage, along with the linked issue of educational background, has been the focus of both efforts to widen access and the allegations of discrimination.[6]

The article draws upon both published sources and my own experience of widening participation work both at the University of Bristol and beyond.[7] It

---

3 See, for example, 'Private Schools Boycott Bristol Over Selection' *Guardian*, 5 March 2003.

4 Sutton Trust, *State School Admissions to our Leading Universities: An Update to 'The Missing 3000'* (2005) 1.

5 'Private Schools Admit No Bias in University Selection' *Guardian*, 17 August 2005.

6 There are, of course, other important access issues in relation, for example, to mature students, students with disabilities, and those from ethnic minorities. Also, intersectionality is particularly relevant to socio-economic disadvantage.

7 My experience at Bristol includes working as a widening participation admissions tutor, being involved in University policy development, coordinating summer schools, teaching school pupils, and devising new outreach initiatives including the Meriton Project. The latter programme involves working with the Meriton Centre, the local teenage mothers' unit, and has been recognized by Universities UK as one of the

begins by briefly examining the problem of low participation and then gives some examples of the range of higher education widening participation policy and practice within the United Kingdom (whilst there are some variations in terms of participation, policy, and practice, the United Kingdom's devolved regions display distinct but similar patterns of educational disadvantage, and widening participation has become a key educational issue in each). The discussion then turns to consider the nature and legality of these policies in the context of the concept of affirmative action and human rights law. Finally, the article reflects upon the effectiveness of widening participation to date and looks briefly to the future.[8]

LOW PARTICIPATION AND BARRIERS TO HIGHER EDUCATION

It is well established that some groups continue to be under-represented in the United Kingdom higher education sector and that this problem is particularly acute in relation to competitive subjects and at 'top' institutions. There are various (overlapping and interconnected) reasons for this but, notably, there is a plethora of research which demonstrates that socio-economic status, along with and linked to educational background, is a key factor associated with higher education participation rates.

Access to the better schools, whether independent or state, is greatly influenced, if not determined, by parental finances and employment histories as well as their experience of (higher) education. Whilst private schools' performance levels vary, on average students from such schools achieve the highest scores in GCSEs and A levels, suggesting the existence of what the Sutton Trust has described as 'a two-nation educational culture'. According to their research, in 2001 '85 of the top hundred schools (in terms of examination results) were independent.'[9] In 1980, research demonstrated that nearly a quarter of pupils from the professional class went to private schools, compared to fewer than 2 per cent from the manual class. The Sutton Trust research reveals that these findings remain relevant and shows that:

> the education of the child tends to resemble that of the parent, and that those who obtained privileged forms of education are also more likely to secure it for their children.[10]

top eleven examples of widening participation good practice in the United Kingdom (out of 141 projects considered). Universities UK and Standing Conference of Principals, *From the Margins to the Mainstream: Embedding Widening Participation in Higher Education* (2005) 124–8.

8 For an alternative approach to these issues, see N. Saunders, 'Widening Access to Higher Education – The Limits of Positive Action' (2004) 16 *Education and the Law* 3.

9 Sutton Trust, *Educational Apartheid: A Practical Way Forward* (2001) 4, 6.

10 A.H. Halsey et al., *Origins and Destinations: Family, Class and Education in Modern Britain* (1980) 53.

Within the state sector, too, not all things are equal. As performance tables and inspection reports demonstrate, where they are available,[11] school performance varies greatly and recent Sutton Trust research shows that children and young people from poor backgrounds lose out to the better off when it comes to both the best comprehensive and the remaining grammar schools.[12] This confirms the observation in 1999 that:

> pupils' chances of gaining a place at grammar school did not depend solely on their intellectual ability but was also influenced by their social origins, the type of primary school they attended and the area in which they lived.

In short, even within the state sector pupils tend 'to be segregated into different types of school by their social class origins'.[13]

However, school achievement and participation in higher education are not solely a matter of the quality of the school attended. Young people brought up by parents with few or no qualifications and no familial experience of further, let alone higher, education tend to have low educational aspirations. More generally, social context can influence young peoples' perceptions of what is and what is not 'for the likes of them'. A study which looked at the attitudes of working-class pupils at an inner city London comprehensive school found that they had a 'deep sense of deficit, of not being "good enough".' Describing themselves as 'dumb', they 'ruled themselves out of post-compulsory (but particularly higher) education, which they constructed as being highly risky and/or impossible'. In this context, it was difficult for teachers or higher education institutions (some of the pupils had attended a university summer school) to change attitudes.[14]

In part, as a consequence of the effect of socio-economic status upon a pupil's schooling and attainment, the 'two-nation educational culture' extends beyond compulsory and 'sixth form' education. Official statistics show that across the United Kingdom regions, over 90 per cent of seventeen year-olds in full-time education attend schools or colleges in the state sector, whereas 86.8 per cent of young entrants to full-time first degree courses in 2003/04 had attended such schools. Moreover, although most institutions take more than 90 per cent of their young entrants to full-time first degree courses from state schools, about one in nine takes 70 per cent or fewer. In addition, although nearly 50 per cent of the population of working age is

---

11 For England, see <http://www.dfes.gov.uk/performancetables/> and <http://www.ofsted.gov.uk/reports/>.

12 Sutton Trust, *Rates of Eligibility for Free School Meals at the Top State Schools* (2005) 2, 8–9.

13 A. Heath and S. Jacobs, *Comprehensive Reform in Britain* (1999) 16 <http://www.crest.ox.ac.uk/papers/p72.pdf>.

14 L. Archer and H. Yamashita, '"That Ain't Never Gonna Happen to Me": Identities, Inequalities and Inner City School Leavers' Post-16 Routes', (paper presented at the Annual Conference of the British Educational Research Association, University of Exeter, England, September 2002), at *EducatiOn-Line* <http//www.leeds.ac.uk/educol/documents/00002317.htm>.

77

classified in socio-economic groups four to seven (the 'low' socio-economic groups), only 28.6 per cent of young entrants to full-time first degree courses come from this section of society.[15]

For those young people who progress to higher education, socio-economic and educational background can also affect the type of institution attended as students from poorer backgrounds are less likely to study at leading universities. According to research published in 2000, a student from an independent school was 25 times more likely to get into one of the leading thirteen universities than a state student from a socially disadvantaged group.[16] Also, a 2004 study found that, whilst 45 per cent of students who obtain the equivalent of an A and two Bs at A level go on to study at a leading university, only 26 per cent of state school students with the same grades do so.[17] The access gap is even more alarming in relation to Oxbridge. In 2001, the Sutton Trust found that 24 per cent of students admitted to these institutions came from the top 100 independent day schools; thus, 'some 3% of schools provide almost a quarter of Oxbridge entrants.'[18]

Under-representation may also, in part, be caused by institutional policies. 'Traditional' higher education admissions criteria and selection practices may lead to the rejection of some exceptionally able applicants from under-represented groups, particularly where leading universities and competitive subjects are concerned.[19] A focus solely or primarily upon high grades, for example, can mean that strong students from poor schools are at an immediate disadvantage and other assumptions about desirable qualities can also mean that applicants from more privileged backgrounds are favoured. Thus, placing great emphasis upon additional qualifications (beyond the standard eight GCSEs and three A levels, or their equivalents) benefits the student who has attended a school or college where taking additional subjects is possible. Expecting relevant unpaid work experience may mean the rejection of students who can ill-afford to work for free and/or do not possess the familial or school contacts to arrange unpaid work. Further, admissions tutors or administrators who look down upon applicants who work, for instance, for fast food companies or in the family business, but look favourably upon those with more 'respectable' employment records tend to select the more privileged student.

---

15 Higher Education Statistics Agency (HESA), *Performance Indicators in Higher Education in the UK 2003/4* (2005), 'Summary' and 'Widening Participation of Under-Represented Groups' <http://www.hesa.ac.uk/pi/0304/home.htm>.

16 Sutton Trust, *Entry to Leading Universities* (2000) 1. The ranking here was based upon the average of newspaper league tables.

17 Sutton Trust, *The Missing 3000: State School Students Under-Represented at Leading Universities*, (2004) 1.

18 Sutton Trust, op. cit., n. 9, p. 4.

19 See, for example, Universities UK, *Fair Enough: Wider Access to University by Identifying Potential to Succeed* (2003) 52 and ch. 3.

The effects of disadvantage continue beyond higher education, as those who have attended independent schools and leading universities have better access to high-status and highly remunerative employment. For example, recent research on the legal profession in the United Kingdom found that the position has not changed significantly in the last fifteen years. Thus, in 2004 three out of four judges, more than two-thirds of barristers at top chambers, and more than half the partners at leading law firms had been educated in the private sector. Indeed, half the current judges had attended boarding schools (which educate fewer than 1 per cent of children). In addition, the research found that judges, top barristers, and top solicitors tend to have attended the 'top' dozen universities and, in particular, Oxbridge.[20]

Such stark evidence of the link between socio-economic and educational disadvantage, leading to inequality of opportunity and declining social mobility, portrays a society where some young people's talent, ability, and potential are wasted. Quite apart from the obvious social injustice that this represents, it also makes little economic sense. For example, it is contrary to the focus upon the value of higher education in terms of increased productivity, economic growth, and the need for a knowledge-based economy in the 2003 White Paper on Higher Education.[21] Also, there is now a recognition that the lack of diversity in terms of socio-economic background in higher education (or, more specifically, in some institutions), within graduate jobs and, in particular, in the professions is problematic. Indeed, the benefits of diversity are now frequently acknowledged in these contexts both in the United Kingdom and elsewhere. In the United States, for example, research has demonstrated the positive effects, in terms of learning, of a student body consisting of people from a variety of different ethnic backgrounds.[22] In the United Kingdom both higher education institutions and the professions are aware of or are at least beginning to acknowledge such benefits.[23] For

---

20 Sutton Trust, *The Educational Backgrounds of the UK's Top Solicitors, Barristers and Judges* (2005). See, further, D. Nicolson, 'Demography, Discrimination and Diversity: A New Dawn for the British Legal Profession?' (2005) 12 *International J. of the Legal Profession* 201.

21 Department for Education and Skills (DfES), *The Future of Higher Education* (2003; Cm. 5735).

22 On the benefits of diversity in the United States, see, for example, A.W. Astin, 'Diversity and Multiculturalism on Campus: How are Students Affected?' (1993) 25 *Change* 44; Y. Amir, 'The Role of Intergroup Contact in the Change of Prejudice and Ethnic Relations' in *Toward the Elimination of Racism*, ed. P.A. Katz (1976); T. Cox, *Cultural Diversity in Organizations: Theory, Research, and Practice* (1993); J.J. Cohen, 'The Consequences of Premature Abandonment of Affirmative Action in Medical School Admissions' (2003) 289 *J. of the Am. Medical Association* 1143; W.G. Bowen and D. Bok, *The Shape of the River: Long-Term Consequences of Considering Race in College and University Admissions* (1998).

23 See, for example, University of Bristol, 'Widening Participation Strategy 2004–2009' 1, at <http://www.bristol.ac.uk/wideningparticipation/strategy/strategy.pdf>. The Admissions to Higher Education Steering Group also recognized the value of a

example, in 2004 the Department of Constitutional Affairs put forward a series of proposals for making the judiciary 'more reflective of society, whilst continuing to make judicial appointments based solely on merit' because '[a] more diverse judiciary is essential if the public's confidence in its judges is to be maintained and strengthened.'[24]

WIDENING PARTICIPATION POLICY AND PRACTICE: OUTREACH, ADMISSIONS, AND STUDENT SUPPORT

Efforts to widen participation in higher education have existed for some time. Indeed, a 1998 study of good practice in the United Kingdom found a variety of initiatives that were already well established.[25] In the late 1990s, however, the Labour government committed itself to increasing diversity in higher education, and widening participation became an important issue for both funding councils and institutions. In 1999, for example, the Higher Education Funding Council for England introduced its plans for widening participation, including mainstream and special funds to support and encourage widening participation.[26] Since then the landscape of widening participation funding and performance monitoring has changed, but the policy focus of increasing access for those from disadvantaged backgrounds continues.[27] Moreover, widening participation is now becoming central to higher education work and a range of national, regional, and institution-specific initiatives have developed, involving the regional funding councils, government education departments and institutions, as well as other organizations.

A variety of different practices, relating to outreach, admissions, and student support, are encompassed within the umbrella of widening partici-pation policy.[28] Outreach activities involve working with communities and schools. They include visits to universities, student-pupil mentoring, summer

diverse student community: DfES, *Fair Admissions to Higher Education: Recommendations for Good Practice* (2004) 6, 31, 76.

24 Department of Constitutional Affairs (DCA), *Increasing Diversity in the Judiciary* (2004) CP 25/04, 8. In addition, the legal profession has acknowledged the business case for diversity: see Nicolson, op. cit., n. 20, p. 216.

25 European Access Network, *From Elitism to Inclusion: Good Practice in Widening Access to Higher Education* (1998).

26 See Higher Education Funding Council for England, 'Widening Participation in Higher Education: Funding Decisions', report 99/24 (1999) at <http://www.hefce.ac.uk/Pubs/index.asp>.

27 For further information on current and future widening participation policy in England, see, for example, <http://www.hefce.ac.uk/widen/>.

28 Not all practices are considered within this article. For example, such work can also involve the creation of new pathways to higher educations such as the University of Bristol's Pathway Certificate Programme, which offers a Foundation Year in Engineering, <www.fen.bris.ac.uk/faculty/pathway/>.

schools, and taster events. These aim, among other things, to raise confidence, aspirations, and attainment in poorly performing state schools and seek to alter elitist perceptions about higher education and sometimes also about particular institutions. Primarily, though, such efforts seek (in the short and long term) to encourage students from under-represented groups to apply to higher education.[29]

In relation to admissions, a variety of policies designed with widening participation in mind have developed with different institutions and, indeed, academic departments developing different methods of selection. However, some common approaches have emerged and there is also recognition of what constitutes good practice. Of these, three approaches are considered here. The first involves contextualizing an application. Here all applicants (whatever their backgrounds) are treated as individuals with their achievement, ability, motivation, and potential being judged in the context of relevant aspects of their background. A contextual approach can, for example, be applied to the assessment of an applicant's non-academic achievements and experiences so that activities associated with a privileged socio-economic and educational background are not preferred. More significantly, grades themselves can be viewed in the context of the schools that an applicant has attended. For example, in the case of an applicant from a particularly poorly performing school (state or independent), grades might be reinterpreted contextually and recognized as a great achievement and an indicator, perhaps, of exceptional ability, motivation, and potential. Thus, available evidence of educational background can be used to allow a more sophisticated reading of a number of aspects of an application and this can be done on an individual basis.

This contextual approach is, of course, by no means new. Applicants from the state and independent sectors who have experienced, for example, ill-health, bereavement or have evidence of other circumstances which have adversely affected their academic performance are also considered in the light of their particular situation. Moreover, the government-commissioned independent review of university admissions which examined the options that English higher education providers should consider adopting in assessing the merit, achievements, and potential of applicants concluded that:

> ... it is fair and appropriate to consider contextual factors as well as formal educational achievement, given the variation in learners' opportunities and circumstances... This is facilitated by 'holistic assessment', or taking into account all relevant factors, including the context of applicants' achievements, backgrounds and relevant skills. 'Broad brush' approaches are generally not appropriate; applicants must be assessed as individuals.[30]

29 Most English and subsequently United Kingdom outreach work is now expected to take place through Aimhigher, which is currently jointly funded by the English Funding Council and the Department of Education and Skills. <http://www.aimhigher.ac.uk/home/index.cfm>.
30 Admissions to Higher Education Steering Group, op. cit., n. 23, p. 6.

In addition, in a 2002 report on widening participation in England, the National Audit Office also recommended that good admissions practice would include 'taking applicants' backgrounds and circumstances into account in assessing likelihood of succeeding in higher education.'[31]

Another influential approach, supported by the findings of a project carried out on behalf of Universities UK, has been to use additional criteria to identify merit.[32] Implicit within the aim of the project was the goal of widening participation within higher education 'by identifying those who have the ability to succeed but whose potential would otherwise be missed.'[33] In particular, the focus was upon the tendency, noted above, to reject able students from under-represented backgrounds when 'traditional' entry criteria were used.[34] Whilst the report did not suggest that examination grades should be abandoned as a criterion, it identified four criteria that could be used within admissions to identify merit (organization, independent working, motivation, and interest) and indicated how these might be identified.[35]

Finally, admissions increasingly involve the use of additional information gathered by setting written work, additional testing or interviews. For example, the Law National Admissions Test seeks to identify merit and aptitude regardless of background.[36] Research suggests that testing and, in particular, scholastic assessment tests may not only assist in distinguishing applicants and identifying potential, but can also be means of identifying able students from less privileged backgrounds.[37] Moreover, adopting a contextual approach, adding new criteria, and seeking additional information are by no means mutually exclusive approaches to admissions. Thus, the Universities UK project, mentioned above, recommended both the use of additional criteria and additional information.[38]

It is well recognized that widening participation work should not end once a student secures a place within higher education.[39] The provision of adequate and appropriate support is important for all students, including those from under-represented groups. This can ensure that students do not feel unwelcome, become marginalized, or find the learning environment intimidating and are not, therefore, deterred or prevented from completing

31 National Audit Office, *Widening Participation in Higher Education in England* (2002) 3.
32 Universities UK, op. cit, n. 19.
33 id., p. 7.
34 id., p. 52 and ch. 3.
35 id., pp. 47–8.
36 See <http://www.lnat.ac.uk/>.
37 A.S. McDonald et al., *A Pilot of Aptitude Testing for University Entrance* (2001).
38 Universities UK, op. cit, n. 19, pp. 47–8.
39 See, for example, M. Yorke and L. Thomas, 'Improving the Retention of Students from Lower Socio-economic Groups' (2003) 25 *J. of Higher Education Policy and Management* 63.

their course. Also, unfavourable student experiences of higher education can undo any work undertaken to shift negative perceptions of higher education or of a particular institution as elitist. Thus, attention has been paid to pastoral care, academic assistance and, particularly in the light of the new variable fee, economic aid. Alongside this, institutional cultures are being studied with the aim of removing or at least seeking to lessen any cultural barriers in terms, for example, of staff and student attitudes to under-represented groups.[40]

Widening participation initiatives also target career progression in order to address any obstacles such individuals might face beyond higher education. Engagement with the professions is a crucial element of this work. Indeed, in some areas professional bodies are already involved in their own widening participation work. For example, both branches of the English and Welsh legal profession now have programmes aimed at encouraging young people to consider a becoming a lawyer.[41]

AFFIRMATIVE ACTION AND WIDENING PARTICIPATION

Having outlined the participation gap in higher education and given an overview of higher education widening participation work, the discussion now turns to consider whether these policies and practices amount to affirmative action. 'Affirmative action' is an umbrella term. Broadly speaking, it refers to programmes that target categories of people in order to redress their inequality as a group. Such practices seek to increase the representativeness of, in the present context, the student body in higher education and, more specifically, in particularly unrepresentative institutions. Affirmative action policies can include positive discrimination in the form of quotas or preferential selection methods, which aim to assist institutions to meet participation targets ('hard' options), but can also involve the use of so-called 'soft' options or 'assistance measures'. For example, limited 'hard' options can be used in United States university admissions. Thus, the Supreme Court recently confirmed that selection decisions could involve a race and ethnicity criterion, as long as this was not the predominant factor and quotas were not used.[42] 'Soft' measures entail the use of positive action to promote equality of opportunity and, thus, seek to assist disadvantaged groups to compete more effectively. They include

---

40 See, for example, University of Bristol, op. cit., n. 23, Objective 1.
41 See <http://www.lawsociety.org.uk/becomingasolicitor/careerinlaw/equalityanddiversity.law> and <http://www.legaleducation.org.uk/Careers/s4s.php>.
42 See *Grutter* v. *Bollinger* 123 US 2325 (2003); *Gratz* v. *Bollinger* 123 US 2411 (2003). For an analysis of the legal significance of these decisions see, for example, C.J. Russo and R.D. Mawdsley, 'American Update: The Supreme Court and Affirmative Action' (2003) 15 *Education and the Law* 263.

outreach work and 'harder' targeted training initiatives. To its critics 'hard' affirmative action measures amount to unjustifiable and unjust discrimination, whilst 'soft' or 'assistance measures' attract little attention or disapproval.[43] In United Kingdom anti-discrimination law, 'soft' measures are permitted or sometimes required. For example, under the Fair Employment and Treatment (Northern Ireland) Order 1998 employers can be directed by the Equality Commission or ordered by the Fair Employment Tribunal to undertake 'soft' affirmative action in relation to workforce under-representation in terms of religious belief and political opinion.[44] In contrast, 'hard' forms of action are unlawful.

At first glance, widening participation policies and practices appear to constitute affirmative action in that they involve the use of 'soft' measures to redress inequality and disadvantage amongst under-represented groups. In addition, some admissions policies might be thought to amount to positive discrimination. However, further analysis reveals that the situation is by no means so straightforward.

Outreach work has, thus far, proved to be an uncontroversial element of higher education widening participation policy and practice. Such activities target under-represented groups; however, this is not to say that all such efforts constitute 'soft' forms of affirmative action. Indeed, some outreach work merely forms a part of institutions' recruitment efforts and should, consequently, be viewed alongside, for example, higher education fairs for potential students, institutional or subject open days, school visits, and overseas recruitment trips. In addition, in the context of increasing student numbers and of recruiting courses, outreach reflects the institutional need to seek new 'student markets' in order to fill additional places or undersubscribed courses. Further, it could also be argued that, in this country at least, some outreach work represents a part of the efforts within public education to improve standards in the public sector; public higher education institutions are contributing to the education system of which they form a part by assisting poorly performing state schools. Some of their involvement with schools and colleges could, thus, be conceived of as part of their educational work and, moreover, their engagement with the local community. However, in so far as institutional involvement in outreach work may be deemed to go beyond general recruitment activities and/or

---

43 See, for example, D.R. Kinder and L.M. Sanders, 'Mimicking Political Debate with Survey Questions: The Case of White Opinion on Affirmative Action for Blacks' (1990) 8 *Social Cognition* 73; J.R. Kluegel and E.R. Smith, *Beliefs about Inequality: Americans' Views of What Is and What Ought to Be* (1986); H.J. Holzer and D. Neumark, 'What Does Affirmative Action Do?' Michigan State University, Institute for Research on Poverty, discussion paper no. 1169-98 (1998) 2, at 59. <http://www.ssc.wisc.edu/irp/>.

44 Fair Employment and Treatment (Northern Ireland) Order 1998, 3162 (NI 21) Arts. 12, 14, 16. See, further, Fair Employment in Northern Ireland Code of Practice, Equality Commission for Northern Ireland, para 6.5.

84

educational work, such initiatives would, of course, constitute 'soft' forms of affirmative action, which aim to promote equality of opportunity. They would not amount to positive discrimination because, as we have seen, outreach initiatives, are primarily aimed at encouraging applications to higher education and generally provide no preference towards a particular applicant in admissions, let alone a guaranteed place.[45]

As we have seen, admissions policies have proved to be the most controversial aspect of widening participation work, with allegations that some institutions have been using positive discrimination to meet quotas. However, there is no evidence to support these accusations.[46] In addition, of the three key approaches to admissions considered above, none amounts to affirmative action. This is because, unlike United States affirmative action admissions policies, they do not use, for example, 'socio-economic disadvantage', 'educational disadvantage' or 'state school sector' as admissions criteria. Rather, they are primarily concerned with identifying merit. Thus, in adopting such approaches, institutions are, first and foremost, looking for more accurate ways of identifying ability and aptitude and selecting the 'best' students without favouring any group of applicants. Indeed, because of this they might more accurately be described as 'widening participation friendly' approaches to admissions rather than specifically 'widening participation admissions policies' (in that they may assist in identifying merit in all students, including those from under-represented groups).

Universities' focus upon pastoral care, academic assistance, hardship grants, institutional barriers and careers may also appear to constitute special consideration and treatment. However, these activities are also not merely a facet of widening participation policy. Having good systems of support, ensuring students do not feel unwelcome, and looking to their future are aspects of universities' work and, indeed, form a part of their duty to their students. The fact that such assistance is considered within widening participation policy constitutes a recognition both that institutions must cater to the needs of all their students and that, in the past, adequate support has often been lacking. More significantly, support is often not targeted at specific groups but at all students. Thus, hardship grants tend to be available to all regardless of socio-economic background and, in particular, parental finances. Similarly, academic sessions such as study skills or essay-writing

45 See, further, n. 58 below.
46 Indeed, rather than finding discrimination against private school pupils in 2002 the National Audit Office, op. cit, n. 31, concluded that in England there was 'widespread activity to raise aspirations and awareness but much less to ensure that applications from people in groups with low representation have a fair chance of succeeding' and, therefore, recommended further action needed to be taken in relation to admissions. In addition, the independent review of admissions concluded that 'across all universities and colleges, and all subjects, admissions processes generally appear to be fair and there is a great deal of good practice within the sector on which to build.': Admissions to Higher Education Steering Group, op. cit., n. 23, p. 21.

tutorials are generally offered to all students. Indeed, those who benefit from attendance are by no means limited to students from under-represented groups. Consequently, only forms of support that are specifically provided for and limited to under-represented groups constitute 'soft' affirmative action.

WIDENING PARTICIPATION AND HUMAN RIGHTS

What then of the legal status of widening participation in the United Kingdom? Thus far, questions about the legality of such policies have only been raised in relation to selection decisions.[47] As we have seen, some pupils, parents, and independent schools, along with some newspapers, have alleged that institutions have unlawfully used positive discrimination to boost the numbers of students from under-represented groups. However, in so far as the widening participation approaches to admissions described above are centrally concerned with better identifying merit, they are easily justified. Selection on the grounds of merit is, after all, the proper business of higher education admissions and the courts have confirmed that this task is best left to individual institutions.[48] Beyond this, there is legal support for specifically widening participation approaches in that they seek to avoid indirect discrimination against those from disadvantaged groups under-represented in higher education. Although discrimination in terms of socio-economic background is not specifically prohibited in the United Kingdom, European human rights might provide some protection for such policies in relation to public universities. Moreover, it is also possible that policies which extend to the use of different treatment or selection methods for students from different groups ('hard' measures) may not only be lawful but also may be required. The following analysis focuses upon legal arguments in support of widening participation in the context of student selection, though similar arguments could be used to justify targeted outreach work and student support.

The European Convention on Human Rights 1950 may provide a justification for efforts to widen access through admissions.[49] Stated simply, the basic argument concerns the right to be free from discrimination (Article

---

47 Admissions to Higher Education Steering Group, id., app. 5. See, also, Saunders, op. cit., n. 8.

48 Selection decisions have generally been assumed to be 'protected' where they involve academic judgements and, as long as procedures are fair and comply with dis-crimination law: see, for example, *R* v. *University College London Ex p. Idriss* [1999] Ed CR 462; *Clark* v. *University of Lincolnshire and Humberside* [2000] ELR 345.

49 This is arguable both in terms of the Convention and the Human Rights Act 1998 as public higher education institutions are most probably performing functions of a public nature in the context of admissions and so are subject to the duty under s. 6(1) of the Act.

86

14) in relation to the right to education (Protocol 1, Article 2). Article 14 states that:

> [t]he enjoyment of the rights and freedoms set forth in this Convention shall be secured without discrimination on any ground such as ... social origin ... property, birth or other status

whilst Article 2, Protocol 1 provides that '[n]o person shall be denied the right to education'. Article 14 can provide protection for those from, for example, economically disadvantaged groups[50] and Article 2 is applicable to higher education provided by the state.[51] Thus, it could be argued that 'traditional' selection methods unjustifiably indirectly discriminate against applicants from poor backgrounds.[52] If this were accepted, it would provide support for policies that seek to prevent such unfairness.

Further, the Convention might provide justification for some level of differential treatment in order to avoid indirect discrimination against socio-economically disadvantaged applicants. Article 14 does not necessarily prohibit a disadvantaged group from being treated differently where the purpose is to assist that group. Indeed, in the *Belgian Linguistics* case the Court stated that:

> Article 14 does not forbid every difference in treatment in the exercise of the rights and freedoms recognised ... [C]ertain legal inequalities tend only to correct factual inequalities.[53]

More recently, the Court has reiterated this view:

> The right not to be discriminated against in the enjoyment of the rights guaranteed under the Convention is also violated when States without an objective and reasonable justification fail to treat differently persons whose situations are significantly different.[54]

In fact, in several cases the Court and Commission have held that different treatment is justified precisely because its purpose is to assist a disadvantaged group. For example, in *Lindsay* v. *UK*[55] the Commission considered legislation that meant that women who were sole breadwinners paid less tax than men in the same position. The government argued that the measure aimed to encourage more women to work, helped overcome male prejudice, and advanced sexual equality. The Commission found that this

---

50 See *Wiggins* v. *UK* (1978) 13 DR 40.
51 The Commission has stated that the right 'includes entry to nursery, primary, secondary and higher education' (quoted in the *Belgian Linguistics Case* 23 July 1968, 22 (merits)). However, there has since been a tendency to prioritize non-advanced studies; see, for example, *X* v. *UK* (1975) 2 DR 50; *Yanasak* v. *Turkey* (1993) 74 DR 14.
52 The argument might also be attempted in relation to state school applicants or state school applicants from poorly performing schools.
53 (No 2) (1968) 1 EHRR 252, 284, para. 10.
54 *Thlimmenos* v. *Greece* (2000) 31 EHRR 411, para. 44.
55 (1986) 49 DR 181.

goal was reasonable and objective as it sought to implement 'positive discrimination' in relation to a disadvantaged group.[56] More significantly, *Wiggins* considered whether economically disadvantaged groups could be treated differently.[57] If this approach was followed in the current context, university admissions criteria that gave some degree of preference to applicants from disadvantaged groups, for example, in a manner not dissimilar to that used in the United States, might be at least permissible under human rights law. However, any such scheme would need to be judged to be proportionate to its aim.[58]

Moreover, a move away from 'traditional' selection methods (possibly to positive discrimination) may also conceivably be found to be required under the Convention. In Strasbourg at least,[59] it might be argued that, since the state is well aware of the problems relating to socio-economic disadvantage, under-representation, and access, and given that there is some evidence that 'traditional' selection methods disadvantage such applicants,[60] there is a positive obligation on the state to do something about this. This obligation would arise out of the Article 2 of Protocol 1 being read in conjunction with the state undertaking in Article 1 as well as Article 14.[61] Thus, in requiring that the Convention right to education shall be secured without discrimination, Article 1 might be taken to impose a positive obligation upon states to take action to remove discrimination.

CONCLUSION

As we have seen, much of widening participation work, including the key approaches to selection, does not amount to affirmative action, although some such activities may constitute 'soft' measures. However, if even 'hard' measures are legally justifiable (if not required), should they be used? One way of assessing this is, of course, to consider whether widening participation is effective. If such policies are deemed to be failing, more radical action may be required in order to narrow the participation gap in terms of socio-economic disadvantage.

---

56 id., p. 191. But see *Van Raalte* v. *Netherlands* (1997) 24 EHRR 503.
57 *Wiggins*, op. cit., n. 50. See, also, for example, *Kilbourn* v. *UK* (1985) 8 EHRR 81; *Gillow* v. *UK* (1986) 11 EHRR 335.
58 Indeed, it has been argued that this could provide a justification for compact schemes (agreements between providers of higher education and secondary or further education) which allow students in partner schools and colleges to receive an advantage in the admissions process, provided they meet the required standards. See Admissions to Higher Education Steering Group, op. cit., n. 23, pp. 38, 73.
59 Article 1 is not translated into United Kingdom law by the Human Rights Act 1998.
60 See, for example, Universities UK, op. cit., n. 19, p. 52 and ch 3.
61 In relation to such positive obligations see, for example, *A* v. *UK* (1999) 27 EHRR 611.

88

Whilst there are some indications that progress has been made in relation to participation in higher education and, in particular, within leading institutions, this is relatively limited. Indeed, arguably little has changed (as the research cited above demonstrates) and the likelihood of continued future progress is uncertain. For example, the latest Higher Education Statistics Agency University Performance Tables, released in September 2005, reveal that the proportion of state school students entering university in each of the devolved regions of the United Kingdom has fallen for the first time in five years. Moreover, the position in relation to some Russell Group institutions is a particular concern, with some institutions falling away from their widening participation benchmarks.[62]

There is also evidence that the effects of disadvantage upon post-higher education employment persist. For example, the Sutton Trust's study of the legal professions found that, while leading law firms took on more partners educated in the state sector in the 1960s, little progress has been made since the late 1980s. Indeed, the findings suggest that the past improvement is unlikely to be lasting as, in 2004, 71 cent of younger partners in leading firms were privately educated.[63] This worrying trend is unlikely to be limited to the legal profession. Indeed, recent research suggests that social mobility in Britain is lower than in other advanced countries and that it is declining. The report concluded that part of the reason for this decline has been that the better off have benefited disproportionately from increased educational opportunity.[64]

In addition, efforts to continue and develop the work to date may be hampered by changes to higher education, particularly in relation to institutional funding and widening participation.[65] For example, given debt aversion, the introduction of variable fees in England in 2006 may understandably deter poorer students from going on to higher education or attending the most expensive universities or courses.[66] Indeed, initial figures for applications made in the 2005–6 cycle, which reveal that early applications from United Kingdom residents are down by over 2 per cent, suggest

62 HESA, op. cit., n. 15.
63 Sutton Trust, op. cit., n. 20.
64 See, for example, J. Blanden et al., *Intergenerational Mobility in Europe and North America* (2005); J.F. Ermisch and M. Francesconi, 'Intergenerational Mobility in Britain: new evidence from the BHPS' in *Generational Income Mobility*, ed. M. Corak (2004), and at <http://www.child-centre.it/>.
65 In relation to England see, for example, Higher Education Act 2004; The Student Fees (Approved Plans) (England) Regulations 2004, 2473; Statutory Letter of Guidance, Secretary of State for Education and Skills to Director of Fair Access, 25 October 2004 <http://www.dfes.gov.uk/hegateway/uploads/OFFA%20final%20 guidance%20letter%20October%202004.pdf>; Higher Education Funding Council for England < http://www.hefce.ac.uk/widen/strategy/>.
66 See, for example, C. Callender, *Attitudes to Debt: School Leavers and Further Education Students' Attitudes to Debt and their Impact on Participation in Higher Education* (2003).

89

that this might be the case.[67] Also, it is unclear how effective the newly created Office for Fair Access will be in its monitoring of widening participation in institutions charging top-up fees.[68]

In the context of this bleak picture, it is important to recognize both that widening participation as a policy is relatively new and that there is only so much higher education as a sector and individual institutions can do to improve participation. For example, adopting a contextual approach within selection and adding criteria can identify some able applicants from groups under-represented in higher education but, without more, the effects of this policy will be limited. Whilst deciding to pursue positive discrimination in this context might provide more impressive results, such a policy would undoubtedly prove to be controversial given recent accusations of discrimination from within the independent schools sector. Moreover, 'hard' measures are unlikely to receive government support. Certainly, the government-commissioned independent review of university admissions was quick to reject this possibility. Its final report stated that 'the Steering Group does not want to bias admissions in favour of applicants from certain backgrounds or schools.'[69] Beyond this, all the evidence of disadvantage and underachievement suggests that action to end under-representation needs to be taken within the compulsory education sector and, more broadly, within society.[70] Poverty and poor schooling are the major contributors to the participation gap in higher education and, if as research suggests social mobility is declining, the problems are likely to become more severe.

However, this is not to say that higher education sector efforts to widen participation should be abandoned. Such work is of crucial importance and can have a life-changing effect upon students from under-represented groups. For example, Paula, a teenage mother taking part in the Meriton Project, an outreach programme run by the University of Bristol, felt that she had greatly benefited from the experience:

> Taking part in the law enrichment scheme was really important to me. I wanted to see what university was like, what students actually did and whether it was how I'd imagined it. I had an idea that all students would be posh, much older and completely different to me... I'm really pleased that I was able to take part in the scheme. It really showed me that university isn't just for other people and it made me more determined to carry on with my education. I would really recommend it to other people ... I definitely want to go to university![71]

67 See Universities and Colleges Admissions Service, 'Figures for 2006 entry', news release, 10 November 2005, at <http://www.ucas.ac.uk/new/press/index.html>.
68 For further information on the remit of the Office, see <http://www.offa.org.uk/>.
69 Admissions to Higher Education Steering Group. op. cit., n. 23, p. 6.
70 A. Furlong and A. Forsyth develop this argument in *Losing Out? Socioeconomic Disadvantage and Experience in Further and Higher Education* (2003).
71 University of Bristol, *Widening Participation at the University of Bristol 2003-2004* Annual Report (2004) 5, at <http://www.bristol.ac.uk/wideningparticipation/strategy/ar.pdf>. For more information on this Project see n. 7 above.

Beyond this, as much of widening participation work looks to the long term, it is arguably too soon to assess its impact. Consequently, higher education widening participation work should continue – but, if any significant changes are to be seen in the future, this should only be one element of efforts to improve the representativeness of the student body within higher education.

JOURNAL OF LAW AND SOCIETY
VOLUME 33, NUMBER 1, MARCH 2006
ISSN: 0263-323X, pp. 92–108

Preferential Treatment, Social Justice, and the Part-time Law Student – The Case for the Value-added Part-time Law Degree

ANDREW M. FRANCIS* AND IAIN W. MCDONALD**

There has been growing pressure to increase diversity in legal education and the legal profession in England and Wales. While this has focused upon the absence of certain groups such as women, ethnic minorities, and the disabled, there has been no specific discussion of part-time law students. Drawing on questionnaires and focus groups with part-time law students across England and Wales, this article examines how their background and experiences may hamper their ability to participate and succeed in higher education and legal practice. In response to the consistent omission of part-time students' needs from attempts to enhance social diversity in universities and the legal profession, it also argues that affirmative action is now necessary and justified in respect of these students. Pragmatic suggestions are made for a contextual approach to affirmative action for part-time law students which adds value to their degree. Finally, the potential effects of affirmative action on part-time law students themselves and upon the gatekeepers to the legal profession are explored.

INTRODUCTION

In recent years, there has been growing pressure to increase diversity in legal education and the legal profession in England and Wales. This has focused upon the absence of certain groups such as women, ethnic minorities, and the disabled, and some progress has been made in improving their position.

* *School of Law, Keele University, Staffordshire ST5 5BG, England*
** *Law Faculty, Frenchay Campus, University of the West of England, Coldharbour Lane, Bristol BS16 1QY, England*
a.m.francis@law.keele.ac.uk   Iain.McDonald@uwe.ac.uk

We would like to thank the students and institutions that participated in this study for their valuable time and cooperation and the Nuffield Foundation, whose funding support made this project possible: Nuffield Foundation Grant Reference SGS/00932/G.

92

However, a group that has so far been overlooked is part-time law students.[1] Part-time students are a diverse cohort whose profile rarely fits that of the 'typical' student, the 'single, geographically mobile 18–21 year old'.[2] Yet there are reasons to believe that they suffer distinct problems in higher education and in achieving access to the legal profession which need particular attention.

Higher education policy has consistently forgotten or overlooked the implications of change for part-time students.[3] The most recent example is the absence of significant debate on this issue during the passage of the Higher Education Act 2004.[4] Under the new scheme for student fees, part-time students will not benefit from the deferred repayment of fees set out in section 41 and are tied into a more onerous payment scheme than their full-time counterparts. In addition, although many students now work part-time to support their studies, this usually cannot be compared to part-time students working full-time while juggling study and caring responsibilities. If research into the experiences of (law) undergraduates continues to overlook the distinctiveness of part-time undergraduates, the significant difficulties that these students frequently face will continue to be ignored.

This article examines the ways in which the background and experiences of part-time students may hamper their ability to participate and succeed in higher education and the legal profession. We draw upon the results of questionnaires distributed to part-time law students across England and Wales in 2004, and of follow-up focus groups, which explored the experiences and aspirations of this cohort. Our argument is that the specific problems of part-time students must be addressed if universities and the legal profession are to succeed in meaningfully widening participation in legal education and in diversifying the future composition of the profession. Indeed, part-time law students may provide a telling litmus test of just how committed these institutions are to achieving equality and diversity. In response to the consistent omission of part-time students' needs from attempts to enhance social diversity in universities and the legal profession, we argue that affirmative action is now necessary and justified in respect of

1 See, for example, P. Harris and M. Jones, 'A Survey of Law Schools in the United Kingdom, 1996' (1997) 31 *Law Teacher* 38; L. Norman, *Career Choices in Law: A Survey of Law Students* (2004); A. Boon et al., 'Career Paths and Choices in a Highly Differentiated Profession: the Position of Newly Qualified Solicitors' (2001) 64 *Modern Law Rev.* 563, at 565. In this paper we focus on those registered on face-to-face qualifying law degrees, rather than those studying through distance learning schemes.
2 R. Maynard, 'Are Mature Students a Problem?' (1992) 17 *J. of Access Studies* 106, at 108.
3 T. Schuller et al., *Part-time Higher Education – Policy, Practice and Experience* (1999) 19–22.
4 The only reference to part-time students is in s. 31, whereby the Director of Fair Access must seek to identify good practice in full-time *and* part-time education. See, also, Baroness Ashton, 662 *H.L. Debs.*, col. 561, 14 June 2004.

93

them. Pragmatic suggestions are made for a contextual approach to affirmative action for part-time law students which adds value to their degree. Finally, its potential effects on part-time law students themselves and upon the gatekeepers to the legal profession are explored.

AFFIRMATIVE ACTION, PART-TIME LAW STUDENTS, AND HIGHER EDUCATION

Any affirmative action policy must expose the existence of discriminatory practices and structures.[5] Only when this has been accomplished can such policies be recognized as enhancing social justice, rather than simply providing preferential treatment for one group at the expense of others.[6] However, many law schools' prospectuses seem to straightforwardly assert (or, at least, imply) that full-time and part-time schemes of study are *equivalent*. This runs contrary to the views of many of our respondents who believed that little progress has been made towards recognizing their distinctive needs:

> I think there's a bit of, and I'll use the word 'discrimination', against us, ... But it's also a case of being treated second-rate ... There just seems to be a bit of an attitude or a mind set that, I guess, that we're secondary – that we come after the full-time students.

Respondents complain about inadequate access to the facilities that full-time undergraduates take for granted, such as pastoral care, careers advice, administrative staff, and key library resources. The conflicting demands of work, study, and family that students face also raise issues about planning that fails properly to consider part-time law students or to respond with appropriate flexibility.

The problem with such claims of equivalence is not that they offer false hope but that they are really only asserting the *minimum* of equivalence – that is, while the part-time law student may study fewer options with less contact time, the course remains a qualifying law degree. This is particularly significant as 64 per cent of our sample planned to continue onto the vocational stage of their legal education after graduation.

By asserting an unquestioned equivalency between part-time and full-time law programmes, universities arguably obscure the role that institutional structures and practices play in the success of its students. In other words, the *result* of a period of higher education (which symbolically lies in the hands of individual students) is emphasized over the *processes* involved in teaching

---

5 A task which is made all the more difficult by the politically controversial status of affirmative action. See, for example, T. Halpin, 'Universities Get Backing for Bias to State Pupils' *Times*, 6 April 2004, 4.
6 C. Bacchi, 'Policy and Discourse: Challenging the Construction of Affirmative Action as Preferential Treatment' (2004) 11 *J. of European Public Policy* 128, at 129.

94

and learning (which involves a much more complex exchange between students, staff, *and* institutional structures).[7]

Moreover, such an approach assumes that entry to the profession is predicated purely on formal levels of qualification. However, recruitment practices suggest that employability will depend on a much broader range of factors.[8] Following Bourdieu, universities are not only sites of formal learning; they are also active participants in the reproduction of class distinctions in society.[9] The law school provides more than just legal knowledge; it is also an important vessel for what Bourdieu describes as cultural capital. Cultural capital encompasses not only formal educational credentials but additionally:

> forms of 'practical knowledge' or 'knowing how things are done' which govern the distribution of rewards, the signs of eligibility for patronage, of 'background' or informal special languages and work-related behaviour.[10]

The law school represents an important site for the initial socialization of future lawyers, not just through the inculcation of legal knowledge, but also through the access they provide to student Law Societies, mooting, Inns of Court dining, careers advice, and contact with the legal profession. However, whereas the full-time law degree provides a wide variety of ways in which to learn how to *behave* like a lawyer, part-time law students are much less likely to be afforded such opportunities. Nearly 66 per cent of our respondents had never taken part in any extra-curricular activity and the lack of careers information is illustrated by the following extract from one of the focus groups:

> If you want to continue into a legal career, they don't give you any help ... I didn't know until recently that law firms recruit two or two and half years in advance. I found that out now, so I am lucky and there is enough time if I want to continue, but otherwise you'd be finishing the grades and wondering what to do next. Whereas the full-timers are told step by step. (Participant 5)

> We are not being told anything, I didn't even know that. That's the first [time I heard] for me. (Participant 2)

Despite the problems of the implied claims of equivalence, an increased provision of part-time law degree programmes could considerably enhance adult learners' opportunities to study law. While over 42 per cent of United Kingdom law schools provide part-time law degrees, these schemes remain

---

7 See M. Prosser and K. Trigwell, *Understanding Teaching and Learning: The Experience of Higher Education* (1999).
8 See H. Rolfe and T. Anderson, 'A Firm Choice: Law Firms' Preferences in the Recruitment of Trainee Solicitors' (2003) 10 *International J. of the Legal Profession* 315.
9 See D. Swartz, *Culture and Power: the Sociology of Pierre Bourdieu* (1997) ch. 8.
10 H. Sommerlad, 'The Gendering of the Professional Subject: Commitment, Choice and Social Closure in the Legal Profession' in *Legal Feminisms: Theory and Practice*, ed. C. McGlynn (1998) 11.

almost exclusively within the new university sector. In fact, only four old universities provide part-time law degrees and of those, two offer only daytime options. Moreover, in contrast to many full-time undergraduates, the existing work and family commitments of many part-time students will severely restrict their ability to move around the country to study or even to choose the best university they can. As such, current levels of provision will only benefit those students fortunate enough to live within commuting distance of a university which offers a part-time law degree already.

For the situation of part-time law students to be significantly improved, changes must address the peripheral position that part-time legal education continues to occupy in many law schools. Furthermore, if affirmative action is to succeed, changes must be clearly directed towards the limitations of the part-time law degree experience rather than generalized assumptions about the deficiencies of part-time law students.

While structural constraints upon universities and part-time students preclude a true equality with full-time schemes of study, these arguments suggest that universities should consider ways to improve the part-time experience of legal education. Given part-time law students' strong motivation to enter legal practice, the success of any affirmative action will depend upon the extent to which it reflects this desire.

AFFIRMATIVE ACTION, PART-TIME LAW STUDENTS, AND THE LEGAL PROFESSION

In recent years professional bodies and the government have taken a closer interest in monitoring the composition of the profession and tackling the under-representation of particular groups.[11] However serious problems remain and there has been sustained criticism concerning the difficulties that women and ethnic minorities face within law firms and at the Bar.[12] Moreover, socio-economic class continues to play a divisive role in the profession, both as an entry barrier and as a dimension of the increasing fragmentation within the profession.[13]

It is our argument that part-time law students are likely to find themselves at the intersection of *multiple disadvantages*. They are older; the majority of

11 D. Nicolson, 'Demography, Discrimination and Diversity: A New Dawn for the British Legal Profession?' (2005) 12 *International J. of the Legal Profession* 201.
12 See H. Sommerlad and P. Sanderson, *Gender, Choice and Commitment: Women Solicitors in England and Wales and the Struggle for Equal Status* (1998); C. McGlynn, *The Woman Lawyer: Making the Difference* (1998); M. Shiner, 'Young, Gifted and Blocked: Entry into the Legal Profession', and S. Vignaendra et al., 'Hearing Black and Asian Voices an Exploration of Identity', both in *Discriminating Lawyers*, ed. P. Thomas (2000).
13 R. Abel, *English Lawyers between Market and State: the Politics of Professionalism* (2003) 150.

96

our sample were over 30, with 38 per cent of our respondents aged between 31 and 40, and a further 18 per cent over 41. By contrast, the average age at entry to the solicitors' roll by direct entry is just 28.[14] Part-time students are more likely to be from an ethnic minority background; a third in our sample, compared with a quarter of all law graduates.[15] They are much more likely to have attended a new university, and our survey suggests that a substantial number will have had a broken educational background, with 40 per cent of our sample not possessing A-levels.[16]

The part-time students we surveyed expressed strong vocational motives, with two-thirds specifically wishing to enter legal practice.[17] As such, the distinctive social composition of part-time law students has the potential to make a significant difference to the diversity of the legal profession. However, just as legal education engages in some problematic assumptions about the 'typical student', there is widespread evidence that the profession makes its own assumptions about the ideal entrant. For the large law firms, the ideal recruit is frequently represented in recruitment brochures as a smiling, attractive twenty-something, surrounded by other smiling, attractive twenty-somethings bent over a computer.[18] Successive research studies suggest that a graduate's chances of becoming a solicitor (and it seems fair to assume that the Bar is the same) are significantly related to their A-level score, the institution they attended, their degree class mark, the school they attended at fourteen, their ethnicity, their work experience, and whether they had relatives in the profession.[19]

The necessity of working full-time to fund their studies means that, for many, vital legal work experience is simply out of the question. Over half of our respondents had not had legal work experience. Interestingly, however, 27 per cent of respondents either worked in or had employment experience of law-related occupations.[20] This group accounts for the vast majority of those with legal work experience and were more likely to have arranged

---

14 B. Cole, *Trends in the Solicitors' Profession: Annual Statistical Report 2003* (2004) 52.

15 id., p. 34.

16 Unfortunately our survey did not elicit further information about grades or schools attended, both of which could further impact on opportunities for entering the profession.

17 Although a recent Law Society study (Norman, op. cit., n. 1, p. 24) suggests that around 80 per cent of all students surveyed expressed a desire to enter the law, this includes nearly 20 per cent who were not sure in which capacity they would work.

18 See R. Collier, '"Be Smart, Be Successful, Be Yourself"? Representations of the Training Contract and the Trainee Solicitor in Advertising by Large Law Firms' (2005) 12 *International J. of the Legal Profession* 51.

19 See E. Duff et al., *Entry into the Legal Professions – the Law Student Cohort Study, Year 6* (2000); T. Goriely and T. Williams, *The Impact of the New Training Scheme – Report on a Qualitative Study* (1996); Rolfe and Anderson, op. cit., n. 8; R. Lee, *Firm Views: Work in and Work of the Largest Law Firms* (1999) 35.

20 Typically this was in an administrative capacity, for example as a legal secretary.

further placements. They were also the only respondents to have secured training contracts. This confirms that the legal profession is more open to those it already knows or recognizes as one of its own.[21]

Whether consciously or subconsciously, recruiters make assumptions about groups of applicants. While the above factors will restrict the entry of certain groups, the multiple disadvantages of part-time law students serve to exclude them in greater numbers. In other words, while a full-time law student may be older, or an Access course entrant or studying at a new university law school, a part-time law student is much more likely to be *all of these things*.

While affirmative action to assist part-time law students continues to be understood in terms of preferential treatment for undeserving individuals, it becomes very difficult politically to advance arguments in favour of it.[22] This is particularly the case within the legal profession. A central dimension of the profession's claims to high status derives in part from its attendant assertion that it guarantees equal access to the law. Related to this is the centrality of formal equality within legal ideology, which sees the legal labour market as a neutral sphere within which individuals succeed by virtue of their own individual merit.[23] This has a significant impact on the way in which the profession claims to be gender, race or class blind and yet ignores the pernicious inequalities that pervade legal practice. As Sommerlad and Sanderson argue in the context of women within the solicitors' profession:

> ... employees [are seen] as autonomous subjects, equal before the law, and requiring minimal legal intervention; ... the legal workplace is represented as an arena in which equal subjects will be treated with impartiality, and where such individuals can make certain choices, whilst in reality it is soaked in the prejudices which underpin gendered difference.[24]

Moreover, the legal profession's historically successful claim to control the market and enjoy higher status was founded:

> on a new basis, that of competence, defined and measured by a [standardised] system of testing ... Elite status was no longer claimed on the basis of identification with the extraneous stratification criteria of 'aristocratic' elites.[25]

Thus, an important part of the profession's status and autonomy derived from the claim that it was equally open to all.[26] Not only do these factors enable the profession to dismiss suggestions of the existence of discrimination and

21 See, generally, Nicolson, op. cit., n. 11.
22 Bacchi, op. cit., n. 6, p. 138.
23 P. Bourdieu, 'The Force of Law: Toward a Sociology of the Juridical Field' (1987) 38 *Hastings Law J.* 805, at 820.
24 Sommerlad and Sanderson, op. cit., n. 12, p. 103.
25 M. Larson, *The Rise of Professionalism: A Sociological Analysis* (1977) 70.
26 id., p. 51. Yet, arguably its status and market control were reinforced by barriers to entry which controlled the numbers of professionals (p. 52).

98

ascribe individuals' positions to their own choices, we would argue that it compounds the difficulty in arguing for the necessity of affirmative action policies.

Affirmative action runs contrary to these long established understandings of merit within the legal profession. Moreover these established conceptions may be difficult to resist if we acknowledge the power of 'habitus' in structuring the behaviour of actors operating within the field.[27] Thus Nelson and Trubek note that the choices that lawyers can make within a particular field are shaped by 'the historically constructed repertoire of "legitimate" or "permissible" professional responses.'[28] In this sense, then, we have to be clear that a crucial dimension of the 'legitimate' responses of lawyers is an insistence upon formal equality. Furthermore, even if affirmative action is reconceptualized as a programme of social justice,[29] this may still prove controversial for it would require the profession to recognize the unequal practices of lawyering and the persistence of discriminatory barriers.[30] Such recognition serves as a direct challenge to the profession's legitimacy and the basis of many of its claims to high status and autonomy.[31]

The challenge of justifying affirmative action is further complicated by the strong sense that the profession's regulatory responsibilities to consumers require that only the 'best' candidates, who demonstrate the highest levels of 'merit' should be permitted access to the profession. Such concerns can be more readily understood if the discursive power of 'affirmative action equals preferential treatment for the undeserving' is acknowledged.[32]

The Law Society's Diversity Access scheme is an example of a 'soft' form of affirmative action. It offers opportunities for non-traditional students to gain work experience, to be put in touch with solicitor mentors and, for a small number of individuals, help with fees on either the Common Professional Examination or the Legal Practice Course.[33] While this is to be welcomed, the scheme is in its infancy and remains relatively restricted in

---

27 Bourdieu, op. cit., n. 23, p. 811.
28 R. Nelson and D. Trubek, 'Introduction: New Problems and New Paradigms in Studies of the Legal Profession' in *Lawyers' Ideals/Lawyers' Practices: Transformations in the American Legal Profession*, eds. R. Nelson et al. (1992) 22.
29 Bacchi, op. cit., n. 6, p. 129.
30 Bacchi, id., is clear that such an approach, in contrast to conception of affirmative action as preferential treatment, will represent a fundamental challenge to the status quo.
31 Arguably as many of the specific supports of traditional professionalism come under increasing threat, the profession may find it derives new legitimacy from a more thorough interrogation of the basis on which access to the profession is premised (see A. Francis, 'Out of Touch and Out of Time: Lawyers, their Leaders and Collective Mobility Within the Legal Profession' (2004) 24 *Legal Studies* 322).
32 Bacchi, op. cit., n. 6, suggests that there is a strong consensus around formal equality of opportunity models which leads even advocates of affirmative action to deploy the language of (necessary) preferential treatment.
33 See, further, <www.lawsociety.org.uk/documents/downloads/DAS-a guide for students.pdf>.

99

scope. Moreover, its limited impact for part-time law students highlights the way in which they may be victims of multiple disadvantages. Their biographical characteristics and their difficult experiences while studying reveal them to be precisely the type of students who would benefit from such a scheme. However, as highlighted earlier, part-time law students face considerable difficulty in finding the time for work experience and in gaining access to services such as careers information, which could alert them to the existence of such schemes.

Despite the good intentions of the Bar Council and the Law Society, there are serious doubts as to the extent to which professional associations can actually speak for and control the recruiting profession.[34] In the context of the solicitors' profession, the largest law firms exercise greater and greater power, with scant regard for the collective concerns of the wider profession. Significantly, these firms are responsible for much of the profession's recruitment. Firms in the range of 27 to 81 plus partners are responsible for 48 per cent of trainee placements, with over half of all these opportunities located in London and the south-east of England.[35] While the Law Society may seek to instil best recruitment practice within these firms, given that such firms are selective (at best) in their treatment of other dimensions of the Law Society's regulatory authority,[36] we would argue that it is extremely optimistic to expect affirmative action polices and a *genuine* commitment to diversity to be inculcated within these firms, merely because the Law Society wishes it.

Thus, it is to the recruiting sector of the profession that we must justify affirmative action, but how is this to be done, given the baggage that the term brings and the specific context of the legal profession? One potentially useful line of argument can be drawn from the justifications offered by the United States Supreme Court when upholding affirmative action programmes. It has focused on the benefits that the diversity produced by such policies can bring to institutional life and to wider society.[37] For example, in the recent decision of *Grutter* v. *Bolinger*[38] the court went further than simply justifying affirmative action in terms of creating a diverse student body and pointed to the leadership role that law graduates play in American society:

> In order to cultivate a set of leaders with legitimacy in the eyes of the citizenry, it is necessary that the path to leadership be visibly open to talented and qualified individuals of every race and ethnicity ... Access to legal education

---

34 See Francis, op. cit., n. 31.
35 Cole, op. cit., n. 14, pp. 43–5.
36 See G. Hanlon, *Lawyers, the State and the Market: Professionalism Revisited* (1999) and J. Griffiths–Baker, *Serving Two Masters: Conflicts of Interest in the Modern Law Firm* (2002).
37 K. Karst, 'The Revival of Forward-Looking Affirmative Action' (2004) 104 *Columbia Law Rev.* 60.
38 *Grutter*, 123 S Ct. 2325 (2003).

(and thus the legal profession) must be inclusive of talented and qualified individuals of every race and ethnicity.[39]

While a legal education has never guaranteed entry to legal practice, these arguments remain a powerful justification for affirmative action and go to the heart of why we should seek genuine diversity within the legal profession.

It may be possible to make an appeal to the profession based on similar premises, for it holds itself out to be an ethical profession, with the protection of justice a fundamental aspect of its professional ideology. However, it will be perhaps strategically necessary to make the case for affirmative action for part-time law students based on business imperatives.[40] Such a business case could still contain elements of social justice. Large corporations, particularly those based in the United States, increasingly demand evidence of corporate responsibility from the law firms eager to secure their business.[41] Perhaps the starkest way in which the business case for affirmative action policies on behalf of part-time law students could be put would be to make clear to the profession that they are potentially ignoring individuals who could become profitable fee-earners. Affirmative action policies which go to the heart of the ways in which merit is determined will go some way towards ensuring that the talent of these individuals is not ignored. Moreover, affirmative action policies should be adopted to alert the profession to the fact that, notwithstanding their necessary heterogeneity, part-time law students are geographically immobile (and so would show loyalty to a locality), have demonstrated extraordinary commitment to the law already, have real life experience, and are likely to possess transferable skills.

The following section will build upon this discussion of the problems facing part-time law students and the difficulties in directing affirmative action arguments towards the legal profession and the universities by developing more concrete proposals for adding real value to part-time legal education. Such suggestions are necessarily targeted at both the legal profession and the universities.

ADDING VALUE TO PART-TIME LEGAL EDUCATION

We argue that it is necessary for providers of part-time law degrees and the profession to scrutinize their own practices and to alter them to bring about a

---

39 id., p. 2341, cited in Karst, op. cit., n. 37, pp. 60–1.
40 However, McGlynn argues that such a strategy may be 'limited and potentially disastrous' in failing to tackle the underlying assumptions of the profession: C McGlynn, 'The Business of Equality in the Solicitors' Profession' (2000) 63 *Modern Law Rev.* 442, at 455.
41 See, generally, Hanlon, op. cit., n. 36, on the client-led nature of professional services, and Karst, op. cit., n. 37, p. 68.

101

more substantive equivalence in their treatment of part-time and full-time students. In addition, such a project should not be seen as momentary assistance for a disadvantaged group, but a much more thorough evaluation of the way in which entry to the profession is controlled. However, any such project of affirmative action would be strengthened by a legal regulatory structure to ensure that progress is made and maintained. Otherwise the persistence of both clients' and employees' prejudices towards particular groups may reward firms who choose not to implement more progressive recruitment strategies.[42] As we have argued, part-time law students frequently find themselves subject to multiple disadvantages. While it is conceptually easier to respond to discrimination on the basis of singular disadvantage, such as race or sex, the law has struggled to articulate an effective legal response to intersectional discrimination.[43]

However, the legal framework established in the Disability Discrimination Act 1995 may provide an innovative way by which institutional responsibility may be mapped onto a regulatory legislative structure for part-time law students. Two important dimensions of the Disability Discrimination Act are that it allows certain discriminatory practices to be justified and also requires more positive steps, or 'reasonable adjustments', to be taken in order to accommodate people who would otherwise be unfairly discriminated against on the basis of their disability. Such positive steps offer a response to discrimination which focuses on equalizing treatment rather than special benefits.

A successful justification of the differential treatment of disabled persons must be 'material to the circumstances of the case and substantial'.[44] In the context of further and higher education, this justification of unfair treatment or the failure to comply with the obligation to make reasonable adjustments is permitted in order to maintain academic standards or standards of another kind.[45] However, the justification offered must be as a result of the assessment of each individual's circumstances and merits. Similarly, the requirement to make 'reasonable adjustments' is directed at an individual's circumstances and is designed to equalize the treatment of disabled and non-disabled persons. In this sense, as Gaston has argued in another context, the meaning of discrimination is reclaimed as

---

42 See G. Massey, 'Thinking about Affirmative Action: Arguments Supporting Preferential Policies' (2004) 21 *Rev. of Policy Research* 783, at 791–2.

43 For example, *Pearce* v. *Governing Body of Mayfield Secondary School* [2003] UKHL 34, where the House of Lords failed to allow an accurate comparator to be used in respect of the harassment suffered by a lesbian teacher. See, also, K. Crenshaw, 'Demarginalizing the Inter-section of Race and Sex: A Black Feminist Critique of Antidiscrimination Doctrine, Feminist Theory and Antiracist Politics' (1989) 89 *University of Chicago Legal Forum* 139.

44 Disability Discrimination Act 1995 s. 28B(7), as amended by the Special Educational Needs and Disability Act 2001.

45 See HMSO, *Post 16 Education Code of Practice* (2002) example 4.27B.

102

'discernment',[46] wherein decisions made are individualized rather than group-based and context-specific rather than generalized.

Thus, notwithstanding the judicial construction of the threshold for justification having been set as 'very low',[47] the framework of Disability Discrimination Act could offer a formula for a more thorough interrogation of the way in which merit is constructed in both universities and the legal profession in the allocation of resources and opportunities. Rather than simply asking for thoughtful reflection, the profession could be directed towards a more explicitly objective construction of merit in the same way that universities must already carefully consider what is meant by academic standards.

It is beyond the scope of this paper to articulate how this might be achieved. However, it is our argument that any such project would have to display a nuanced approach to understanding and identifying both discrimination and disadvantage. Such an approach consciously avoids preferential treatment in favour of a broader focus on social justice by focusing on the *social* good to be derived from an interrogation of the prejudicial effects of the profession's current practices. Thus, rather than emphasize 'special treatment' to enable candidates to meet existing conceptions of 'merit', the focus on 'reasonable adjustments' and more individualized constructions of merit will ensure that entry to the profession is premised on genuinely fair and transparent criteria. This could, for example, involve the profession being directed to make 'reasonable adjustments' to the operation of their applications criteria when assessing part-time law students. Such an approach challenges the profession to think about the way in which 'merit' is constructed. This could run alongside more effective targeting of existing programmes such as the Diversity Access scheme, which could increase the profession's awareness of the quality that may be found within the part-time cohort. Moreover, this process might additionally require the imposition of harder-edged short-term policies of affirmative action, perhaps through the insistence on quotas and targeted hiring for under-represented groups including part-time law students.

Moving the focus from legal practice, there are a number of key actions targeted within universities which could immediately enhance part-time law degree programmes and make a real difference to these students' experiences of studying law and their subsequent opportunities within the legal profession.

The commitment of the new universities to widening participation in higher legal education has a long and creditable history.[48] However, the level

---

46 P. Gaston, 'Reflections on Affirmative Action: Its Origins, Virtues, Enemies, Champions and Prospects' in *Diversity Challenged: Evidence on the Impact of Affirmative Action*, ed. G. Orfield (2001) 290.

47 *Heinz* v. *Kenrick* [2000] IRLR 144 (EAT).

48 P. Leighton, 'New Wine in Old Bottles' (1998) 25 *J. of Law and Society* 85.

of provision of part-time law degrees amongst the old university sector must be dramatically improved in order to tackle the geographical immobility of many aspiring adult learners that stands in the way of their higher education. Moreover, the challenge of bringing diversity and equality to the legal profession must be the responsibility of *all* law schools. While part-time law students remain overwhelmingly located within the new university sector, the profession's entrenched notions of merit are left unchallenged, as the talent and potential that exists within this cohort will continue to be ignored. In the short- to medium-term, a commitment from the old university sector to part-time and non-traditional law students may play a pivotal role in establishing a more inclusive vision of professionalism for recruiters, as well as for the next generation of lawyers we are currently producing.

Once embarked upon a part-time law degree, students will require meaningful access to a range of university facilities. For example, while many libraries are moving to 24-hour opening during term time, this will be of primary benefit to those who do not have home or family commitments. Moreover, a recurring complaint amongst respondents to our questionnaire was access to key materials in short-loan collections. In most libraries, such materials may be taken out overnight or over the weekend. This, in itself, is of limited assistance to part-time law students who may not be able to return to the library the following morning. Moreover, in most cases, such materials will already have been issued to full-time students earlier in the day. Therefore, the introduction of longer loan periods for part-time law students might appear to be 'preferential treatment' but is, in fact, a means of increasing substantive fairness in terms of access to resources. The limited time that part-time law students have in the library could also be compensated by supporting students' photocopying costs. Alternatively, part-time law students could receive thorough and integrated training in e-resources, such as Westlaw and Lexis/Nexis. Any such move would, of course, have to consider fully the IT needs and resources of part-time students, as well as the possibility of providing bursaries to support students without home computer equipment and internet access.

Access to the law school office for inquiries and assistance should be enhanced. Improved opening hours, even on an occasional basis, would assist in making part-time students feel a part of the law school, rather than an inconvenience to its smooth running. Moreover, such moves could also ameliorate common practices which frequently indirectly discriminate against part-time students by demanding that coursework is submitted and collected in person and within certain times.

If the part-time law degree is truly to offer added value, it should reflect the vocational drive of students and, as far as it is acceptable to do so, the priorities of legal recruiters. Responses to our survey of part-time law students indicate that access to careers advice and awareness of recruitment criteria is patchy. Moreover, there are often insurmountable barriers to gaining legal work experience, frequently a key factor in obtaining training

104

contracts. While our survey suggests that many part-time law students are unable to participate in extra-curricular activities, the importance with which these activities are regarded by the profession demands that law schools think more creatively about how such activities and contact with the legal profession might be incorporated into the part-time experience of law school. Mooting, other legal advocacy skills, and clinical legal education could be incorporated into the curriculum and the importance of personal development planning stressed. Indeed, more input from the profession or firm-sponsored prizes specifically for part-time law students could enable the profession to identify potential in this often overlooked group.

Finally, in that part-time considerations are so often peripheral to planning and resourcing decisions, the representation of these students should be encouraged and accommodated, perhaps through ensuring that some key meetings take place at times convenient to their involvement.

THE IMPACT OF AFFIRMATIVE ACTION POLICIES ON PART-TIME LAW STUDENTS

1. Individual effects of part-time study and the impact of affirmative action

An emerging theme of our current research is the effect of involvement in part-time legal education on the students themselves.[49] It is important to note that a significant number of our respondents have noted an increase in self-esteem. Interestingly they also reported an enhanced respect and admiration from friends, family, and work colleagues.

Respondents reported clear benefits, ranging from '[the part-time degree has helped me develop] a determination I didn't know I had' to '[a] tremendous sense of personal achievement and self-pride'. Interestingly, participants in focus groups also discussed the study of law in terms of self-empowerment; they felt better equipped to deal with their employers in particular and were more confident in asserting their 'rights'. This was particularly true of the one student who self-identified as disabled (somebody who might otherwise be said to occupy a further distinct position of disadvantage, even as against other part-time law students):

> I'm doing employment law this year, and I had concerns with my employer because I'm classed as disabled. And I had to explain about the Disability Act and employment law and the alarm bells just rung. I've never seen my employer move so fast ... I enjoy working there, but you know [in the past] issues have been raised and it's taken a couple of years. But as soon as I said I was doing employment law, it's like 'Woah! OK!' So yeah, it does work to your advantage at times.

---

49 See A. Francis and I. McDonald, 'Part-time Law Students: The Forgotten Cohort?' (2005) *Law Teacher* (forthcoming).

However, we would be concerned as to whether adding value to a part-time degree as a strategy of affirmative action would continue to enhance students' self-esteem or would instead have detrimental effects.[50] Their achievements may in fact be coloured by their status as targets of affirmative action strategies.[51] Bacchi is clear that such deleterious impacts flow from the construction of affirmative action as preferential treatment.[52] Radin suggests that the prevailing perception of affirmative action is that it 'gives benefits to people who are less qualified or less deserving than white men or indeed are wholly unqualified or undeserving'.[53] Sadly, such discursive power leads many marginalized groups to distance themselves from affirmative action policies and to reassert that they wish only to be judged 'on the merits'.[54] Clearly we should be reluctant to pursue strategies that undermine some of the existing success of part-time legal education, notwithstanding the deeper problem of why affirmative action can be so problematic for the very groups for whom it is intended to secure justice.

This concern about the risk of stigmatization is perhaps supported by our findings that two-thirds of our respondents believe that they *should not* be treated differently from full-time students. This in itself may not be surprising given the predominance of the ideas on the equivalence of part-time and full-time degrees, and an attendant reluctance to be identified or to self-identify as a student or group in need of 'special treatment'. Even within the focus groups, when we were able to explore the point about different treatment more fully, while all students were vocal in expressing dissatisfaction at their status as second-class citizens within the law school, the proposals they suggested were not so much different treatment, as to be treated with *real* equivalence to the full-time cohort. These responses suggest that a properly articulated policy of affirmative action, which stresses fairness (or 'accommodation') over preferential treatment, could find greater acceptance from the group targeted.

2. External effects of part-time law degrees and the impact of affirmative action

While possession of a law degree encompasses part of the necessary cultural capital[55] for entry into the profession, other ascribed attributes would still leave many part-time law graduates with the difficulty that they do not resemble lawyers in terms of attributes, background or experiences valued by

---

50 See S. Carter, *Reflections of an Affirmative Action Baby* (1992).
51 However, for a contrary view, see W. Bowen and D. Bok, *The Shape of the River: Long-term Consequences of Considering Race in College and University Admissions* (1998).
52 Bacchi, op. cit., n. 6, p. 132.
53 M. Radin, 'Affirmative Action Rhetoric' (1991) 8 *Social Philosophy and Policy* 130, at 134–6.
54 Bacchi, op. cit., n. 6, p. 135.
55 P. Bourdieu, *An Outline of a Theory of Practice* (1977) 187.

106

the profession. Similar problems are highlighted by work, such as Sommerlad and Sanderson's, which reveals the ways in which notions of 'commitment' and 'professionalism' are constructed within legal practice.[56]

Given that the recognition of appropriate cultural capital is not automatic within the legal field, we might question whether having a value-added law degree will assist part-time law students and address the present deficiencies which place disproportionate emphasis on criteria (or attributes) beyond the control of the individual – for example, choice of school or university, the ability to do well in A-levels, poorly resourced schools, gender, ethnicity, and so on. Is it possible that a value-added law degree, however conceived, will contribute to the development of the cultural capital necessary to achieve entry to the profession?

Arguably, in a least worst-case scenario, affirmative action could have a negligible impact on their cultural capital. However, would it, in fact, confirm their outsider status to the legal profession? The possession of a value-added part-time degree, the recipient of 'special treatment' or 'affirmative action' may lead the profession to ascribe certain attributes, which have negative value in the professional marketplace.

Cultural capital involves complex and arguably not even always conscious processes of socialization and informal learning. If it was felt that such socially validated attributes had only been 'artificially' developed through a programme of affirmative action, given the discursive baggage with which the term is saddled, this is likely to further undermine the extent to which part-timers' attributes will be recognized. The difficult context of the legal profession requires, first and foremost, a pragmatic response for affirmative action to succeed. Therefore, we argue that some of the harder-edged policies of affirmative action outlined here must be time-limited in order to focus the attention of the profession upon its own practices of recruitment, rather than helping to confirm any misconceptions that part-time law students require 'special treatment'.[57]

Although the biggest law firms and most prestigious sets of chambers represent the largest section of the recruiting profession, we should be careful not to valorize these sectors. Clearly not every part-time law graduate will wish to work in these fields. Moreover, the cultural capital valued by the profession is not consistent across an increasingly heterogeneous legal marketplace. This suggests that part-time law graduates may find their attributes and experience more highly valued and socially validated in some discrete fields of the fragmented profession, for example, high-street practices or in crime and family where life experiences might be more highly valued.[58] At present, where part-time graduates do enter the profession, we would argue (and it

---

56 Sommerlad and Sanderson, op cit., n. 12.
57 See Bacchi, op. cit., n. 6, p. 133.
58 However, compare T. Williams and T. Goriely, *Recruitment and Retention of Solicitors in Small Firms* (2003) 13.

appears to be borne out anecdotally at least) that it is more likely to be in the lower-status areas. While such limited evidence suggests that sections of the profession can accommodate part-time law graduates, our central argument remains that the profession's scrutiny of its own definitions of merit requires a continuing project of reflection so that part-time law graduates are not limited by the recruiting profession's blinkered conception of the ideal recruit.

CONCLUSION

However difficult it may be to make a policy of affirmative action work for part-time law students, this should not be taken to absolve universities or the profession of responsibility for these students and social diversity more generally. Moreover, we argue that the preconceptions that part-time students are 'messy, complex and problematic'[59] could contribute to the misconception that part-time graduates are somehow 'less than whole', regardless of the diversity of their life experiences. Such negative images blot out the positive attributes that part-time law students can possess – their commitment, their sacrifices, and their ability to manage conflicting responsibilities successfully – which will eclipse the typical full-time student's experience. In fact, we should be asking why is the appeal of part-time law graduates not more widely recognized?

The danger of pursuing a policy of affirmative action to add further value to the part-time law degree is that this may be only a momentary action which further confirms the idea of them as a group needing special assistance and help. This creates an approach which is premised on a group's 'deficiencies' rather than something that will be transformative of institutions and the professions. The longer such policies remain in place, the stronger the argument will become that part-time law students are messy because the underlying issue will not have been resolved.[60] Therefore, to succeed, such policies must be coordinated between institutions and the profession and aimed at cultural and attitudinal changes. As suggested above, it may also be necessary to encourage such change through legislative force. As Fredman recognizes, 'affirmative action needs to be only one part of a broad based and radical strategy, which does more than redistribute privileged positions; but refashions the institutions which continue to perpetuate exclusion.'[61] Only in this way will the pejorative image of the 'part-time law graduate' be replaced by the person who has simply graduated through a part-time route.

59 P. Davies, 'Half Full, Not Half Empty: A Positive Look at Part-time Education' (1999) 53 *Higher Education Q.* 141, at 144.
60 Bacchi, op. cit., n. 6, p. 132, points out that 'the problem becomes those described as "damaged"; they are the ones who must change.' Moreover, any failure following the implementation of the policy is seen to lie firmly at the feet of the targeted group.
61 S. Fredman, *Discrimination Law* (2002) 160.

JOURNAL OF LAW AND SOCIETY
VOLUME 33, NUMBER 1, MARCH 2006
ISSN: 0263-323X, pp. 109–25

Affirmative Action in the Legal Profession

DONALD NICOLSON*

This article examines whether the legal profession should use quotas and decision-making preferences in recruitment and promotion in favour of women, ethnic minorities, and those from socially disadvantaged backgrounds. It argues that this is necessary to eradicate current patterns of discrimination and disadvantage. It also argues that quotas and decision-making preferences do not necessarily conflict with appointment or promotion on merit, and hence that consequent unfairness to other applicants is more apparent than real. Moreover, any potential stigmatization of the beneficiaries of affirmative action is outweighed by the advantages in reversing the under-representation of women, ethnic minorities, and those from socially disadvantaged background, thereby challenging perceptions of their inferior qualities as lawyers. Finally, practical problems in the implementation of affirmative action are considered and argued to be insufficiently serious to stand in the way of its introduction.

INTRODUCTION

For centuries, the legal profession constituted an exclusive club of white, middle-class men. Although the last few decades have seen a dramatic increase in female and ethnic minority entrants, research shows that a successful legal career is far from being equally open to all. This raises the question whether affirmative action should be introduced by the legal profession.

A positive answer has implications extending beyond legal practice. This is because the advanced educational qualifications, and the intellectual and other skills required of entrants, which are thought to guarantee high quality

* Law School, University of Strathclyde, Stenhouse Building, Glasgow G4 0RJ, Scotland
donald.nicolson@strath.ac.uk

I would like to thank Amanda Benstock, Harry Dematagoda, Julie Donaldson, and Adrienne Shepherd for their research help.

109

services to clients, mean that appointing and promoting on merit is regarded as particularly important in professional and other skilled occupations. Showing that merit is not compromised by affirmative action in the legal profession thus assists the case for affirmative action in all such occupations. Nor is it inappropriate to use the legal profession as a test case given the readership of this collection. Indeed, it can be argued that legal academics have a special duty to ensure that those they purport to admit to law school on merit and prepare for practice do not later find their career prospects hampered by their social background. In addition, for those wishing to ensure a more general acceptance of affirmative action, persuading the legal profession that it is just and practicable is a useful starting place, since lawyers are better placed than most occupational groups to secure an end to the current legal prohibition on 'strong'[1] forms of affirmative action. This is recognized by the Bar Council[2] which, along with the Law Society of England and Wales, also accepts that, given the profession's *raison d'être* in ensuring access to justice and upholding 'people's rights without fear and favour', lawyers should 'take a lead on issues of equality and fairness'.[3] To this end, they have already introduced detailed measures designed to eradicate discrimination and promote diversity, including 'weak' forms of affirmative actions.

In arguing that the Anglo-Welsh[4] professional bodies should contemplate strong forms, I will concentrate on recruitment and promotion quotas, and decision-making preferences, which require members of previously excluded groups to be recruited or promoted if regarded as equally or almost as capable as their competitors (what I will call 'tie-break' and 'ballpark' preferences, respectively). I will also limit discussion to the position of women, ethnic minorities, and those from socio-economically disadvantaged backgrounds. This is not to deny that other groups have justifiable claims for affirmative action. However, because of space constraints, and the fact that the problems of sexuality, age, and religion seem less extensive than those of class, gender, and race, whereas disability requires and is to some extent already receiving[5] unique forms of affirmative action, I will only discuss the 'big three', leaving it to others to apply relevant insights more extensively.

---

1 That is, those forms of preferential treatment which require selection panels to choose recruitment or promotion candidates solely or partly because of their group membership, rather than simply take action to put some in a position where they might be more likely to be chosen (such as targeting them in terms of recruitment publicity or access to training).

2 The General Council of the Bar, *The Stephen Lawrence Inquiry Report: Response by the Bar Council* (1999) 15.

3 Bar Council, *Equality and Diversity Code for the Bar* (2004); The Law Society, *Delivering Equality and Diversity: A Handbook for Solicitors* (2004) 2.

4 The Scottish and Northern Irish branches are not discussed because there is very little information on their demographic background and they have done little to address discrimination.

5 See n. 3 above.

110

Finally, I will concentrate on arguing that affirmative action is justified as necessary to ensure distributive justice and equal opportunities in legal practice since alternative justifications are far less likely to be convincing in the United Kingdom,[6] if at all,[7] or do not independently justify the extensive demographic changes that distributive justice might.[8] This justification runs as follows:

1. The legal profession is morally and, as far as gender and race are concerned, legally obliged not to discriminate in distributing jobs and promotions;
2. Currently the legal profession does so discriminate;
3. Existing measures are unlikely to eradicate such discrimination even in the medium term;
4. If appropriately designed and implemented, quotas and decision-making preferences can reverse patterns of exclusion;
5. Consequently, unless there are strong countervailing considerations or insurmountable practical problems, they should be introduced into legal practice.

Given that the first step of this argument is uncontroversial and that the fourth is supported by the experience in other jurisdictions and in other occupations,[9] the rest of the article will seek to establish that hard affirmative action is necessary, not otherwise objectionable nor irredeemably impractical.

6 Compare A. McHarg and D. Nicolson, 'Justifying Affirmative Action: Perception and Reality', pp. 9–11 in this issue, regarding the argument that affirmative action should be introduced to compensate for past discrimination.
7 Compare Dworkin's unpersuasive argument that a more diverse legal profession will reduce social tension: R. Dworkin, *Taking Rights Seriously* (1977) 228.
8 See D. Nicolson, 'Demography, Discrimination And Diversity: Legal Ethics And Social Background' (2005) 12 *International J. of the Legal Profession* 201, regarding the arguments that a demographically diverse legal profession will improve legal services to the community, and that the greater presence of lawyers from previously excluded backgrounds, particularly in promoted positions, may act as role models, encouraging later generations to aspire to a career previously seen as unattainable, and are likely to ensure greater challenges to unthinking expressions of prejudice and greater reform of discriminatory practices. See at pp. 117–8 and 121, below, where they are used in support of the distributive justice argument.
9 For example, R. Kennedy, 'Persuasion and Distrust: A Comment on the Affirmative Action Debate' (1986) 99 *Harvard Law Rev.* 1327, at 1329; J. Edwards, *When Race Counts: The Morality of Racial Preference in Britain and America* (1995) chs. 5 and 6; D.A. Farber, 'The Outmoded Debate Over Affirmative Action' (1994) 82 *California Law Rev.* 893, at 913.

A few decades ago, the existence of a discriminatory profession was clear from the almost total exclusion of women, ethnic minorities, and those from socially disadvantaged backgrounds. Today, while there appears to be little change to the legal profession's class background, female recruits have steadily increased to the point where numerical parity is not far off, whereas the number of ethnic minority lawyers exceeds their general social distribution. These figures, however, hide gender and race discrimination. Women still face greater difficulty in obtaining pupillages and tenancies, training contracts, in negotiating the transition from trainee to qualified solicitor if they have children, and possibly also in obtaining the same starting salaries as men. Ethnic minority lawyers face similar difficulties in obtaining training contracts and the same starting salaries as their white counterparts.

However, it is after qualification that demographic differences really begin to bite. While there have been no British studies on the effect of class on legal careers, elsewhere it has been shown to have a lasting impact. British research does however reveal that a gender gap in solicitor' salaries and barristers' earnings increases incrementally with time, that the award of silk and partnerships are equally affected by gender, and that ethnic minorities find it more difficult to obtain partnerships. This glass ceiling can no longer be dismissed as a temporary stage on the road to equality. Thirty years after large-scale female entry into legal practice, and twenty years after that of ethnic minorities, the expected 'trickle up' has not materialized and women and ethnic minorities with appropriate levels of experience still tend to work in less lucrative areas of practice and more generally to fail to match white men in career progression. Moreover, qualified lawyers report that they continue to face discrimination on the grounds of gender, race, and class, whereas women also report sexual harassment.

Thus, the legal profession can still be criticized for not ensuring that a successful legal career is equally open to all. The Anglo-Welsh professional bodies are, however, likely to assert that their recently introduced anti-discrimination and pro-diversity measures go beyond anti-discrimination law and require time to work before strong affirmative action can be said to be necessary to remedy this situation. Admittedly, these measures are detailed and are based on a relatively sophisticated understanding of, and a sincere attempt to eradicate, discrimination. However, their reflection of the law's formal rather than substantive approach to discrimination[11] and various other flaws undermine their ability to ensure equality of opportunity.

At a basic level, many of these provisions, particularly those involving 'weak' affirmative action, are undermined by confusion as to their precise

10 See the fuller discussion in Nicolson, op. cit., n. 8, where detailed statistics and supporting references can be found.
11 See S. Fredman, *Discrimination Law* (2001) ch. 5.

requirements, are recommendatory rather than mandatory, and, even when mandatory, lack clear sanctions for breaches. Furthermore, some are patchy in their application. For example, the Law Society has set recruitment targets for ethnic minorities but not for other groups[12] and requires equal pay reviews for women but only recommends them for ethnic minorities.

Such flaws can be easily remedied. More problematic is the failure to adequately address some of the underlying causes of discrimination. Thus, one of the biggest obstacles to career progression for women lies in the fact that legal practice is based on the work patterns of lawyers unencumbered by domestic responsibilities. By taking substantially more time out of work than men, female lawyers are not only less able to show their qualities, but also less available for the long hours, and after-hours socializing and practice development regarded as important for advancement. The professional bodies have partially addressed this problem by recommending maternity leave longer than the statutory minimum, but have done nothing to make parenting cost-free for promotion prospects and hardly anything to encourage male lawyers to take more responsibility for childcare.

The limited nature of the anti-discrimination provisions is most apparent in their failure to address the fact that class is now the greatest obstacle to qualification and progress in legal practice, especially because of the increase in places going to women and because of the over-representation of ethnic minorities amongst the less privileged social groups. Most obviously, the cost of qualifying remains daunting, especially because of reduced state funding, and especially for aspiring barristers who must still survive many years of unremunerative practice. Fear of debt might prompt law students to work part-time, which in turn might affect academic performance and the ability to gain the unpaid work experience which is so important for recruitment, or may even deter some from a legal career altogether. Yet, financial support for aspiring lawyers tends to go to those who least need it.

Perhaps more importantly, class interacts with the selection criteria used by professional gatekeepers to discriminate indirectly against those from less privileged backgrounds. Thus, parental access to financial capital may place children onto an escalator of privilege by enabling them to attend fee-paying schools, which, when combined with the social capital represented by the atmosphere, expectations, and parental support in middle-class homes, substantially increases the chances of middle-class children choosing a legal career and obtaining the academic results necessary to enter law school, especially a prestigious one. Attendance at the latter, in turn, increases the chances of obtaining a good degree and hence progression to the vocational stage of legal education. Good degree results (and, in the case of training contracts, also school results, and the educational institution attended) substantially enhance the chances of obtaining work experience, pupillages, and

---

12 The Bar has dropped targets for chambers, perhaps because ethnic minority recruits to the Bar now exceed overall ethnic minority distribution.

training contracts, especially in the more prestigious, better paying firms, and apparently also continue to enhance career progression after qualification. Furthermore, a privileged family background and attendance at the better academic institutions provide the social connections and 'old boy' networks that facilitate finding work experience, training contracts, pupillages, and post-qualification employment. Thus, even after 'objective' criteria like academic results and work experience are held constant, having graduate or professionally qualified parents, and attending an independent school and/or elite law school substantially increase the chances of obtaining pupillages and training contracts, especially in the City and large provincial firms.

But even if these flaws and omissions in the profession's current anti-discrimination measures were to be addressed, they are unlikely by themselves to ensure equality of opportunity. This is because many of the problems faced by previously excluded groups lie not in directly or even indirectly discriminatory recruitment or promotion criteria, but in the fact that the hegemonic form of cultural capital[13] in legal practice is that of white, upper middle-class men. Possession of such cultural capital is particularly important because the surplus of qualified candidates for legal positions means that more subjective selection criteria and an instinctive judgement about candidates' 'fit' play a crucial role in recruitment and promotion. It is also important because 'personalist' or 'clientist' relationships 'underpin power hierarchies and key decision-making' in legal practice.[14] Thus, lacking the right cultural capital, women, ethnic minorities, and those from socially disadvantaged backgrounds are less likely to receive mentoring, patronage, and training and to be allocated the sort of work useful for promotion. This 'fraternal contract'[15] also characterizes lawyer-client relationships, hence affecting the ability to gain and retain clients. But both intra-professional and lawyer-client relationships tend to be forged in settings in which women, ethnic minorities, and perhaps also those from socially disadvantaged backgrounds feel uncomfortable and sometimes even in male-only settings. Finally, while the performance of all previously excluded groups is likely to be more closely monitored and harshly judged by those who assume their inferior competence, women face the particular problem that, whatever the reality, their real or assumed commitment to family will be interpreted as a concomitant absence of commitment to work – which is *the* criterion for recruitment and for obtaining mentoring, training and favourable work allocation.

The Anglo-Welsh professional bodies seem to understand some of these problems and have warned against practices such as asking women about

---

13 Defined as a 'permanent disposition, a durable way of standing, speaking, walking and thereby of feeling and thinking': P. Bourdieu, *The Logic of Practice* (1990) 69–70.
14 H. Sommerlad and P. Sanderson, *Gender, Choice and Commitment: Women Solicitors in England and Wales and the Struggle for Equal Status* (1998) 7.
15 M. Thornton, *Dissonance and Distrust – Women in the Legal Profession* (1996).

family plans or assuming that lawyers will welcome visits to the pub, and have recommended the provision, for instance, of areas for prayer. However, while legal practice, and particularly its upper echelons, continues to be dominated by white, upper middle-class men, attitudes will take years to change. Even soft affirmative action measures will do little to address the stubborn fact that social disadvantage prevents most working class members, many ethnic minorities and some women from meeting the educational and entrance criteria. For instance, it is no use advertising jobs in socially deprived or ethnic minority areas if members of those communities do not attend the schools and universities, gain the grades, and have the social and cultural capital necessary to succeed in the increasingly competitive market for training contracts and pupillages.

It is thus arguable that it is only by increasing the numbers of socially disadvantaged recruits and promoting more female and ethnic minority lawyers that challenges to assumptions about the unsuitability of these groups to legal practice, existing standards of recruitment, and the hegemonic form of cultural capital can be expected to increase. Consequently, unless one is prepared to wait for a painfully slow 'trickle-in' and 'trickle-up', it would seem that hard forms of affirmative action are justified as the only means of ensuring distributive justice and equality of opportunity.

IS STRONG AFFIRMATIVE ACTION OBJECTIONABLE?

1. *The argument from merit*

Lawyers, however, seem resolutely opposed to such measures, primarily because they are thought to be incompatible with appointing and promoting on merit.[16] Given the strength of this belief and the professional bodies' apparent determination to eradicate discrimination, it is probably not enough to note the irony, if not the hypocrisy, of lawyers trumpeting a principle which so many continue to disregard, not to mention the bigotry of the assumption that those from previously excluded groups are inherently inferior.

Instead, it is necessary to refute the argument that, by contravening the merit principle, hard affirmative action is unfair to unsuccessful applicants and causes a lowering of professional standards.[17] Even assuming for the present that current selection criteria ensure the best possible recruits, the

16 See, for example, Law Society, op. cit., n. 3, at pp. 3, 5, 29, 42; views reported in R.L. Abel, *English Lawyers Between Market and State: The Politics Of Professionalism* (2003) 127, 130–1, 150, 155–6; H. Rolfe and T. Anderson, 'A Firm Choice: Law Firms' Preferences in the Recruitment of Trainee Solicitors' (2003) 10 *International J. of the Legal Profession* 315, at 328–9.

17 See, in relation to legal practice, L.A. Graglia, 'Special Admission of the "Culturally Deprived" to Law School' (1970) 119 *University of Pennsylvania Law Rev.* 351.

115

spectre of falling standards need not materialize. By definition, tie-break preferences do not effect the quality of recruits and, if suitably defined, ballpark preferences need make little difference, whereas quotas can be confined to those with the necessary minimum qualifications and required abilities. Nor is it plausible to argue[18] that hard affirmative action will reduce the incentives for recruitment and promotion candidates to study and work hard because affirmative action beneficiaries will think that they will succeed, and non-beneficiaries that they will fail, anyway. The former still have to compete with fellow beneficiaries, whereas non-beneficiaries will have to compete more fiercely with other non-beneficiaries in the case of quotas or, in the case of hiring and promotion preferences, ensure that they vastly outperform beneficiaries.[19]

Thus, if affirmative action is unlikely to cause existing standards to drop to unacceptable levels, the argument from merit must establish that it nevertheless illegitimately prevents selection of the best recruitment or promotion candidates. There are two routes this argument can take.[20] The first is that candidates adjudged to be the best have a moral right or claim to the relevant position. However, there are two problems with seeing merit in terms of moral desert. One is that recruitment decisions are not based on candidates' past performance, except to the extent that it reveals their future potential, whereas rewarding past performance through promotion is unlikely if it is not expected to continue. Secondly, even if one does look solely to past performance in assessing candidates, one cannot really say that the selected candidate has greater moral worth than her competitors. Although effort plays an important role, so does natural ability and social privilege, and no one seriously maintains that inherited advantages are morally deserved.

---

18 See, for example, S. Steele, *The Content of our Character: A New Vision of Race in America* (1990).
19 M. Selmi, 'Testing For Equality: Merit, Efficiency, and the Affirmative Action Debate' (1995) 42 *UCLA Law Rev.* 1251, at 1305–9; A. Freeman, 'Racism, Rights and the Quest for Equality of Opportunity: A Critical Legal Essay' (1988) 23 *Harvard Civil Rights-Civil Liberties Law Rev.* 295, at 380; D.B. Wilkins and G.M. Gulati, 'Why Are There So Few Black Lawyers in Corporate Law Firms? An Institutional Analysis' (1996) 84 *California Law Rev.* 496, at 602–3.
20 The following critique is based on Edwards, op. cit., n. 9, especially pp. 198–217; Freeman, id., pp. 380–4; T. Mullen, 'Affirmative Action' in *The Legal Relevance of Gender: Some Aspects of Sex-based Discrimination*, eds. S. McLean and N. Burrows (1988) 252–4; M. Cavanagh, *Against Equality of Opportunity* (2002), especially ch. 2; R.H. Fallon, 'To Each According to His Ability, From None According to His Race: The Concept of Merit in the Law of Antidiscrimination' (1980) 60 *Buffalo University Law Rev.* 815; T. Nagel, 'Equal Treatment and Compensatory Discrimination' (1973) 2 *Philosophy and Public Affairs* 348; S. Sturm and L. Guinier, 'The Future of Affirmative Action: Reclaiming the Innovative Ideal' (1996) 84 *California Law Rev.* 953. See, also, C. McCrudden, 'Merit Principles' (1998) 18 *Oxford J. of Legal Studies* 543, who persuasively argues that the meaning of merit is so contested that more is lost than gained by its use in debating affirmative action.

116

Consequently, it is sometimes argued that the best candidates have a legitimate expectation, rather than a moral claim, to the position. But even if such expectations are not illegitimate in being dependent on the sort of prior bias which still benefits white middle-class men, they merely establish that affirmative action requires advance warning and sufficient publicity so as to warn aspirant lawyers of changed opportunities. Furthermore, it is question-able whether aspirant lawyers can complain of being misled into working hard towards a legal career by the expectation of more available posts than later materialize. Professional recruiters certainly do not regard themselves as morally prohibited from reducing recruitment in response to economic downturns.

It is thus widely agreed that the merit argument depends on the material benefits to be gained from recruiting and promoting the best candidates. If these benefits only accrue to lawyers themselves, it would be difficult to argue that this should defeat the moral case for addressing discrimination and disadvantage. However, it can be argued that clients will also benefit from more effective lawyers and, therefore, if current methods of evaluating merit are both objective and effective, they should be retained notwithstanding their role in maintaining the advantages of those with privileged access to the educational and other attributes required by the profession.

The problem is that these methods are neither objective nor particularly effective. For one thing, recruitment can never be based solely on factors like educational performance and work experience, nor promotion decisions on factors like billing hours and 'rainmaking'. As we have seen, particularly because of the personalist and clientist nature of legal practice and the intense competition for positions, more subjective criteria play an important role. As a result, selection and promotion panel members are likely to favour, at least subconsciously, those who look, sound, and behave like themselves.

But even if recruitment and promotion decisions could be based on criteria which are capable of objective evaluation, current indicators of merit have a discriminatory impact which reflects a subjective choice. For ex-ample, the ability to obtain work placements often depends on social contacts, while favourable work allocation, mentoring, and training is not allocated on objective grounds. Those who receive these advantages are therefore not objectively better than their competitors. As regards factors like intellectual intelligence, rainmaking, and zealous representation, their prominence can be said to involve a subjective choice which reflects the mindset and ethical orientation of those who have dominated legal practice. Expanding the perception of a good lawyer to include, for instance, emo-tional intelligence, supportive client care, and a willingness to act ethically would clearly result in a different conception of merit and different recruit-ment and promotion decisions. Indeed, it is sometimes argued that women, ethnic minorities, and those from socially disadvantaged backgrounds have a

117

predisposition to display such qualities.[21] This link is not, however, beyond doubt, nor likely to be impervious to professional socialization and institutional constraints. Yet even the profession itself supports demographic diversity on the grounds that recruits from different backgrounds may bring different ways of thinking and new ideas, thus enhancing legal services.[22] The latter may also occur because many clients may prefer or even insist upon being represented by someone like themselves, who is familiar with their accent, way of speaking, social milieu, and the problems associated with their common background. Such greater understanding may also reduce the chances of lawyers imposing unwanted and harmful solutions on clients because of a failure to comprehend their different world-views. While the profession sees these advantages in financial terms as opening up new markets, they also implicitly challenge traditional conceptions of good lawyering.

Finally, even if one regards such traditional conceptions to be objective, research suggests that current methods of assessing recruitment candidates on the basis of academic results, references, an interview, and sometimes also paper and pen ability tests and simulated exercises fails accurately to predict their ability to be effective lawyers.[23] This is likely to increase in today's economy which increasingly requires flexibility, problem solving, and team work.

No doubt, persuading the profession that traditional means of identifying the best candidates are neither objective nor particularly effective is likely to be an uphill struggle. Fortunately, this is not essential because quotas or decision-making preferences do not necessarily prevent the appointment or promotion of the best candidates even as traditionally understood and evaluated.

Here one can rely on Aristotle's insight that distributive justice requires treating different people differently as much as treating equal people equally, and Lyndon Johnson's analogy that there is no equal opportunity if you remove the shackles from a runner half way through a race[24] to argue that if previously shackled runners tie, or only just lose races, they deserve to be treated as having won. In other words, if despite the disadvantages of gender, race or class, an applicant for a position has equal or nearly equal credentials to a rival lacking such disadvantages, she must in fact have greater ability.[25]

---

21 See the discussion and references cited in Nicolson, op. cit., n. 8.
22 See Law Society, op. cit., n. 3, pp. 2, 22–3, 52, and section 3; Bar Council, op. cit., n. 3, para. 1.64, Annex H.
23 See Sturm and Guinier, op. cit., n. 20, pp. 968–87 and 1003–8.
24 See, for example, G. Pitt, 'Can Reverse Discrimination Be Justified?' in *Discrimination: The Limits of the Law*, eds. B. Hepple and E.M. Szyszczak (1992) 294.
25 Compare H. Jones, 'Fairness, Meritocracy, and Reverse Discrimination' (1977) 4 *Social Theory and Practice* 211; L.C. Harris and U. Narayan, 'Affirmative Action as Equalizing Opportunity: Challenging the Myth of "Preferential Treatment"' in *Ethics*

118

This justifies decision-making preferences in favour of those from previously excluded groups by showing that white, middle-class males who are not selected are not prejudiced by reverse discrimination, but are simply prevented from benefiting from the advantages conferred by their backgrounds.

It is even possible to argue that quotas do not create the alleged 'innocent victims' of anti-affirmative action rhetoric. According to Fiscus, distributive justice requires that individuals should receive the employment positions they would have attained if they had been allocated under fair conditions.[26] Moreover, in an ideal non-discriminatory world, he argues, every social group would be represented in all activities in numbers proportionate to their distribution in society as a whole or at least within relevant localities.[27] To deny this either evidences bigotry in suggesting that women, ethnic minorities, and those from socially deprived backgrounds are inherently inferior, or naivety in thinking that their different career aspirations are unaffected by discrimination and disadvantage. Admittedly, as Fiscus's critics argue,[28] it is impossible to know what the exact proportion of each group's representation in particular social activities is likely to be in an ideal world, especially as innocuous cultural differences might explain such variations. Such cultural differences do not, however, explain the marked patterns of difference based on gender, race, and class. These patterns can be regarded as presumptive evidence of discrimination to be remedied by quotas. If they result in slightly too many – or indeed, too few – members of previously excluded groups gaining positions than they would have in an ideal world, that seems a small (and theoretical) price to pay for a position far fairer than that at present. Moreover, according to Fiscus, quotas are not unfair to those who are not selected. All they do is ensure that candidates compete with those who have faced similar obstacles or privileges. A privileged candidate who does not obtain a position because he is not the brightest and best amongst other privileged candidates is not unfairly treated even though formally better qualified than the brightest and best of less privileged candidates, because it is only privilege which creates his apparent superiority.

---

in Practice: An Anthology, ed. H. LaFollette (2002) especially 451–4; R.D. Kahlenberg, 'Class-Based Affirmative Action' (1996) 84 California Law Rev. 1037, at 1066.

26 R.J. Fiscus, The Constitutional Logic of Affirmative Action: Making the Case for Quotas (1992).

27 See, also, Selmi, op. cit., n. 19, especially p. 1291.

28 Edwards, op. cit., n. 9, pp. 174–5, 189; W. Feinberg, On Higher Ground: Education and the Case for Affirmative Action (1997) 62 ff. See, also, M.E. Levin, 'Reverse Discrimination, Shackled Runners and Personal Identity' (1980) 37 Philosophical Studies 139 for a similar objection to the shackled runners' analogy.

119

2. Reverse discrimination and the 'stigma' of affirmative action

While it can be argued that appropriately formulated decision-making preferences and quotas are compatible with the merit principle, a more worrying problem is that they use the very categories that anti-discrimination campaigns seek to render socially irrelevant. Moreover, in doing so, they may confirm existing social prejudices and engender feelings of inferiority on the part of those from previously excluded groups.[29]

There are various responses to the idea that 'one gets beyond racism [and sexism and class prejudice] by getting beyond it now'.[30] One is that, '[i]n order to get beyond racism, we must first take account of race'[31] and there is a big difference between distinctions made for bigoted reasons and those made to address the effects of bigotry.[32] It would be a great irony to allow continuing assumption about the inferiority of women, ethnic minorities, and members of the 'lower classes' to prevent the means necessary to allow them to prove these assumptions wrong. Furthermore, sexism, racism, and class prejudice are probably reinforced far more by the image of a legal profession dominated by white, upper middle-class men than by the fact that some women, ethnic minority or socially-deprived lawyers may owe their positions to affirmative action.[33] Finally, it is important to keep in mind that individuals who benefit from affirmative action limited to recognizing the difference between raw talent and its socially constructed indicators will only rarely be less able than their more privileged counterparts.[34] By publicly recognizing and reiterating this fact, professional leaders can go some way to addressing the alleged stigma attached to 'affirmative action babies'.[35]

Nevertheless, it is possible that the whisperings of those predisposed to seeing women, ethnic minorities, and working-class lawyers as inferior will filter through to their targets.[36] Some might be able to reassure themselves

29 See, for example, Graglia, op. cit., n. 17; Steele, op. cit., n. 18; M.B. Abram, 'Affirmative Action: Fair Shakers and Social Engineers' (1986) 99 *Harvard Law Rev.* 1312; W. van Alstyne, 'Rites of Passage: Race, the Supreme Court and the Constitution' (1978-9) 46 *University of Chicago Law Rev.* 755; S. Carter, *Confessions of an Affirmative Baby* (1992).
30 van Alstyne, id., p. 809.
31 *Regents of the University of California* v. *Bakke* 438 US 265, 407 (1978).
32 For example, A. Aleinikoff, 'A Case for Race-Consciousness' (1991) 91 *Columbia Law Rev.* 1060; T. Campbell, 'Sex Discrimination: Mistaking the Relevence of Gender' in McLean and Burrows, op. cit., n. 20, especially pp. 31–3; J.W. Nickel, 'Preferential Policing in Hiring and Admissions: A Jurisprudential Approach' (1975) 75 *Columbia Law Rev.* 534, at 550–3.
33 Harris and Narayan, op. cit., n. 25, p. 457; Kennedy, op. cit., n. 9, p. 1331.
34 Harris and Narayan, id., p. 456.
35 Carter, op. cit., n. 29.
36 Compare anecdotal evidence from E. Herman, 'Committee Targets Retention of Minorities at Big Law Firms' (1995) 18 *Chicago Lawyer* 13; M.J. Radin, 'Affirmative Action Rhetoric' (1991) 8 *Social Philosophy and Policy* 130; D.B. Wilkins, 'Two

120

that they know their own worth better than their detractors do.[37] Others may take the view that the stigma of obtaining a position because of their group membership is preferable to the stigma of not obtaining such position.[38] However, it is possible that some beneficiaries of affirmative action will suffer psychologically. Consequently, before those not affected in this way conclude that this is a price worth paying, it is important to consult as widely as possible with the relevant groups. Here it is instructive to note that many ethnic minorities in the United States deny feeling stigmatized by affirmative action, and, like some in the United Kingdom,[39] continue to support it.[40] It should also be remembered that, while affirmative action might be a necessary evil, it should only be a temporary one.[41] Thus, the sight of previously excluded groups becoming more visible and successful is likely to have a 'multiplier effect'[42] persuading others that a legal career is possible, thus countering the symbolic effects of earlier exclusion and generally creating an atmosphere hostile to the expression of prejudice. Similarly, the possibility that initial recipients of affirmative action are regarded as having side-stepped the merit principle is likely to be forgotten over time as they make their mark.[43]

IS STRONG AFFIRMATIVE ACTION PRACTICABLE?

However, even if hard affirmative action can be justified, a number of practical questions remain. Perhaps the easiest to address is the appropriate temporal duration of such measures. Given that affirmative action is best justified as a form of distributive justice, it seems obvious that it should continue until discrimination has clearly ceased.

A more difficult question relates to whether evidence of continuing discrimination should be gauged from the success rate of particular groups in entering and progressing within legal practice as compared to their overall

Paths to The Mountaintop? The Role of Legal Education in Shaping the Values of Black Corporate Lawyers' (1981) 45 *Stanford Law Rev.* 2004.

37 Wilkins and Gulati, op. cit., n. 19, p. 604.
38 See D.L. Rhode, 'Perspectives On Professional Women' (1988) 40 *Stanford Law Rev.* 1163, 1197, 1200; W.F. Menski, 'The Indian Experience and Its Lessons for Britain' in Hepple and Szyszczak, op. cit., n. 24, pp. 336–7.
39 S. Vignaendra et al., 'Hearing Black and Asian Voices – An Exploration of Identity' in *Discriminating Lawyers*, ed. P. Thomas (2000) 145.
40 See, for example, Aleinikoff, op. cit., n. 32, p. 1091; Kennedy, op. cit., n. 9, pp. 1332-3; Nickel, op. cit., n. 32, pp. 554–5.
41 For example, B. Parekh, 'A Case for Positive Discrimination' in Hepple and Szyszczak, op. cit., n. 24, p. 278; R.H. Fallon Jr. and P.C. Weiler, 'Firefighters v. Stotts: Conflicting Models of Racial Justice' [1984] *Supreme Court Rev.* 1, 37.
42 P. Brest and M. Oshige, 'Affirmative Action for Whom?' (1995) 47 *Stanford Law Rev.* 885.
43 A prediction supported by research: Sturm and Guinier, op. cit., n. 20, p. 1029.

social distribution, distribution in a particular locality, or in the pool of applicants. The same problem arises in relation to the setting of quotas.[44] The fairer and more practical option seems to be to consider actual applicants. Otherwise, the fact that women and ethnic minorities are now becoming qualified at rates exceeding their overall social distribution will rule out affirmative action from the outset, notwithstanding recruiters' continuing prejudice. It also seems sensible to assess the success rate of applicants within broad geographical localities in both professional branches.

Another practicality involves defining ethnicity and social class. As regards the former, it is only necessary to distinguish white from black and Asian lawyers. Although the various ethnic minority groups might be associated with different levels of socio-economic disadvantage, this factor should be considered independently of ethnicity. Defining socio-economic class is likely to prove controversial, particularly if account is taken of its many gradations. However, there are numerous workable models which can be adopted.[45]

The most complex practical question is likely to involve choosing which form of hard affirmative action is most appropriate. In the abstract, both have advantages and disadvantages, which more or less mirror each other. Thus quotas are relatively simple and hence efficient to operate, especially if they ignore the relative disadvantage suffered by different socio-economic social stratas and the multiple disadvantages suffered by some individuals. But if these complexities are ignored, quotas may be thought to be too crude a tool for remedying discrimination and disadvantage.[46] On the other hand, if quotas do reflect relative socio-economic advantage and multiple disadvantage, there might have to be more categories than applicants for some positions. Moreover, quotas can be said to exacerbate the problems always associated with basing remedies on group membership, namely, that some individuals may obtain an advantage despite having escaped discrimination or disadvantage,[47] or that the impact of one of form of disadvantage (such as ethnicity) is overridden by overwhelming advantages (such as that conferred by social wealth and connections). Finally, quotas are far more likely to be perceived as contravening the merit principle, causing unfairness and lowering standards. While this is not necessarily the case if certain minimum standards are maintained, setting such standards is not easy and certainly far harder than operating decision-making preferences.

The latter have other advantages. They can give effect to relative and multiple disadvantages in a flexible and sophisticated manner. For example,

---

44 For detailed discussions, see Edwards, op. cit., n. 9, pp. 31–3; Fiscus, op. cit., n. 26, pp. 85–92.
45 Kahlenberg, op. cit., n. 25, pp. 1073–83.
46 See Nickel, op. cit., n. 32, pp. 555–8, regarding the problem of having to weigh the advantages of efficiency against the disadvantages of simplicity.
47 Compare E. Phillips, 'Positive Discrimination in Malaysia: A Cautionary Tale for the United Kingdom' in Hepple and Szyszczak, op. cit., n. 24, pp. 353–4.

an increasing numbers of preference points can be awarded for multiple disadvantages and for subtle differences within forms of disadvantage (such as the difference between being lower middle-class and upper lower-class), while points can be subtracted for overriding wealth advantages. On the other hand, such schemes will be resource- and time-intensive. Other practical problems include having to define what differences in ability can be condoned by ballpark preferences, and the possibility of candidates exaggerating or concealing information relating to family background. But while no group-based social scheme can escape similar problems, a more serious objection to decision-making preferences is that they may lead to women and ethnic minorities being selected in numbers vastly exceeding their social distribution or even distribution in the pool of applicants. Indeed, particularly if generous ballpark preferences are applied, they may obtain all positions, especially in small practice settings. Conversely, and partly because of the fear of such results, decision-making preferences may have very little effect at all. Given the inevitable inclusion of subjective factors in such decisions, continuing prejudice and the current professional distaste for affirmative action, it is very possible that white, middle-class men will unconsciously, if not consciously, be over-evaluated in order to avoid triggering decision-making preferences.[48] Indeed, some lawyers might even consciously ignore the equal or even superior claims of members of previously excluded groups on the grounds that recruiting or promoting a few is 'affirmative action enough'.[49]

Consequently, quotas might on balance be the more appropriate and effective means of ensuring a quick reversal of patterns of discrimination and disadvantage. If they lead to some female, ethnic minority or economically deprived applicants gaining more of an advantage than their past record or potential seems to merit, such 'fortunate beneficiaries' are likely to be far fewer than the countless mediocre white middle-class men who have benefited from centuries of discrimination and privilege. Given this, and the fact that quotas are designed to end rather than sustain discrimination, accepting their inevitable inaccuracies seems justifiable.

But while quotas might in general be the most appropriate form of hard affirmative action, they are not universally necessary or realistic. Thus, the fact that women and ethnic minorities are now entering legal practice in numbers exceeding their overall social distribution, and do not face discrimination in all practice settings, suggests that recruitment quotas are not required throughout legal practice, nor for anything other than a brief period.

By contrast, class-based quotas might be required in perpetuity. However, the profession is likely to argue that, unlike society as a whole, they have no obligation to engage in 'social engineering' and assist those who are

---

48 Compare Mullen, op. cit., n. 20, p. 260.
49 Radin, op. cit., n. 36, p. 137.

prejudiced by factors beyond professional control.[50] Admittedly, the Anglo-Welsh branches have accepted a positive duty to accommodate pregnancy, parenting responsibilities in general, and certain cultural differences, but this remedies the indirect discrimination involved in modelling working practices on the needs of white men. By contrast, indirect discrimination on class grounds is legally condoned and lawyers are unlikely to see recruiting and promoting candidates on educational and other 'objective' grounds as objectionable.[51] In response, one can point to the substantial material and other rewards which accompany professional status. Whether adopting the Marxian premise that all social wealth is based upon the exploitation of the poor, sometimes aided and abetted by lawyers themselves, or the Rawlsian premise that the opportunity to share in social goods should be equally open to all, one can argue that the legal profession should be obliged to ensure that the rewards of professional status are not reserved for those who are already socially advantaged.[52] Otherwise, arguments for affirmative action for women and ethnic minorities might play into the hands of those who oppose affirmative action as not reaching those most in need.[53] While this objection is unpersuasive and possibly cynical in illogically suggesting that no affirmative action is better than some, it is not the logic but the vehemence of objections to affirmative action which may carry the day.

The problem, however, is that class-based recruitment quotas would radically alter the profession's traditional class profile and almost definitely be perceived as substantially undermining standards. Consequently, they are likely to be fiercely resisted by the profession itself as well as by politically and media literate middle-class parents not prepared to see their children's opportunities for a legal career reduced. This suggests that recruitment targets might be as much as can be achieved. However, if a case for class-based decision-making preferences can be successfully argued, it might be regarded as limited to recruitment and the decision to keep on trainee solicitors and pupils. Thereafter, those who originally suffered from social disadvantage might be thought to have had sufficient opportunity to show their potential.[54] On the other hand, the possibility of residual unconscious prejudice, and the importance of possessing the right cultural capital for

---

50 Abel, op. cit., n. 16, p. 154; Rolfe and Anderson, op. cit., n. 16, pp. 328–9.
51 Compare the views of Martin Mears, then Law Society President, quoted in (1995) 39 *Solicitors' J.* 1111.
52 Compare Cavanagh, op. cit., n. 20, pp. 16-7, who argues that moral obligations to meet social needs appropriately fall disproportionately on those who are most capable of meeting them.
53 See Abram, op. cit., n. 29, p. 1323; Menski, op. cit., n. 38. Consequently, Kahlenberg, op. cit., n. 25, argues that affirmative action should only be class-based, thus assisting only the most needy women and ethnic minorities. This, however, ignores the effects of sexism and racism, and particularly the gendered nature of parenting, which operate over and above social disadvantage: see, for example, Feinberg, op. cit., n. 28.
54 Kahlenberg, id., p. 1070, who argues that this also applies to lateral recruitment of established practitioners.

obtaining mentoring, training, and favourable work allocation suggest that tie-break preferences remain justified, at least up until the point that its beneficiaries reach proportionate representation in promoted positions. The same might be said to apply to ethnic minorities. By contrast, the substantial impact of the gendered nature of legal practice, and particularly the fact that the costs of parenting and perceptions about consequent commitment to career fall disproportionately on female lawyers, suggests that there is strong case for promotion quotas, at least in practice settings involving more than a few promotion candidates.

CONCLUSION

Many of the questions of detail raised by the various possible ways in which quotas and decision-making preferences may attempt to deal with the complex patterns of discrimination and disadvantage in legal practice may benefit from more detailed attention than that provided here. The important point, however, is that such questions are complicated but not irresoluble if the general case for hard affirmative action in the legal profession is accepted. Hopefully this article will go some way to ensuring such acceptance.

But it is not just lawyers who need to be persuaded. Some commentators argue that affirmative action is ultimately prejudicial to equal opportunities by detracting attention away from the potentially more effective strategy of challenging current conceptions of occupational merit.[55] Admittedly this is an important task, which is avoided by my central argument that hard affirmative action need not conflict with prevailing standards of merit. However, given that convincing lawyers of the latter, rather moderate point is likely to be far from easy, there seems little hope at present of a radical challenge to traditional conceptions and methods of assessing professional merit. Indeed, prospects for such a challenge seem likely to be enhanced rather than diminished by using affirmative action to ensure that women, ethnic minorities and those from deprived socio-economic backgrounds use their increased visibility throughout the profession and especially in leadership roles to model alternative legal attributes. Furthermore, as affirmative action is intended as a relatively short-term remedy for discrimination and disadvantage in legal practice, any distraction from more radical approaches to equal opportunities should be short-lived.

---

55 See, for example, Sturm and Guinier, op. cit., n. 20; D.A. Bell Jr., 'Bakke, Minority Admissions, and the Usual Price of Racial Remedies' (1979) 67 *California Law Rev.* 3; R. Delgado, 'Affirmative Action as a Majoritarian Device: Or, Do You Really Want to be a Role Model?' (1991) 89 *Michigan Law Rev.* 1222.

125

JOURNAL OF LAW AND SOCIETY
VOLUME 33, NUMBER 1, MARCH 2006
ISSN: 0263-323X, pp. 126–40

Rethinking the Merit Principle in Judicial Selection

KATE MALLESON*

Against the background of the continuing lack of diversity in the make-up of the judiciary in England and Wales, this article explores the reasons behind the consistent rejection of affirmative action policies in relation to the judicial appointment process. It examines the relationship between affirmative action and the merit principle in this context and argues that the belief that the two are inherently in tension rests on implicit assumptions about both which are open to question.

'I would like, obviously, the judiciary to be as diverse as we can get it. But that must not interfere with the fundamental principle that we have got to choose the best man for the job.'[1]

The concept of affirmative action has attracted very little support in the United Kingdom as a means of promoting diversity in the selection processes of public and professional life. The belief that affirmative action results in unfairness to individual applicants and a reduction in the overall quality of those selected has led to a general consensus that such policies are incompatible with selection systems based on merit. This view is particularly strongly entrenched in relation to the judicial selection process. While there is increasing acceptance amongst members of the judiciary, government, the legal profession and academia that the lack of diversity in the composition of the judiciary has a corrosive and damaging effect on the work of the courts,[2]

* *Department of Law, Queen Mary, University of London, 339 Mile End Road, London E1 4NS, England*
k.malleson@qmul.ac.uk

1 Lord Lloyd of Berwick, evidence to the Constitutional Affairs Committee, First Report, *Inquiry into the Provisions of the Constitutional Reform Bill*, 2003–4, HC 48-II.
2 The main arguments in support of a more diverse judiciary focus on the damaging effect that the current make-up of the bench has on public confidence, the loss of potential judicial talent through the absence of well-qualified lawyers from non-traditional backgrounds, and the danger that those appearing before the courts will feel they are being judged by a society to which they do not belong. See, for example, Department for Constitutional Affairs, *Increasing Diversity in the Judiciary* (October 2004) 14 and C. Banner and A. Deane, *Off with their Wigs* (2003) 129–37.

there is widespread agreement that affirmative action should not form any part of the solution to that problem. This consensus has held firm despite the limited success of a range of official efforts going back more than a decade to ensure that more women and minority lawyers are appointed to the bench.

This article examines the basis for this rejection of affirmative action policies by analysing the relationship between the concepts of affirmative action and merit. It considers how the two concepts interact in the context of the judiciary and argues that the belief that the merit principle and affirmative action are inherently in tension rests on implicit assumptions about both which are open to question.

AFFIRMATIVE ACTION AND THE SOVEREIGNTY OF MERIT

The strength of the antipathy towards affirmative action in the United Kingdom can only be understood with reference to the very narrow definition which is applied to the term. The concept is generally understood as describing a range of policies which contemplate the possibility of the selection of a less qualified over a more qualified candidate on the basis of her or his membership of an under-represented target group.[3] In contrast, the range of policies and programmes which are defined as affirmative action in many other countries, particularly the United States of America where the concept originated, tends to encompass mainstream equal opportunities policies which have been in place in the United Kingdom for over 30 years.[4] In its broader context, the term affirmative action can be used to describe any policy or programme directed at addressing the under-representation of members of those groups which have been identified as having been denied equal access to the allocation of educational opportunities, employment positions or public office as a result of direct discrimination in the past. While the identification of these target groups is a dynamic process, expanding in response to changing political awareness of different forms of discrimination, the common factor which distinguishes affirmative action policies from other equality policies is that they do not require evidence of discrimination on an individual basis but rest on the identification of past group-based discrimination.

The earliest and least controversial affirmative action policies were those designed to remove factors such as gender and race as considerations, both positive and negative, from selection processes. Under the overarching requirements of the Sex Discrimination Act 1975 and Race Relations Act 1976, appointment processes for positions in both private and public life articulated the need for selection to be made free from direct discrimination on grounds of sex and race. In addition, and more controversially at the time,

---

3 T. Sowell, *Affirmative Action Around the World* (2004) 2.
4 See C. Burton, *Redefining Merit* (1988); F. Holloway, 'What is Affirmative Action?' in *Affirmative Action in Perspective*, eds. F. Blanchard and F. Crosby (1989) 9–19.

127

selection processes were required to ensure that they avoided indirect sex discrimination, whereby treatment which is apparently neutral in practice disproportionately disadvantages one sex more than the other. Such forms of affirmative action represent the first stage in the development of policies designed to address the effects of discrimination on the basis of group characteristics. More recently the trend has been to move beyond this prohibitive approach to encompass more positive action, requiring selection processes to engage proactively to encourage more applications from under-represented groups. Such policies include, for example, efforts to seek out and encourage applications from women and members of minority ethnic groups as well as providing them with training and other opportunities to improve their ability to apply for promotion.

These more proactive policies are still, however, generally understood in the United Kingdom context as forms of equal opportunities policies rather than affirmative action. The reason is that neither prohibitive nor positive action of the type described above is envisaged as being in conflict with the merit principle. Both are firmly based on the premise that membership of an under-represented target group can never 'trump' merit so that the best-qualified candidate will always be appointed regardless of their membership of any particular group. The development of proactive policies to encourage a more diverse range of candidates into a recruitment or promotions pool is intended to increase the chances that candidates from under-represented groups can compete equally in the selection process, but ultimately they will be measured against all other candidates on the basis of merit. For this reason the application of proactive policies poses no threat to the fairness of the selection system as between individual candidates because they do no more than put unfairly disadvantaged candidates in the same position as advantaged candidates. Nor do they run the risk of undermining the merit principle by reducing the quality of those appointed. Indeed, by encouraging more qualified applicants to come forward and so expanding the recruitment pool, such policies should increase the competition for places and thus the quality of those ultimately appointed.

The conclusion that prohibitive and proactive approaches to countering the effects of group discrimination are consistent with a merit-based selection is strongest when the selection process adopts a 'maximalist' approach to the merit principle. This holds that there is always one best candidate in any particular selection decision who must be appointed regardless of any other considerations.[5] For this approach to be applied, the qualifications for any particular position must be objectively measurable so that candidates can be ranked in terms of qualifications. In practice, of course, the identification of the best candidates in a selection process is not always so easy. Different selectors within a merit-based selection process can quite legitimately

---

5 See, for example, Sir Thomas Legg, 'Judicial Appointments and a Supreme Court', written evidence to the Constitutional Affairs Committee, op. cit., n. 1, para. 8.

disagree about how to rank the relative merits of different candidates. This is particularly true in relation to the allocation of highly sought after positions which require the performance of varied and complex functions and where the general quality of the candidates is high. This requires a comparison between candidates who occupy a relatively narrow range on the qualification spectrum. In such circumstances the maximalist approach may be modified to allow for the possibility of the application of a 'tie-break' approach to merit. This arises where two or more candidates are identified as equally qualified and one is from an under-represented group such as a woman; the latter's disadvantaged status then serves as a 'tie-breaker' giving her the advantage.

Although the tie-break approach is rejected by strict maximalists on the grounds that it poses a threat to the merit principle, it shares with the maximalist approach a commitment to the fundamental principle that less qualified candidates will never be appointed over those who are more quali- fied. Neither approach, therefore, falls within the more radical definition of affirmative action. In practical terms, this key distinction is reflected in the differentiation between the use of targets and quotas. The former, whereby a selection system seeks to make a certain proportion of appointments from under-represented groups, is consistent with merit-based approaches because such targets are essentially aspirational. The targets will not be met if the only way to achieve them would be to appoint less qualified over more qualified candidates. In contrast, and for the same reason, the compulsory nature of quotas represents the practical articulation of fully-blown affirmative action since such a system must allow for the possibility that, to be met, a less qualified candidate will be appointed over one who is more qualified. For this reason, the use of quotas represents the Rubicon of affirmative action.

This is the case despite the fact that quota systems remain primarily merit- based in that, where possible, the most qualified candidates will always be chosen. This principle is only modified when and if it proves impossible to meet the quotas by applying the traditional approach. Moreover, the selection of the candidates within each quota group will still be made on the basis of merit. In addition, many quota-based systems adopt a 'minimalist' approach to merit whereby for any candidate to be appointed they must achieve a certain standard of qualification, and it is only when this standard is achieved by more than one candidate that priority is given to members of the target group. But despite these moderating factors, the quota system has been widely rejected in the United Kingdom as representing a fundamental erosion of the sovereignty of the merit principle since the appointment of a less qualified candidate will result in unfairness to the more qualified individual who is passed over, and a reduction of the overall quality of the body than would have been if the more qualified had been appointed.[6] For

---

6 A. Phillips, *The Politics of Presence* (1995) 58. See, in relation to the use of quotas in the judiciary, Banner and Deane, op. cit., n. 2, pp. 129–37 and S. Kentridge, 'The Highest Court: Selecting the Judges' (2003) 62 *Cambridge Law J.* 55.

critics of affirmative action, therefore, quotas overstep the line between *reversing* discrimination and *reverse* discrimination.

The history of the development of affirmative action programmes in the allocation of positions in public and professional life in the United Kingdom is one of a gradual move along the spectrum from the prohibition of positive discrimination to the introduction of proactive policies to widen recruitment pools. In most selection processes a maximalist approach has been retained, though there is evidence of a greater willingness to consider the use of tie-breakers in some areas where progress in achieving diversity has been particularly slow. To date, the line has been firmly held in most selection processes against the introduction of any form of quota system. However, the application of short-listing and other quota systems for women candidates in the 1997 and 2005 general elections and the elections to the Scottish and European Parliaments and the Welsh Assembly constitutes a key moment in this history, representing the first foray over the affirmative action Rubicon. For the time being, though, the new legislation is limited to the legalization of voluntary quotas which political parties may choose to use or not. It remains to be seen whether the United Kingdom will follow the example of some other European countries in introducing compulsory electoral quotas.[7]

AFFIRMATIVE ACTION IN THE JUDICIARY

As a relatively closed and homogeneous institution, it might be expected that the appointments system for the judiciary in England and Wales would have lagged behind those of other public and professional selection processes in adopting proactive policies to encourage greater diversity in its composition. In fact, increasing public criticism of the under-representation of women and minority lawyers on the bench has led to the development and implementation of a wide range of policies designed to encourage applications from lawyers who do not come from the traditional candidate pool. Since the 1980s, successive Lord Chancellors and senior judges have actively supported the goal of increasing diversity. In 1992 Lord Taylor, when Lord Chief Justice, stated that:

> The present imbalance between male and female, white and black in the judiciary is obvious ... I have no doubt that the balance will be redressed in the next few years ... Within five years I would expect to see a substantial number of appointments from both these groups. This is not just a pious hope. It will be monitored.[8]

Lord Justice Auld, in his 2001 report on the criminal courts, similarly urged the Lord Chancellor's Department to adapt to the needs and working

7 See A. McHarg, 'Quotas for Women! The Sex Discrimination (Election Candidates) Act 2002' in this issue, pp. 141–59.
8 Lord Taylor, *The Judiciary in the Nineties*, Richard Dimbleby Lecture (1992) 9.

arrangements of all lawyers in order to ensure diversity on the bench: 'It is not enough to wait for the professions to present the Lord Chancellor's Department with suitably "visible" as well as qualified candidates for appointment.'[9] The Lord Chancellor's Department in turn commissioned research to identify the reasons why women and minority lawyers might be deterred from applying for judicial office and looked at alternative appointments processes with better records in achieving a more diverse judicial composition.[10] In its new incarnation as the Department for Constitutional Affairs, the Department took forward this process through the introduction of proactive measures such as the revision of judicial job specifications, the introduction of salaried part-time posts, and greater flexibility in the requirement for High Court judges to travel for long periods on circuit. These sorts of changes are intended to ensure that the judges' work is more compatible with the lives and experiences of non-traditional judicial candidates such as solicitors and women with family responsibilities. At the same time, changes to the appointments process designed to increase the openness and objectivity of the system have included advertising of posts, the introduction of interviews and, most recently, the use of assessment centres as part of the selection process. These internal efforts have been reinforced by the strong criticism of the existing appointments process from the Commission for Judicial Appointments. Having fully scrutinized the system, it concluded that the 'trickle-up' approach would not, by itself, result in sufficient diversity and that proactive measures were needed.[11]

These varied efforts to encourage greater diversity in the judiciary have had a considerable cumulative impact on the operation of the judicial appointments process but have not affected the traditional understanding of the role of merit in the selection process. Almost without exception, official expressions of support for proactive measures to encourage diversity have been qualified by a statement of commitment to a strict application of the merit principle.[12] The effect of this has been the maintenance of a strong maximalist approach to merit and a clear divide between the idea of positive action to encourage a wider candidate pool and the sacrosanctity of the role of merit in selecting between those candidates. In the early 1990s, Lord Taylor raised the possibility of adopting a tie-break approach as a means of maintaining the sovereignty of merit whilst promoting greater diversity. The fact that even this very modest adaptation of the merit principle found few

---

9 Lord Justice Auld, *Review of the Criminal Courts of England and Wales* (2001) para. 84.
10 K. Malleson and C. Thomas, *Judicial Appointments Commissions: The European and North American Experiences and the Possible Implications for the UK* (1997).
11 The 'trickle-up' approach is based on the expectation that the changing composition of the legal profession will naturally and automatically result in much greater numbers of women and minority lawyers being appointed to the bench. See Commission for Judicial Appointments, *Annual Report* (2003) 4.
12 See, for example, evidence given to Constitutional Affairs Committee, op. cit., n. 1.

supporters is evidence of the degree of commitment in the judicial appointments process to maintaining a strict interpretation of selection on merit.

This approach is not, of course, unique to the judiciary. But the strength and consistency of that commitment is arguably stronger than many other public and professional selection processes because of the particular role and function of judges. The argument that selecting a less qualified over a more qualified candidate is unjust to the candidate passed over applies to the allocation of all positions in a selective appointments system. But the extent of the unfairness is affected by the particular type of position being allocated. Where the allocation is of a position occupied at an early stage of a person's education or career, the injustice to the better qualified individual who is rejected is mitigated by the fact that the time and effort which they have invested to obtain the position will be less substantial and they are likely to be able to realise this investment in alternative employment opportunities. In contrast, where a position is the culmination of a person's career, the ultimate goal aspired to after many years of focused input, the injustice in being passed over by a less qualified person will be more acute. Moreover, the chance of acquiring an equivalent position in the future is much reduced for a pinnacle position of this kind. Being a judge is the final achievement in a legal career so that the judiciary sits at the far end of this spectrum. Being effectively a second career, it is consequential to and dependent on a high degree of investment of time and effort over a long period. If a lawyer has shaped his or her career over many years so as to fulfil the qualifications required to be appointed to the bench and then is passed over in favour of a less qualified candidate, the unfairness is clearly greater than it would be for many other positions.

Equally, the quality argument against compromising the merit principle can be said to be stronger in relation to the judiciary than many other positions. The extent of the efficiency cost in terms of the reduction in the quality of performance as a result of the appointment of a less qualified over a more qualified candidate will depend on two factors. The first is the nature of the responsibilities undertaken by those appointed to the position. The greater their impact on others, the less acceptable any drop in quality will be. The work of surgeons, for example, has a direct effect on the health and life of other individuals. Even a small drop in the quality of surgeons may have an immediate and devastating effect on people's lives and would therefore represent a high efficiency cost. Although judges do not, like surgeons, literally hold lives in their hands, the indirect impact of their work is arguably just as great. They are required to make decisions on a daily basis which fundamentally affect people's liberty, livelihood, and reputation. The influence they have both on the lives of individuals and society generally is therefore at the high impact end of the spectrum.

The second factor which affects the efficiency cost of any compromise in the merit principle is the extent of the gap in qualifications between the less qualified person appointed and the more qualified who is passed over. Again,

132

there is a difference here between positions at an early and late stage of candidates' educational and career development. The reason why the imposition of gender quotas in all co-educational schools is considered uncontroversial, even amongst those schools with selective entrance requirements, is that the difference in qualifications between girls and boys entering schools is marginal, so that gender equality can be achieved with relatively little quality cost. Therefore the fact that gender quotas in school undoubtedly lead to more qualified individuals of one sex (usually girls) losing out to a less well-qualified individual of another (usually boys) is accepted because the efficiency cost is relatively low compared to the gain to society of educating boys and girls equally. In contrast, the differentiation in the qualifications of female and male candidates competing for positions at the latter stages of their professional careers is far greater as a result of the impact of the cumulative effect of differential gender patterns in careers and unequal division of labour in society at large. For the judiciary to impose, for example, a requirement for an equal gender balance in the judicial appointments process in the same way as is done in schools would require that at least some male candidates with much higher qualifications than their female equivalent would have to be passed over.

The combination of these efficiency and justice arguments against any diminution of the merit principle in the judicial appointments process are compounded by the effects of the principle of judicial independence. The requirement that judges are free from external pressure in order to preserve their impartiality has guaranteed the judiciary an unparalleled degree of job security. Although judges can, in theory, be dismissed for poor performance, in practice they are almost unsackable. This means that the public may suffer the effects of a judge's poor performance for many years without any realistic possibility of removal. In addition to this direct potential efficiency cost there is also an indirect judicial independence argument against compromising the merit principle. One important reason why a strict merit principle has been applied in the judiciary is the fear that if any other background factors were allowed to be taken into account in the selection process, this could be manipulated for purposes other than the promotion of greater diversity. The executive, as well as many different interest groups, will always have a vested interest in securing, if possible, the appointment of judges who share their views or values. One way of guarding against the danger that the selection decisions will be driven by values, rather than by ability, is to limit the scope for consideration of the background and characteristics of the appointees beyond their strictly professional skills and experiences.

The fear that any weakening of a strictly merit-based system may undermine judicial impartiality and independence explains why such a sharp distinction has traditionally been drawn between the forms of affirmative action which might be appropriate for the selection of politicians and for judges. Until relatively recently there was general agreement that the roles of

133

the two branches of government were absolutely distinct, and that a clear divide could be drawn between the formation and implementation of policy by elected representatives and its interpretation by independent judges who reached their decisions with reference solely to the law. This differentiation explains why the adoption of quotas in election candidacies has not, as yet at least, given rise to any debate about the applicability of such methods in promoting diversity in judicial appointments. However, as the power of senior judges has grown, it has become more difficult to sustain this bright line between the functions of judges and politicians. The emergence of the judiciary as the third branch of government, checking and scrutinizing the executive, has narrowed the gap between the functions of the senior judiciary and elected politicians. Judges are not politicians in wigs but they are increasingly required to reach decisions in relation to politically controversial issues which cannot be resolved without reference to policy questions.

As the differentiation between law and politics blurs, the efficiency arguments against the use of methods such as quotas to bring about greater diversity become less compelling and the benefits to be gained from a more diverse judiciary in terms of democratic legitimacy and public confidence grow. The evidence for this trend is clearly visible in relation to other powerful Constitutional Courts and Supreme Courts, such as in the United States, South Africa, and Canada. The political power of the judges in these courts (long-standing in the United States, more recent in other countries) has given rise to intense debate over the composition of the judiciaries and the extent to which they are reflective of society.[13] In practice, quotas in different forms, whether formal or informal are widely used in top courts around the world. It would be very hard for any United States President today to appoint to the Supreme Court without ensuring that it included at least one woman and one black judge. As the Hispanic population and power base grows, it is likely that in future it will also be necessary to ensure one judge of Hispanic origin. In Canada, where gender equality has a particularly high profile and four out of nine Supreme Court judges, including the Chief Justice, are women, it is doubtful whether there could, in the foreseeable future, be fewer than two women on the Supreme Court bench. In South Africa the importance of reflecting the 'rainbow nation' in the institutions of the new constitution is reflected in the make-up of the Constitutional Court to a degree unprecedented in other countries.[14]

For the new United Kingdom Supreme Court, it is likely that the question of diversity will come to be equally pressing. The first signs of this have already appeared. The tradition of including at least one judge from Scotland

---

13 See K. Malleson and P. Russell, *Appointing Judges in an Age of Judicial Power: Critical Perspectives From Around the World* (2005).
14 The inclusion of two disabled members of the South African Constitutional Court is explicitly identified in South Africa as an example of the high level of diversity awareness in the judicial selection process.

and one from Northern Ireland in the House of Lords will undoubtedly continue in the Supreme Court given that it is a statutory requirement that the judges of the new court will have knowledge of, and experience in, the law of each part of the United Kingdom.[15] But the need for geographical diversity is as much if not more about ensuring the legitimacy of the court as about its technical legal skills. Similarly, there is little doubt that the new Supreme Court Judicial Appointments Commission will be under considerable pressure to appoint a second and third woman to the Court in the near future as well as appointing its first minority judge.

THE CONSTRUCTION OF MERIT AND THE CANDIDATE POOL

Although the growing political pressure for greater diversity in professional and public appointments may increase the priority given to widening the recruitment pool in areas such as the judiciary, changing practice is unlikely to have an impact on the underlying conception of the merit principle on which such appointments processes rest. Despite the almost universal failure across a wide range of public and professional appointments systems to produce more than marginal changes in the composition of those appointed, advocates of change have generally argued that the problems do not lie within the concept of merit itself but rather with the failure of selection processes to apply it. A strong consensus still holds that full and proper application of the merit principle in the allocation of positions in education, employment or public life would lead naturally and automatically to the requisite degree of diversity in the appointments made.[16] Even those who advocate more radical alternatives such as quotas justify them as a temporary fix needed to reverse the effects of past discrimination before re-establishing a genuine merit-based system.[17]

A key feature of a strict merit-based system is that the determination of the relevant qualifications for each position should be derived solely on the basis of the functions to be fulfilled.[18] The most qualified person is the one whose characteristics and abilities are such that they will be most likely to perform those functions effectively. Critics and supporters of existing selection systems generally agree that in order for the determination of what constitutes merit to be free from prejudice it must be constructed without taking into account the background of the members of the potential candidate pool.[19] The rationale for this view is the recognition that traditional

---

15 Constitutional Reform Act 2005 s. 27(8).
16 See, for example, evidence given to the Constitutional Affairs Committee, op. cit., n. 1.
17 Sowell, op. cit., n. 3, pp. 2–7.
18 See, for example, Burton, op. cit., n. 4, p. 1.
19 See, for example, Department for Constitutional Affairs, *Increasing Diversity in the Judiciary, Responses to the DCA Consultation Paper CP 25/04* (2005).

135

selection processes have constructed merit around the needs of certain preferred groups in a way which has unfairly advantaged them.

This claim is no longer a controversial one. The belief that it can be solved by requiring that merit be constructed without reference to the candidate pool is, however, highly problematic. The function of a merit-based selection system is the selection of the most qualified amongst those who are willing and able to occupy the position. In order for the notion of merit to be translated from an abstract principle into a set of concrete qualifications which can be used to achieve this result, there must be an assessment of the nature of the potential candidate pool. Without knowledge about who the potential candidates are likely to be, selection systems would regularly and inevitably devise qualifications which would be pitched either too high or too low. The result would be either a failure to appoint any or enough candidates or a failure to attract sufficiently highly qualified candidates.

For selection systems in which appointments are made on a regular basis, this process of translating merit into job qualifications and selection criteria in a way which pitches appropriately to the available candidate pool is relatively unproblematic. The matching of qualifications to the pool is an ongoing process derived from knowledge gained of the likely applicants in recent selection decisions. In stable conditions, those who operate the selection process will be familiar with the candidate pool and so able to judge how to construct merit in each case so as to be able to select the best from the available pool. As the pool gradually changes over time, resulting in qualifications being set too high or too low, small changes will be made to future selection rounds to match more closely the pool and achieve the optimum selection. These changes may involve lowering or raising the formal qualifications. More often, they require a change in the interpretation of the selection criteria. What is meant, for example, by criteria such as 'significant experience' or 'strong communications skills' will be adapted to reflect the characteristics and experience of those in the pool. Without that reflexive engagement, it would be impossible for any selection process to determine where to pitch the definition of merit so as to appoint the best from the available pool.

Occasionally an unanticipated and sudden instability in the candidate pool arises which brings a sharp correction to this process and demonstrates very clearly the close relationship between the make-up of the potential candidate pool and the definition of merit. Such a change arose during the Second World War when the absence of large numbers of men left many posts to be filled by women. The definition of merit for a wide range of positions from manual labourers to senior managers had to be reconstructed very rapidly in response to the make-up of the new potential candidate pool. Equally, it changed back just as quickly after the war to exclude them and draw back in the returning male workforce. Had the men never returned, the new definition of merit would inevitably have remained in place. This example simply

136

demonstrates in an exaggerated way due to the compressed timescale the dynamic process which goes on in all selection processes over a longer period. Change may not always be as radical as in the war example, but each new cohort of candidates can never be an exact replication of the old. Their experiences, skills, life choices and attitudes inevitably change.

Furthermore, the process of constructing merit with reference to the potential candidate pool is dynamic, not just in the sense that the definition of merit adapts as the pool changes, but also in that the characteristics of the potential pool are influenced by changes in the definition and interpretation of merit. Individuals who perceive, on the basis of previous selection decisions, that they have the potential to be included in the candidate pool will develop and invest in those qualities which are required. Others, who perceive that they are less likely to be included in the pool, are more likely to choose to focus on acquiring and developing other skills and experiences, and so drop out of the pool. The boundaries of the potential pool therefore move according to the preconceptions of both selectors and potential candidates as to which people with what characteristics are likely best to perform the functions of the position. The more desirable the post and so the more competitive the selection process, the larger the potential pool will be and the more responsive it will be to the changing definition of merit.

The conclusion that it is not possible to determine what constitutes merit in any particular case without reference to the potential candidate pool undermines the claim that merit is derived solely from the functions of the position which in turn can be disconnected from the people who will occupy the position. If we accept that the functions of a position, the candidate pool, and the definition of merit are interdependent then we must accept that there is no possibility of disengaging the construction of merit from the question of who might be appointed. From this it follows that, in all cases where there is competition for a position or positions, the selection process must formulate the definition of merit through the expression of preferences for certain types of candidates over others. The critical issue therefore becomes the basis on which those preferences are formed. On what basis do selectors determine that certain types of candidate are likely to demonstrate merit? The crude answer is that it is those who are most similar to people who are already judged to be successfully fulfilling the functions of the post. In selection systems such as for the judiciary, where those doing the job are part of the selection process, the preference constitutes both replication and self-replication.

The notion that selection processes unfairly advantage candidates who are most similar to past appointees and the selectors themselves is not a novel one. But this is usually understood as a prejudicial process which comes into play so as to distort the proper application of a pure merit principle rather than an inherent feature of the way in which merit is constructed. If this alternative analysis is accepted, the problem becomes at once harder and easier. It is harder because the hope that diversity will follow automatically if

137

the holy grail of a pure merit system is adopted must be abandoned. But it also provides a way out of the otherwise irresolvable dilemma produced by the belief that affirmative action is inherently in tension with the merit principle. If merit can only be constructed in a dynamic process with reference to the candidate pool then the primary principled objection to affirmative action falls away. The claim that the incorporation of mechanisms designed to give preference to the characteristics of certain groups within the selection system inherently conflicts with merit is no longer sustainable.

THE CONSTRUCTION OF MERIT IN JUDICIAL SELECTION

The judicial appointments process provides a particularly effective case study to illustrate the way in which the construction of merit is a dynamic process which can only be carried out with reference to the qualifications of the potential candidate pool. In common with many other appointments processes, the lack of diversity in the appointments made has consistently been attributed to a failure properly to apply the merit principle.[20] The historical existence at various times of formal and informal bars on certain groups such as women, Jews, blacks, Catholics, and gay men provided sound empirical evidence for this view. Inevitably and understandably, attention has focused on removing these obvious barriers to a merit-based selection system. However, one effect of the presence of these relatively crude and direct forms of discrimination in the judicial appointments process has been to obscure the more complex interaction between the definition of merit and the candidate pool. A review of the history of the construction of merit in the judicial appointments process shows a particularly close and explicit relationship between the definition of merit and the qualifications of certain groups. Although the eligibility requirements for judicial office are broad enough to include a wide range of different lawyers, in practice the senior judiciary has traditionally been recruited from an extremely narrow group consisting of white, male barristers drawn from a small number of commercial chambers in London. The structural relationship between the bench and Bar, whereby judges have maintained strong links with their chambers, combined with the key role judges play in the selection system through the consultations process has meant that barristers joining such elite chambers as pupils have found themselves on a 'golden road' to judicial office.[21] They have been, effectively, the beneficiaries of a particularly pervasive and entrenched form of reverse affirmative action.

20 See id. and evidence given to the Constitutional Affairs Committee, op. cit., n. 1.
21 A term used by a judge to describe his career path from an elite chambers to the bench. See K. Malleson and F. Banda, *Factors Affecting the Decision to Apply for Silk and Judicial Office* (2000) 29.

The judicial appointments process also clearly illustrates the dynamic nature of this relationship. As the make-up and experiences of the recognized candidate pool changed over the years, so the construction of merit adapted accordingly. When once, for example, military service was common (even when no longer obligatory), successful service as an officer was taken to provide sound evidence of desirable judicial characteristics. As military service lost its popularity and upper-middle-class education and career patterns changed, the link between military experience and judicial merit disappeared. A similar relationship can be seen in the development of a requirement that those appointed to the bench serve a period as part-time judges while still in practice. This form of judicial apprenticeship, unknown in many other parts of the world, was constructed around barristers' working patterns since it necessitated the flexibility of self-employed status to be able to sit as a judge from time to time when required. Solicitors in partnership have always found that such part-time sittings are difficult to reconcile with the pattern of their working lives. Had solicitors rather than barristers emerged from the Victorian period as the senior branch of the legal profession and therefore the natural recruitment pool for the judiciary, there is no doubt that a requirement which was incompatible with their working arrangements would not have been a key step on the career path to the bench. Similarly, the requirement of many years of advocacy in the higher courts would not have been perceived as a prerequisite for appointment. Rather, the skills, experiences, and career patterns of elite groups of solicitors would instead have been taken as reflecting the desirable characteristics of a judge. Ability to negotiate with clients and management of an office, for example, might have been highly valued as evidence of judicial aptitude. Indeed, there is evidence that exactly this process of changing construction is taking place. In recent years, as the economic, political, and social influence of the solicitors' branch of the profession has grown, the 'junior' branch of the profession has lobbied successfully for changes to the appointments process which reorientate the definition and interpretation of merit towards them. The effect of this power shift has been a reconceptualization of what is needed in a judge which is directly influenced by the nature of the potential candidate pool rather than the nature of judicial office. The primacy of advocacy skills, for example, has been removed, not because judges' functions have changed, but as a consequence of the dynamic relationship between the construction of merit and the nature of who is perceived to be in the candidate pool. If the power of the solicitors' branch continues to grow, the definition of judicial merit is very likely to continue to change in turn.

CONCLUSION

The development and application of effective affirmative action programmes in public and professional selection processes has been paralysed by the fear

139

that such action will corrupt the merit principle. Decades of painfully slow progress in changing the composition of powerful institutions have failed to undermine this tenet of faith. The recognition that the definition of merit developed and adapted in systems such as the judicial appointments process has, inevitably and unavoidably, been constructed with reference to the career paths, skills, interests, life choices, experiences, and culture of particular groups has been taken to be evidence of the failure of the system to apply the merit principle. The dominance of the idea of merit as a pre-existing standard defined solely with reference to the functions of the position and without reference to the potential candidate pool has meant that affirmative action policies are doomed to failure. Within this framework they are understood, even by their supporters, as a regrettable necessity grafted onto systems which frustratingly and persistently fail to adopt a pure merit approach.

The result is that only those programmes which do not impact on the core of the merit-based system – the construction of what is meant by merit – can claim to have legitimacy, yet only those which fully engage with the construction of merit have any hope of being effective. This dilemma lies at the heart of the current affirmative action debate. The first step in its resolution lies in the recognition that the construction of merit always and inevitably is carried out with reference to the potential candidate pool. Affirmative action which seeks to articulate merit in response to the characteristics of a target group or groups is therefore no more than one particular expression of a process which is intrinsic, ongoing, and essential if a merit-based system is to achieve its goal of appointing the most qualified candidates from amongst those able and willing to do the job.

Recognizing the inevitability of this dynamic process is significant in that it legitimizes the concept of affirmative action in a merit-based system but it provides no guidance on how to assess the validity of the relative claims of different potential candidate groups. It is one thing to conclude that the historically privileged position given to white male barristers from elite chambers in the judicial appointments process was a consequence of the power relations of the legal profession of the twentieth century. But this does not tell us which groups sharing which particular characteristics should influence the construction of judicial merit today. Opinions will reasonably differ as to what mix of experience, skills, and characteristics are desirable and how they should be ranked one against the other. The construction of what constitutes merit for any particular position must continue to be contested as it has always been. The change in approach advocated in this article does no more than allow us to accept that the answer to that question can only be sought with reference to the nature of the potential candidate pool. Affirmative action is a radical development not because it threatens the merit principle but because it seeks to counter the weight traditionally given to power, similarity, and familiarity in determining what constitutes merit.

140

JOURNAL OF LAW AND SOCIETY
VOLUME 33, NUMBER 1, MARCH 2006
ISSN: 0263-323X, pp. 141–59

Quotas for Women! The Sex Discrimination (Election Candidates) Act 2002

AILEEN MCHARG*

The Sex Discrimination (Election Candidates) Act 2002 is unusual in two respects. First, it is a rare example of the permissible (though not mandatory) use of affirmative action in the United Kingdom, in this case to reduce gender inequality in the selection of election candidates. Secondly, the Act contains a sunset clause and will expire in 2015 unless extended. This article examines the background to the legislation, the forms of affirmative action it permits, and the use so far made of it by political parties. It also considers the justifications for affirmative action to increase women's political representation, asking what sets this apart from other contexts in which women are under-represented, and whether the temporary nature of the legislation is appropriate.

INTRODUCTION

The Sex Discrimination (Election Candidates) Act 2002 (hereafter SDECA) is a doubly unusual piece of legislation. First, it represents a rare – and in relation to gender, unique – departure from the United Kingdom's typical 'symmetrical' approach to anti-discrimination law, its purpose being to remove doubts about the legality of positive action, including reverse *discrimination*, to reduce gender inequality in the selection of election candidates. Although affirmative action is normally highly controversial, SDECA was nonetheless enacted remarkably easily. All parties, except the Ulster Unionists, officially supported the Bill in the House of Commons, and there was so little opposition in the Lords that it was not even debated after its second reading. However, given that all speakers, including the few opponents, agreed that increasing women's political representation was an important objective, it is perhaps unsurprising that most were prepared to

* *School of Law, University of Glasgow, Stair Building, 8 The Square, Glasgow G12 8QQ, Scotland*
a.mcharg@law.gla.ac.uk

contemplate special measures, since this is an area in which simply removing legal obstacles has clearly been insufficient to ensure real equality. Although one of the earliest contexts in which formal sex equality was achieved – women gained the right to stand for Parliament in 1918[1] and even earlier for local government[2] – they still constitute a mere fifth of MPs (see table). Moreover, even that figure has only been reached because of the 'all-woman shortlists' (AWS) policy adopted by the Labour Party for the 1997 and 2005 elections. Women constitute a similarly low proportion of United Kingdom MEPs, local councillors and Northern Ireland Assembly members. Whilst much higher in the Scottish Parliament and National Assembly for Wales (NAW) (the latter in fact being the only elected body in the world to have achieved gender parity), these too are achievements which are partly attributable to affirmative action.[3] British experience thus confirms evidence from abroad that significant levels of female electoral representation are almost impossible to achieve without special measures.[4]

Women's Political Representation in the UK

Institution	Most Recent Election	Number of Members	Number of Female Members	Percentage of Female Members
United Kingdom Parliament	May 2005	646	127	19.7%
Scottish Parliament	May 2003	129	51	39.5%
Welsh Assembly	May 2003	60	30	50.0%
Northern Ireland Assembly	November 2003	108	17	15.7%
United Kingdom MEPs	June 2004	78	19	24.4%
London Assembly	June 2004	25	9	36.0%
Local government (excl. N. Ire)	2001[5]	–	–	25.5%

1 Parliament (Qualification of Women) Act 1918.
2 Gradually extended between 1870 and 1907.
3 The absence of an 'incumbent effect' in these new institutions was also crucial.
4 See, for example, J. Squires and M. Wickham-Jones, *Women in Parliament: a Comparative Analysis* (2001) 13. The type of electoral system used is also an important determinant – see further below.
5 The most recent year for which figures are available. Source: Fawcett Society, *Women's Representation in British Politics*, available at <www.fawcettsociety.org.uk>.

142

Nevertheless, SDECA cannot be read as a straightforward endorsement of the legitimacy of affirmative action. For one thing, the legislation is permissive only.[6] To some extent, therefore, it merely shifts debates about the appropriateness of special measures to the parties themselves, where the issue continues to be controversial. In addition, the Act's second unusual characteristic is that it contains a sunset clause – it will expire at the end of 2015, unless extended by ministerial order[7] – a feature which normally indicates that the affected legislation is somehow exceptional and only of qualified legitimacy.

This article therefore attempts to answer three questions. First, on what basis can affirmative action to increase female electoral representation be justified? Second, what, if anything, distinguishes political representation from other contexts in which women are under-represented? Third, is the temporary nature of the legislation appropriate? Before addressing these issues, however, it is necessary to outline the background to SDECA's enactment, its legal effect and the use made of it so far.

THE LEGISLATION

1. Background

Affirmative action to address women's political under-representation began in the United Kingdom in the 1980s, when all major parties adopted limited measures such as special training and support for aspiring women candidates[8] and education for party selectors. The first to take stronger steps was the Social Democratic Party (SDP), which included in its 1981 constitution a rule (later retained by the Liberal Democrats) that, wherever a woman applied for selection as an election candidate, at least one should be shortlisted.[9] However, it was the Labour party that took the issue most seriously, influenced by feminist party members and socialist parties elsewhere, but also by the desire to counteract its 'masculine' image and hence the significant gender gap amongst its voters.[10] Thus, the party adopted the SDP's compulsory shortlisting rule in 1988 and, in 1989, passed

---

6 Some countries require parties to promote gender parity, or even reserve a proportion of legislative seats for women – see P. Norris, *Electoral Engineering: Voting Rules and Political Behaviour* (2004) 191–8.
7 Subject to affirmative resolution – s. 3 SDECA.
8 Permitted by ss. 47–8 Sex Discrimination Act 1975.
9 D.T. Studlar and I. McAllister, 'Candidate Selection and Voting in the 1997 British General Election: Did Labour Quotas Matter?' (1998) 4 *J. of Legislative Studies* 72, at 74.
10 See C. Short, 'Women and the Labour Party' and S. Perrigo, 'Women and Change in the Labour Party 1979–1995', both in *Women in Politics*, eds. J. Lovenduski and P. Norris (1996).

143

a conference resolution committing it to securing gender parity in the parliamentary party within ten years. Nevertheless, whilst these measures did ensure that more female candidates were selected, they had only a limited impact on the number actually elected,[11] since women were disproportionately concentrated in unwinnable seats.[12] Accordingly, following the 1992 election, and analysis showing that had Labour attracted as many female as male voters it would not only have won that election, but would have been in power continuously between 1954 and 1979,[13] the party decided in 1993 to adopt AWS for the 1997 election. The policy was to apply to half the seats with a retiring Labour MP and half the party's target seats. Thirty five women were eventually selected from AWS, all of whom were subsequently elected. The policy therefore made a substantial contribution to the record 101 female Labour MPs elected in 1997, which doubled the overall percentage of women MPs from 9.2 to 18.2 per cent.

The AWS policy was, though, brought to a premature[14] end in 1996 when, in *Jepson & Dyas-Elliott* v. *the Labour Party*,[15] an industrial tribunal held that it amounted to direct discrimination against men contrary to section 1(1) of the Sex Discrimination Act 1975 (SDA). Labour sought to rely on section 33, which exempted 'any special provision for persons of one sex only in the constitution, organisation or administration of the party.' However, this applied only to Part III SDA, relating to services, whereas *Jepson* held that candidate selection fell within Part II, relating to employment: being an MP constituted a 'profession' and candidate selection fell within section 13, prohibiting discrimination by an 'authority or body which can confer an authorisation or qualification, which is needed for, or facilitates, engagement in a particular profession or trade.' Since the tribunal decision had no precedential value, Labour chose not to appeal for fear of compromising those women already selected. Nevertheless, *Jepson* was effectively confirmed by the Employment Appeal Tribunal in 1999 in *Sawyer* v. *Ashan*,[16] brought under equivalent provisions in the Race Relations Act 1976 (RRA), though *Sawyer* was itself subsequently overruled by the Court of Appeal in *Triesman* v. *Ali*,[17] shortly before SDECA was enacted.

Although Labour was forced to abandon AWS, *Jepson* did not end affirmative action altogether. Having undertaken (along with the Liberal Democrats) in the Scottish Constitutional Convention (SCC) to promote gender parity in the Scottish Parliament,[18] Labour adopted a policy of

---

11 Having remained static at around 3 to 4 per cent from 1945 to 1983, the number of women MPs began to rise in 1987, to 6.3 per cent, and again in 1992, to 9.2 per cent.

12 J. Lovenduski, *Feminising Politics* (2005) 116–17.

13 M. Russell et al., *Women's Political Participation in the UK* (2002) 36.

14 The target had been for AWS to be employed in 40 seats.

15 *Jepson & Dyas-Elliott* v. *the Labour Party* [1996] IRLR 116.

16 *Sawyer* v. *Ashan* [2000] ICR 1.

17 *Triesman* v. *Ali* [2002] ECR 1026.

18 SCC, *Scotland's Parliament, Scotland's Right* (1995).

'twinning' (whereby pairs of constituencies were obliged to choose a male and female candidate between them) for the 1999 Scottish and Welsh elections and the 2000 London Assembly elections. Plaid Cymru also used its top-up lists to achieve a degree of gender balance amongst its Welsh Assembly members, and the Liberal Democrats 'zipped' their English regional lists for the 1999 European elections (that is, put men and women in alternate places). Nevertheless, the adverse precedents clearly cast a shadow over the parties' ability and willingness to promote female candidates. Although designed to minimize the legal risks, twinning and zipping (and, indeed, shortlisting quotas) still potentially constituted unlawful indirect discrimination,[19] and further legal challenges were in fact threatened.[20] These did not ultimately materialize, but they were sufficient to persuade the Liberal Democrats to renege on their SCC commitments[21] and nearly caused Labour to do so too.[22] Moreover, neither zipping nor twinning was feasible for Westminster elections, given the nature of the electoral system and the high number of incumbent candidates. Hence, for the 2001 election the only special measures adopted were shortlisting rules in the Labour and Liberal Democratic parties, the former requiring equal numbers of men and women to be shortlisted, and the latter at least one third of each gender. Consequently, the number of female MPs elected in 2001 actually fell, from 120 to 118. Anticipating this result, Labour pledged in its manifesto to reverse *Jepson*.

2. Scope

The legal effect of SDECA is, superficially, very straightforward. It simply adds a new section 42A to the SDA[23] stating that nothing in Parts II–IV shall be construed as affecting or rendering unlawful arrangements by a registered political party which:

> (a) regulate the selection of the party's candidates in a relevant election, and
> (b) are adopted for the purpose of reducing inequality in the numbers of men and women elected, as candidates of the party, to be members of the body concerned.

Relevant elections are to the United Kingdom Parliament, the European Parliament, the three devolved assemblies, and local government (excluding mayoral races). Accordingly, parties appear to be permitted to adopt any measures they see fit, as long as they only seek gender parity amongst their

---

19 See R. Ali and C. O'Cinneide, *Our House: Race and Representation in British Politics* (2002) 68–9.
20 M. Russell, *Women's Representation in UK Politics: What Can Be Done Within the Law?* (2000) 9–10.
21 Russell et al., op. cit., n. 13, p. 29.
22 Russell, op. cit., n. 20, p. 14.
23 And a parallel provision to the Sex Discrimination (Northern Ireland) Order 1976.

own candidates, and do not, for example, attempt to compensate for inaction by other parties by selecting more women than men.

Nevertheless, uncertainty remains in two respects. First, SDECA was intended to leave unaffected the prohibition of *negative* discrimination in the candidate selection process. However, *Triesman* throws this into doubt.[24] Although it held that candidate selection was potentially covered by section 25 RRA, prohibiting discrimination against (aspiring) members of private clubs, the SDA has no equivalent provision. Its only potentially applicable provision is section 29, which prohibits discrimination in the provision of 'goods, facilities or services' to members of the public. However, *Triesman* doubted whether candidate selection could properly be so described.[25]

Secondly, there is uncertainty about what precise *positive* measures SDECA authorizes. The Joint Committee on Human Rights, in its report on the Bill,[26] argued that candidate selection fell within the Equal Treatment Directive (ETD)[27] and Article 3 Protocol 1 (the right to vote),[28] read with Article 14 (non-discrimination) of the European Convention on Human Rights (ECHR), both of which permit positive action to achieve substantive gender equality, but only to the extent that such measures are proportionate. Hence, though the Committee regarded the Bill as a whole as proportionate, particularly because of its permissive nature and the sunset clause (international law only permits temporary affirmative action),[29] it concluded that parties would still need to ensure that any measures they adopted also passed this test. For instance, in a coded reference to AWS, the Committee suggested that a policy which automatically and unconditionally gave priority to women over equally qualified men would not be permitted by the ETD.[30] Similarly, though AWS might be justifiable under the ECHR, given the difficulty in a first-past-the-post system of using less intrusive measures,[31] this might still prohibit policies which favour women excessively, such as parties allocating all their winnable seats to them.[32]

---

24 See M. Russell and M. O'Cinneide, 'Positive Action to Promote Women in Politics: Some European Comparisons' (2003) 52 *International and Comparative Law Q.* 587, at 595.
25 See, also, H. Davis, 'All Women Shortlists in the Labour Party' [1995] *Public Law* 207, at 212.
26 Joint Committee on Human Rights (JCHR), Fourth Report, 2001–02, HL 44, HC 406.
27 Directive 76/207/EEC, OJ L 39/40, 14 February 1976.
28 Which includes the right to stand as a candidate: see, for example, *Mathieu-Mohin and Clerfayt* v. *Belgium* 10 EHRR 1, 1987.
29 See, particularly, the Convention on the Elimination of Discrimination Against Women 1249 UNTS 13 (1979), Art 4.
30 JCHR, op. cit., n. 26, para. 20.
31 Russell and O'Cinneide, op. cit., n. 24, p. 612.
32 JCHR, op. cit., n. 26, para. 15.

146

Neither of these conclusions is, however, incontrovertible. Meg Russell has persuasively argued (and the government agrees)[33] that candidate selection does not in fact fall within the ETD.[34] Quotas for women's representation are widely used in other member states without challenge under Community law, and they typically consider candidate selection to be a matter of constitutional rather than employment law, hence falling outwith Community competence – a view accepted by the European Commission.[35] Similarly, the ECHR's applicability in domestic law depends upon either regarding political parties as public authorities within section 6 of the Human Rights Act 1998 (HRA), or reading a proportionality requirement into SDECA under section 3 HRA, both of which (particularly the former)[36] are open to question. Nevertheless, SDECA has clearly not succeeding in removing all legal risk from the use of affirmative action in candidate selection.

3. Practical impact

Despite this, the Labour Party lost no time in reinstating the AWS policy for the 2003 Scottish and Welsh elections,[37] local government elections from 2004, and the 2005 Westminster election. In fact, for the latter, the policy was even more radical than previously, since AWS were imposed in two-thirds of seats in which sitting Labour MPs announced their retirement before Christmas 2002, and nearly all seats in which retirements were announced thereafter. To avoid opposition, though, the policy was not applied in Scotland, where the abolition of thirteen seats meant that competition for selection was more than usually fierce. It was also highly contentious in Wales; in Blaenau Gwent, a former party member who stood as an independent in protest at the imposition of an AWS succeeded in overturning a 19,000 Labour majority.[38] Nevertheless, the policy was again vindicated by its results; whilst 47 Labour MPs lost their seats in 2005 overall, four more women were elected, increasing their proportion of the Parliamentary Labour party to 27.5 per cent.

33 See Lord Williams of Mostyn, 629 *H.L. Debs.*, col. WA 56 (28 November 2001); 630 *H.L. Debs.*, col. WA 31 (17 December 2001).
34 Russell, op. cit., n. 20, pp. 41–5.
35 Written Question No 1556/98 by Nel van Dijk to the Commission, OJ 354/111, 19 November 1998.
36 Relying on United States case law, the JCHR considered that parties are covered by s. 6 HRA. However, United Kingdom political parties have historically been regarded as private associations, and the government's view was that candidate selection is a private act, not a public function: Lord Williams, op. cit., n. 33.
37 Twinning was no longer feasible, given the presence of incumbents. The Scottish Socialist Party and Plaid Cymru also used quotas for these elections.
38 Quotas for local government elections also produced discontent – see 'Council Female Quota Angers MPs' *Guardian*, 23 May 2003.

Neither of the other main United Kingdom parties has, however, yet been prepared to follow Labour's example.[39] In 2001, the Liberal Democrats rejected a proposal to adopt AWS and, in 2002, in fact resolved to abandon zipping for European elections. Instead, the party established a Gender Balance Task Force charged with designing positive action policies to encourage and support women seeking selection, although it has retained its rule that at least a third of shortlisted candidates should be female.[40] Despite leadership proposals,[41] the Conservatives have been unwilling to adopt even these minimal positive discrimination measures. They have therefore relied on reforming procedures for access to their approved candidates list, to ensure men and women are treated equally, and equal opportunities training for local selection committees, who retain the final say in selection.[42] Although the Liberal Democrats' measures have proved reasonably success-ful – the party gained four female MPs in 2005, increasing their proportion of women to 16.1 per cent – Conservative women MPs remained virtually static at 8.6 per cent.[43] More female Conservative candidates were selected, but again they were concentrated in hopeless seats.[44] Nonetheless, the fact that both parties have felt obliged to address the issue of female representation may be evidence of the beginning of the 'contagion effect' witnessed in other countries, where the adoption of quotas by one party (usually on the Left) gradually spreads to others.[45] Indeed, demands for stronger measures continue to be raised within the Liberal Democrats.[46]

JUSTIFYING AFFIRMATIVE ACTION IN THE POLITICAL SPHERE

The existence of a contagion effect suggests that political parties' main *motivation* for adopting quotas for women in politics may be to gain (or neutralize) electoral advantage, and there is some evidence that female voters are more likely to vote for female than male candidates.[47] However, electoral considerations are not a legitimate reason for employing normally suspect gender categorizations. Instead, to return to the first question posed

39 Though the Scottish National Party at its 2004 Spring conference agreed to an unspecified plan to ensure 'a balanced list of candidates, particularly in regard to gender.'
40 See Fawcett Society, *Liberal Democrat Candidates – Where are the Women?*, available at <www.fawcettsociety.org.uk>.
41 Squires and Wickham-Jones, op. cit., n. 4, p. 74; Lovenduski, op. cit., n. 12, p. 70.
42 See T. May, 'Women in the House: the Continuing Challenge' (2004) 57 *Parliamentary Affairs* 844.
43 They gained only three women out of 33 new MPs.
44 Fawcett Society, *Conservatives Candidates – Where are the Women?*, available at <www.fawcettsociety.org.uk>.
45 See Squires and Wickham-Jones, op. cit., n. 4, p. 36.
46 Lovenduski, op. cit., n. 12, p. 75.
47 P. Norris et al., *Gender and Political Participation* (2004) 9.

in the Introduction, there are two main arguments used to justify affirmative action to increase women's representation. One is an argument from fairness: that this is necessary to ensure that women have an equal chance to stand for election. The other is an argument from democracy: that elected assemblies cannot truly represent women without an increase in female members. Though sometimes invoked together, these arguments carry rather different implications for the second and third questions posed above about the distinctiveness of political representation and the appropriate duration of affirmative action.

1. Fairness

The fairness argument was most commonly relied upon during parliamentary debates on SDECA. The contention is that women are currently unable to compete for selection on equal terms with men. Accordingly, *temporary* special measures are necessary to help them overcome their disadvantages and create a level playing field.

Explanations for why there are fewer female than male candidates focus on both supply- and demand-side factors – those which deter women from *seeking* selection and those which prevent them being *chosen*. The most benign supply-side explanation is that women are simply less interested in seeking political office. There is indeed evidence of a modest gender gap in political activism, at least as regards party political activity,[48] which in turn means that women are less likely to have gained the necessary party contacts and experience to make them credible candidates for selection. However, one problem with this explanation is that the activism gap may itself reflect structural gender inequalities.[49] For example, the unequal distribution of caring responsibilities means that women have less time for political activities. They are less likely to be employed in jobs that give them a high sense of political efficacy, confidence in public speaking, and so on; and their weaker economic position means that they have less access to the resources necessary for political participation and influence – particularly for engaging in costly selection campaigns. Finally, women may be deterred by the masculine face and adversarial style of politics. In fact, evidence from abroad suggests that the activism gap disappears as more women are elected.[50] In any case, it is not sufficiently wide to explain the disparity in the numbers of men and women selected as candidates. In practice, except perhaps in the Conservative party, there does not seem to be any real problem in finding sufficient women to put themselves forward.[51] And even when equal numbers of men and women are available for selection, men are

48 id.
49 See, for example, id., ch. 4.
50 id., pp. 23–5.
51 Lovenduski, op. cit., n. 12, p. 71.

149

still more successful: female candidates secured only 10.3 per cent of winnable Labour seats for the 2001 election, despite the balanced shortlisting rule.

Recent research has therefore focused upon demand-side factors. Studies conducted by the Fawcett Society[52] and the Equal Opportunities Commission,[53] which were influential in securing the passage of SDECA, uncovered substantial evidence of discrimination by selection committees. At the extreme, this included (particularly in the Labour and Conservative parties) overtly hostile or patronizing comments and sexual harassment. For instance, one women reported that 'you are told things like "your children are better off with you at home" ', whilst another was asked 'if she ... was in Westminster during the week, what would her husband do for sex?'[54] More covert, but widespread discrimination consisted of inconsistent questioning, particularly about family responsibilities, and double standards being used to judge male and female candidates. In addition, the studies uncovered a problem of 'favourite sons' (again more prevalent in Labour and the Conservatives), whereby certain male candidates received additional help, sometimes in breach of party rules, to virtually guarantee their selection. For some women, the experience was so bad as to put them off applying for another seat, and it probably sends a message that deters others from trying at all.[55]

At this point it might be argued that a case has been made for weaker forms of affirmative action, such as special encouragement, training, and possibly even financial support for potential women candidates, alongside rigorous enforcement of anti-discrimination law, but not for stronger forms, which seek to guarantee that women are selected, since they interfere with the appointment of candidates on merit, thereby discriminating against men and patronizing women.[56]

One response might be to question whether notions of objective merit have much role to play in the context of elected representatives. Indeed, the fact that no-one really knows what the qualifications for office should be means that selection decisions are particularly liable to be based on judgements about *who* candidates are rather than *what* skills they offer.[57] Secondly, leaving aside whether the SDA actually applies to candidate selection, there are reasons to think that a standard anti-discrimination

---

52 L. Shepherd-Robinson and J. Lovenduski, *Women and Candidate Selection in British Political Parties* (2002).
53 J. Elgood et al., *Man Enough for the Job? A Study of Parliamentary Candidates* (2002).
54 Shepherd-Robinson and Lovenduski, op. cit., n. 52, pp. 15, 29.
55 Lovenduski, op. cit., n. 12, p. 71.
56 See, for example, Lord Lester of Herne Hill, 630 *H.L. Debs.*, cols 397–402 (20 December 2001); A. Widdecombe, 373 *H.C. Debs.*, cols. 352-4 (24 October 2001); Elgood et al., op. cit., n. 53, pp. 102, 107–9.
57 Compare A. Phillips, *The Politics of Presence* (1995) 61.

150

approach might be particularly ineffective in this context. For instance, the involvement of local party members in candidate selection makes it difficult to adhere to best recruitment practice,[58] as does the infrequency of the process, especially in safe seats. Realistically, also, since candidacies, again especially in safe seats, are scarce resources, it will always be difficult to ensure complete fairness in their allocation. Equally, disappointed candidates may be particularly unlikely to complain about discrimination for fear of undermining their chances in future.

Thirdly, experience suggests that weaker forms of affirmative action, which seek to place female candidates on an equal footing with males, are simply not sufficiently effective. What this seems to indicate is the persistence of a deep-seated cultural expectation that politicians are men.[59] Centuries of political theory have constructed the political sphere as an exclusively male space,[60] an attitude which continues to be reflected in, for example, hostile media coverage of women politicians,[61] and in the 'institutionally sexist' environment of the House of Commons.[62] Further, the male norm is reinforced by the incumbency bias of party selectors – the tendency, in the absence of reliable data about voter preferences, to favour incumbent candidates or ones who resemble those who have previously been successful – which particularly affects single-member constituencies where there are no countervailing pressures to present a balanced ticket.[63] Hence, the view persists (especially amongst Liberal Democrat selectors) that female candidates are an electoral liability,[64] despite consistent polling evidence to the contrary.[65]

Thus it can be argued that strong affirmative action is both necessary and justified to break the grip of sexism in politics. True political equality requires not only showing that women can be as good as men, but normalizing the idea of female politicians. By deliberately promoting female candidates, the expectation is that they will act as role models and help make their parties and elected institutions more female-friendly places, thereby encouraging other women to enter politics.

However, the fairness argument does indeed offer only a temporary justification for affirmative action. It is essentially a pragmatic rationale

---

58 Russell, op. cit., n. 20, p. 49.
59 Compare Elgood et al., op. cit., n. 53, pp. 78–82; Shepherd-Robinson and Lovenduski, op. cit., n. 52, pp. 29–30, 41, 49.
60 See, for example, C. Pateman, *The Sexual Contract* (1988).
61 See, for example, A. Sreberny and K. Ross, 'Women MPs and the Media: Representing the Body Politic' in Lovenduski and Norris (eds.), op. cit., n. 10.
62 Lovenduski, op. cit., n. 12, pp. 47-56; see, also, K. Ross, 'Women's Place in "Male" Space: Gender and Effect in Parliamentary Contexts' (2002) 55 *Parliamentary Affairs* 189; 'Women MPs Bullied and Abused in Commons' *Guardian*, 7 December 2004.
63 Norris, op. cit., n. 6, p. 182.
64 Shepherd-Robinson and Lovenduski, op. cit., n. 52, pp. 40–1.
65 See, for example, Studlar and McAllister, op. cit., n. 9.

151

which involves overlooking less favourable treatment of men in order to eradicate discrimination against women. It follows, therefore, that special measures are permissible only so long as they remain necessary to ensure a level playing field. An equal opportunities approach does not permit insistence upon end-state equality, and unequal outcomes do not provide conclusive proof of ongoing discrimination. Moreover, the validity of the fairness argument is premised upon the assumption that affirmative action policies are actually effective in eradicating discrimination. Paradoxically, this may mean that stronger measures are *more* defensible than weaker ones. For example, compulsory shortlisting rules may be counter-productive, because they create the perception that women are gaining special favours without guaranteeing that any more will be chosen,[66] while also causing resentment amongst aspiring women candidates, who spend time and money on unwinnable campaigns.[67] On the other hand, stronger measures carry greater risk of backlash. For example, the extensive press criticism of Labour women MPs after the 1997 election was at least partly attributable to the controversy surrounding AWS.[68] A pragmatic approach therefore suggests that special measures should be discontinued if there is evidence that they are *not* working in practice. But it also runs the risk that the commitment to affirmative action may be overridden if it conflicts with other pragmatic goals, without being given a proper chance to work. All this begs the questions, which will be addressed further below, how to judge whether affirmative action has been effective or not, and whether the timescale set by SDECA is likely to be realistic.

A more problematic aspect of the legislation from a fairness perspective was articulated by Virginia Bottomley MP: '[m]y worry is what the public will make of our passing legislation that is specifically for Members of Parliament when we are not prepared to pass similar legislation for other professional groups.'[69] In other words, the equal opportunities rationale would appear to justify affirmative action in any context in which women face endemic discrimination,[70] and where the potential benefits outweigh the potential costs. In fact, in so far as women's political disadvantage is linked to general economic disadvantage, it makes little sense to single out candidate selection for special legal treatment.

However, as noted above, part of the legal justification for SDECA was precisely that election candidacies should *not* be equated with employment. What, then, explains the distinctiveness of political representation? One possibility is the operation of a public/private distinction: we expect higher

---

66 Squires and Wickham-Jones, op. cit., n. 4, p. 87.
67 Shepherd-Robinson and Lovenduski, op. cit., n. 52, pp. 21–2, 44–5, 51.
68 See Lovenduski, op. cit., n. 12, pp. 153–8.
69 V. Bottomley, 373 *H.C. Debs.*, col. 347 (24 October 2001).
70 J. Squires, 'Quotas for Women: Fair Representation?' in Lovenduski and Norris (eds.), op. cit., n. 10, p. 78.

standards of equality in the public than in the private sector. The history of female emancipation shows that formal equality has usually been achieved in the public sector first; similarly, foreign experience tells us that affirmative action is often required in the public sector before the private.[71] Nevertheless, even if we accept that political parties are properly classified as public, this begs the question *why* should we expect higher standards from public bodies, and is vulnerable to the counter-argument that they owe stronger duties not to violate *men's* rights, as well as to uphold women's rights.

Two arguments do, however, give some substance to this implicit public/private distinction. First, achieving equality in political representation has symbolic value as an indicator of women's social standing that makes it more important than other contexts. Second, it has a genuine vanguard status as a means to securing equality in other areas of life.[72] Empirically, both are contestable claims. In the Nordic countries, for example, it has been suggested that women were allowed into parliament only when real power had shifted elsewhere,[73] and labour markets there are the most segregated in Europe despite high levels of female political representation.[74] Nevertheless, these arguments are significant because they begin to move the case for affirmative action away from fairness towards the democratic rationale. In other words, it is not just about ensuring equal rights for women to compete for a desirable career,[75] but about responding to a democratic imperative.

2. Representation and diversity

There are weaker and stronger versions of the argument from democracy. The weaker is that increased women's presence is necessary to improve the legitimacy of representative institutions, since they cannot be fully democratic unless they reflect the diversity of the electorate. The stronger claim is that this will make a substantive difference to the quality of representation provided, because women have a different political style to men and/or because they have different interests and perspectives which are not being adequately considered. Although relatively few supporters of SDECA relied on these democratic arguments, and some rejected them entirely, if sustainable, they offer clear grounds for distinguishing political representation from other social contexts. They also provide a defence to the

---

71 C.L. Bacchi, *The Politics of Affirmative Action: 'Women', Equality and Category Politics* (1996) 16.
72 Squires and Wickham-Jones, op. cit., n. 4, p. iii; Declaration of the 4th UN World Conference on Women Women in Power and Decision-Making (Beijing, September 2005).
73 Phillips, op. cit., n. 57, p. 183.
74 Lovenduski, op. cit., n. 12, p. 97.
75 A. Phillips, 'Democracy and Representation, Or, Why Should it Matter Who Our Representatives Are?' in *Feminism and Politics*, ed. A. Phillips (1998) 230–1.

153

criticism that affirmative action is unfair to men, because it is not about benefiting particular women candidates, but a question of justice to the *electorate* in being represented fairly.[76] Hence, they potentially supply a longer-term rationale for special measures, not merely to secure equality of opportunity but to entrench a model of 'parity democracy'.

However, the claim that women are not properly represented by male-dominated institutions is highly contested. One problem is that it rests on a conception of representation that is arguably incompatible with our democratic traditions.[77] The prevailing view is that elected representatives speak on behalf of their whole constituency, not for particular demographic groups. They are chosen according to their competing interpretations (mediated by political parties) of their constituents' interests. Hence the key issue is to ensure proper representation of the diversity of *opinions* held by the electorate, rather than diversity amongst the representatives themselves.[78] Furthermore, it has been considered important that voters should have a free choice between competing candidates. By contrast, the claim that women are 'under-represented' appeals to a 'microcosmic' or 'descriptive' conception of representation which requires representatives to share their constituents' characteristics.

It must be emphasized that SDECA does not in fact interfere with voter choice; parties are free to field, and voters to choose, candidates of either gender. However, as regards the conflict between what Anne Phillips calls the 'politics of ideas' and the 'politics of presence',[79] political theorists generally prefer the former to the latter. One reason is that a representative body which perfectly mirrors the electorate's social characteristics is neither achievable in practice, given size constraints, nor desirable in theory. For instance, few dispute the appropriateness of membership restrictions relating to age, mental capacity or criminal convictions, and the unusual demands of a political career mean that it inevitably appeals to a socially-atypical group.[80] Secondly, as Hannah Pitkin points out, microcosmic representation focuses attention on *who* the representatives are rather than *what* they do.[81] Representation, she argues, is an activity, not a status, which requires that representatives be responsive to their constituents; if they are not sufficiently responsive, the answer lies in improving their accountability, rather than changing their identity.

However, these criticisms arguably present an overly simplistic view of both our representative traditions and the nature of the concept. In fact, multiple versions of representation, including microcosmic, have been

---

76 Squires, op. cit., n. 70, p. 75.
77 See House of Lords Constitution Committee, Third Report, 2001–02, HL 42.
78 Phillips, op. cit., n. 57, p. 6.
79 id.
80 A.H. Birch, *Representation* (1971) 57.
81 H. Pitkin, *The Concept of Representation* (1967).

invoked at different historical periods, elements of which survive in contemporary democratic practice.[82] The Labour party, particularly, has a history of representing group interests, one purpose of the trade union link being to produce more working-class MPs. There is also a strong tradition of geographical representation, reflected both in the drawing of constituency boundaries and in the existence of regional parties. Similarly, many women MPs do see themselves as 'acting for women',[83] just as Muslim MPs are sometimes treated as representating the Muslim community. Indeed, A.H. Birch argues that there is no single correct meaning of representation, because we require the concept to perform multiple functions.[84] Since one is to maintain popular support for governing institutions, the inclusiveness of their membership is highly relevant, especially where excluded groups have historically been deemed incapable of governing.[85] Moreover, even Pitkin concedes that a representative's characteristics may be relevant to the extent that they affect how she or he acts.[86] Thus, microcosmic representation is likely to find support wherever social characteristics are thought to have political significance.[87]

However, the suggestion that gender is politically significant raises a second problem: that of essentialism. It is far from clear either that women do have distinct interests and perspectives which are better represented by other women or that female politicians act differently from men. Research shows that party is a stronger indicator of attitudes on most issues than gender.[88] Arguably, also, where women adopt distinctive political styles (for example, a preference for working behind the scenes),[89] this is driven more by pragmatic responses to context (the desire to avoid attracting hostility) than by innate gender differences.[90] Accordingly, it may be positively undesirable to base the case for increased women's representation on such claims, since they may perpetuate gender stereotypes and create a double

---

82 Squires, op. cit., n. 70, pp. 79–80; Birch, op. cit., n. 80.
83 S. Childs 'In Their Own Words: New Labour Women and the Substantive Representation of Women' (2001) 3 *Brit. J. of Politics and International Relations* 173; 'Hitting the Target: Are Labour Women MPs "Acting For" Women?' (2002) 55 *Parliamentary Affairs* 143. There is also a women's party – the Northern Ireland Women's Coalition – which has held seats in the Northern Ireland Assembly and in local government.
84 Birch, op. cit., n. 80, pp. 105, 107.
85 Phillips, op. cit., n. 57, p. 39; J. Mansbridge, 'Should Blacks Represent Blacks and Women Represent Women? A Contingent "Yes"' (1999) 61 *J. of Politics* 628, at 628.
86 Pitkin, op. cit., n. 81, p. 142.
87 Birch, op. cit., n. 80, p. 59.
88 Squires and Wickham-Jones, op. cit., n. 4, pp. 91–2.
89 id., pp. 97–9.
90 Compare Ross, op. cit., n. 62, p. 191; E. Breitenbach, 'The Women's Movement in Scotland in the 1990s' in *Women and Contemporary Scottish Politics: An Anthology*, eds. E. Breitenbach and F. MacKay (2001) 83–4.

155

bind for female politicians: ghettoizing them in 'softer' policy areas, whilst providing ammunition to be used against them if they fail to make a difference.[91] In 1997, for instance, female Labour MPs were particularly criticized for not rebelling over cuts in lone-parent benefits.

Yet gender is clearly not wholly irrelevant politically. Social and biological differences mean that there are some issues which *in practice*, even if not inevitably, affect men and women differently, and surveys do show some modest gender differences in political attitudes, particularly on gender-related issues.[92] Moreover, anecdotal evidence suggests that increased women's presence does have an effect on policy output and working practices, albeit this is difficult to prove conclusively.[93] In fact, though, Phillips argues,[94] it is precisely *because* 'women's interests' cannot be determined objectively, coupled with the fact that representatives in practice enjoy considerable autonomy, that it is important to have more female politicians. If interests are clear, it matters little who represents them, so long as they can be held accountable to the group in question. However, where these conditions are not met, selecting decision makers who share the group's characteristics provides an alternative reassurance, although not a guarantee, that they will also share the group's concerns. Thus, to the extent that women do have distinct interests and perspectives, the presence of more female representatives *increases the chances* of these being articulated. The politics of presence is not, therefore, simply about ensuring descriptively accurate representation, but about providing the best advocates for the interests of previously excluded groups. Further, the more women that are present, the greater the likelihood of reflecting the diversity *amongst* them, as well as their differences from men.[95]

Do these democratic arguments therefore justify affirmative action? On the one hand, they clearly add weight to the fairness argument, since they provide further reasons for challenging monolithic perceptions of appropriate representatives. On the other hand, given the tentative nature of the democratic case and the fact that it is also premised upon redressing discrimination, it does not seem to supply an independent justification for affirmative action, such as to sanction special treatment for political

---

91 Compare R. Voet, *Feminism and Citizenship* (1998) 95.
92 Squires and Wickham-Jones, op. cit., n. 4, pp. 91–2; R. Campbell, 'Gender, Ideology and Issue Preference: Is There Such as Thing as a Political Women's Interest in Britain?' (2004) 6 *Brit. J. of Politics and International Relations* 20.
93 See, for example, Squires and Wickham-Jones, id., pp. 92–7; Childs, op. cit., n. 83; S. Childs and J. Withey, 'Women Representatives Acting for Women: Sex and the Signing of Early Day Motions in the 1997 British Parliament' (2004) 52 *Political Studies* 552; P. Chaney and R. Fevre, 'Is there a Demand for Descriptive Representation? Evidence from the UK's Devolution Programme' (2002) 50 *Political Studies* 897.
94 Phillips, op. cit., n. 57; Phillips, op. cit., n. 75.
95 Mansbridge, op. cit., n. 85, p. 363.

representation, or to permit permanent gender quotas. Moreover, it raises a further question about the legitimacy of SDECA, namely, why should it only be women who benefit? Thus there have been calls for affirmative action to be extended to other politically under-represented groups,[96] and the use of AWS in constituencies with large non-white populations has caused extra resentment when this has excluded prominent male ethnic minority activists. Gender and ethnicity do not raise identical issues in this context, and it is harder to design appropriate measures to boost ethnic minority representation, not least because of the diversity of Britain's ethnic minorities themselves.[97] However, Labour and the Liberal Democrats already have special shortlisting rules for ethnic minorities, and it is difficult to see why the RRA should not be similarly amended to allow parties to adopt such measures as are feasible.

Finally, the democratic arguments also potentially add to the costs associated with affirmative action. The risk of essentialism is avoidable in theory, but real in practice. In addition, there is a danger of promoting one form of diversity at the expense of others. For instance, the AWS policy has been accused of promoting middle-class women at the expense of working-class men, and has also failed to produce a single ethnic minority candidate.[98] Similarly, the centralization of selection procedures necessary to implement gender quotas may reduce diversity of opinion within party groups. Again, therefore, judgements have to be made about whether the benefits of increased descriptive representation outweigh the costs.[99]

CONCLUSION

This article has argued that the legalization of affirmative action to increase women's political representation, including positive discrimination measures such as AWS, is justified on both fairness and democratic grounds. Moreover, SDECA must be regarded as setting an important precedent in favour of the extension of strong affirmative action in the United Kingdom, not only to increase the political presence of other under-represented groups, but also to other contexts in which women or others face endemic discrimination.

It has also been argued that, in principle, the temporary nature of the legislation is appropriate. However, it remains to be discussed whether the thirteen-year timescale laid down by SDECA (which allows for three

96 See, for example, Ali and O'Cinneide, op. cit., n. 19; Cheney and Fevre, op. cit., n. 93.
97 See Phillips, op. cit., n. 57, pp. 94–9; Ali and O'Cinneide, id., pp. 61–73.
98 See, for example, H. Muir, 'Where Race Meets Gender' *Guardian*, 10 December 2004.
99 Compare Mansbridge, op. cit., n. 85, p. 654.

157

electoral cycles for each of the bodies covered by the Act) is likely to be sufficient to enable meaningful progress to be made. This appears to have been an essentially arbitrary decision[100] and, although the Act may be continued in force beyond 2015, it contains no criteria by which to determine whether to do so.

The most obvious measure of the success of affirmative action is whether it produces a significant increase in the number of women representatives. It is already clear that equal representation will not be achieved for all the United Kingdom's democratic institutions by 2015. For example, it has been estimated that even if half of all vacant safe seats were to be filled by female candidates at each election it would take six or seven electoral cycles for women to achieve equal representation at Westminster.[101] However, it is widely claimed that once women reach around 30 per cent of any representative body, they achieve a 'critical mass' which both allows them to make a real impact on policy making and makes further increases in their numbers self-sustaining. This figure has, of course, already been exceeded for the Scottish Parliament and the Welsh Assembly. But even by this lower standard, SDECA's success is doubtful, thanks to its voluntary nature. Since the recent improvements in women's representation are largely attributable to the Labour party, any further decline in its electoral fortunes means that additional progress is unlikely, and that the numbers may even decrease. For instance, at the current rate of increase, it will take an estimated 400 years to achieve gender equality amongst Conservative MPs.[102]

In any case, the accuracy of critical mass theory has been questioned,[103] and the empirical record suggests that numbers alone are not the key to long-term change. For example, 33 per cent of seats in the Soviet Chamber of People's Deputies were reserved for women, but at the first democratic elections for the Russian Duma in 1990, men secured 95 per cent of the seats.[104] In other words, without accompanying efforts to challenge stereotypical assumptions about women's role in the political sphere and practical measures to accommodate them, quotas alone are unlikely to be effective.[105] From this perspective, it is disappointing that women's gains in the devolved institutions do not seem to have had any spill-over effects for

100 A. Whitehead, *H.C. Debs.*, Standing Committee A (8 November 2001).
101 J. Ashley, 'Revealed: How Labour Sees Women' *New Statesman*, 4 February 2002.
102 Fawcett Society, 'Record Numbers of Women MPs', press release 6 May 2005.
103 See, for example, D.T. Studlar and I. McAllister, 'Does a Critical Mass Exist? A Comparative Analysis of Women's Legislative Representation Since 1950' (2002) 41 *European J. of Political Research* 233.
104 N. Shvedova, 'The Challenge of Transition – Women in Parliament in Russia' in *Women in Parliament: Beyond Numbers*, ed. A. Karam (1998) 58.
105 Compare J. McKay, 'Women in German Politics: Still Jobs for the Boys?' (2004) 13 *German Politics* 56. See, also, N. Busby, 'Sex Equality in Political Candidature: Supply and Demand Factors and the Role of the Law' (2003) 66 *Modern Law Rev.* 245, who argues that the uncertain application of the SDA to discrimination *against* women in the political context is a particular problem in this regard.

other elected bodies, and that Labour's record of selecting women in non-AWS seats is little better than the other parties.[106] Similarly, the reversal in January 2005 of relatively modest attempts to normalize Westminster's working hours – viewed as symbolic of its commitment to inclusiveness – suggests that women politicians still have a long way to go before they are accepted on equal terms with men.

Accordingly, it is probable that special measures will continue to be needed well beyond 2015. If so, international law is unlikely to prevent SDECA from being extended for a further temporary period. Nevertheless, if by then there is no significant change in the willingness of parties other than Labour to employ strong affirmative measures, it might be more appropriate to consider alternative strategies. One option might be to impose compulsory gender quotas, as in France and Belgium. However, this raises more difficult issues concerning the maintenance of free voter choice and freedom of association for parties which advocate traditional gender roles, and hence is likely to provoke greater resistance than SDECA. The other proven alternative is the adoption of proportional representation. Although this does not guarantee high levels of women's representation, there is a strong correlation in practice between the two, since proportional systems with multi-member constituencies and/or party lists encourage parties to balance their candidate lists and allow quotas to be implemented more easily than under a first-past-the-post system.[107] Thus, if Labour is serious about improving the inclusiveness of the United Kingdom's democratic institutions, this should strengthen its commitment to further electoral reform.

POSTSCRIPT

In December 2005, the new Conservative party leader, David Cameron, announced a positive action programme to increase the number of female, ethnic minority, and disabled Conservative MPs. The programme requires all Conservative-held and target seats to select from a priority list of candidates, at least half of whom will be women (although constituencies will still be permitted to add to the list in exceptional circumstances). This will be supplemented by headhunting and mentoring of potential female and ethnic minority candidates. The programme will be reviewed after three months and further action taken if necessary. Whilst there is room for scepticism about the likely effectiveness of these measures, the announcement nevertheless represents a significant change in Conservative policy, in accepting both the importance of improved diversity and the need for special measures in order to achieve it.

106 Fawcett Society, op. cit., n. 102.
107 See, generally, Norris, op. cit., n. 6, ch. 8.

159

JOURNAL OF LAW AND SOCIETY
VOLUME 33, NUMBER 1, MARCH 2006
ISSN: 0263-323X, pp. 160–80

Minority Business Enterprise Programmes in the United States of America: An Empirical Investigation

MARTIN J. SWEET*

Affirmative action in the United States has generated no shortage of academic, legal, and popular analysis. Yet few ever ask, let alone test, the most fundamental question about affirmative action – whether it actually works. This article provides an historical overview of affirmative action in the United States, briefly reviews its legal status, and then tests the effectiveness of one type of affirmative action in three American cities between 1981 and 2000. It finds that affirmative action in government contracting does not significantly increase minority employment and is statistically insignificant in eradicating discrimination in contracting.

ORIGINS AND AIMS OF MINORITY BUSINESS ENTERPRISE PROGRAMMES

Less than a decade after the Supreme Court dismantled the 'separate but equal' framework of American racial apartheid in *Brown* v. *Board of Education*,[1] leading United States politicians began to come to terms with the inadequacy of formalized constitutional equality. Although the Constitution had provided for equal protection under the law since the middle of the nineteenth century, political practice and social views lagged far behind throughout much of America for the next century. Realizing that inaction resulted in status quo race relations, President Kennedy in 1961 issued executive order 10925. This mandated that federal contractors 'take affirmative action' towards guaranteeing that their employees would not be discriminated against on the basis of race, colour, creed or national origin.[2]

* *Honors College, Florida Atlantic University, 5353 Parkside Drive, Jupiter, Florida 33458, United States of America*
msweet4@fau.edu

1 347 US 483 (1954).
2 T. Jacoby, *Someone Else's House: America's Unfinished Struggle for Integration* (1998).

Soon thereafter, Congress passed the Civil Rights Act of 1964, expanding these earlier efforts to encompass private action.[3]

At the 1965 Howard University commencement address, President Johnson aided the transformation of the civil rights vocabulary from equality of *opportunity* to equality of *result*. He said:

> You do not take a person who, for years, has been hobbled by chains and liberate him, bring him to the starting line of a race and then say, 'you are free to compete with all the others' and still justly believe that you have been completely fair.[4]

He continued:

> It is not enough just to open the gates of opportunity. All our citizens must have the ability to walk through those gates ... We seek ... not just equality as a right and a theory, but equality as a fact and as a result.[5]

Thus the key principle of equality became transformed into a more pragmatic measuring device – equal results. Within two years, President Johnson issued executive order 11246 establishing the 'Philadelphia Plan,' which required federal contractors, first in Philadelphia and later in 55 other cities, to utilize minority employees as a precondition for the receipt of federal contract dollars.

Under the guidance of President Nixon, the United States first instituted a requirement on federal contractors to have affirmative action plans containing both minority and female hiring goals. Thus by the time President Carter came to office in 1977, these programmes that were at their core designed to remedy inequities against African-Americans ironically covered a majority of the United States population.[6] Competition between and among disadvantaged groups would prove to be one of the legacies of American affirmative action.[7] Federal efforts toward eradicating racial disparities began to take hold in state and local governments as well. Towards the end of the 1980s, more than 200 separate state and local government programmes existed nationwide, on top of over 100 similar federal programmes.[8] Admittedly, these programmes were often limited to contracting. But even narrow programmes were far-reaching. It is estimated that approximately 25 per cent of the entire American workforce is employed by

---

3 H. Graham, *Collision Course: The Strange Convergence of Affirmative Action and Immigration Policy in America* (2002).
4 T. Edsall and M. Edsall, *Chain Reaction: The Impact of Race, Rights, and Taxes on American Politics* (1991).
5 Jacoby, op. cit., n. 1.
6 T. Bates and D. Williams, 'Do Preferential Procurement Programmes Benefit Minority Business?' (1996) 86 *Am. Economic Rev.* 294.
7 Graham, op. cit., n. 3.
8 G. La Noue, 'The Impact of Croson on Equal Protection Law and Policy' (1997) 61 *Albany Law Rev.* 1.

firms from which the *federal* government alone contracts.[9] And annually, governments nationwide spend more than $450 billion in procurement contracts, with state and local governments spending more than half of this amount.[10] As power continually devolves from the federal government to state and local governments, and as privatization of government services increases, it is widely expected that the contracting dollars at stake here will continue to increase over time.

As most people know it, affirmative action typically encompasses preferences by virtue of membership to a particular race or ethnicity – though women, veterans, and the disabled have also been the beneficiaries of some particular affirmative action programmes. Most programmes fall into one of three areas: education, employment, or government contracting. Benefits for members of protected groups could include lower admissions requirements for schools, different standards used for hiring, promotion, and retention in the workplace, or government contracts in which members from a class receive more favourable treatment than non-members from the class.

Government contracting affirmative action programmes – the subject of this article – are termed 'minority business enterprise' (MBE) programmes. These typically provide favourable treatment for minority-owned businesses in the bidding process for government contracts, which can range from the building of a new sports arena or convention centre, to the purchase of office supplies or automobile parts, to the selection of accounting or legal services. Whenever the government seeks to purchase a service or a good, there is nearly always an opportunity to contract with an MBE. The favourable treatment of MBEs range from 'set-asides' or 'sheltered markets' whereby only targeted groups can compete for the government contracts, to 'bid enhancements' whereby the bids submitted by MBEs are not directly compared to the otherwise lowest qualified bid, to 'goals' programmes whereby the government attempts to contract with minority-owned businesses without using set-asides or bid enhancements – most often requiring prime contractors to make good-faith efforts in subcontracting with MBEs. Nearly every level of government uses MBE programmes. Yet despite their prevalence, they are both constitutionally dubious and, as I will show, probably inefficacious in achieving their economic goals.

LAW AND AFFIRMATIVE ACTION

The constitutionality of affirmative action in the United States is a mixed story, ebbing and flowing across time and across areas: education,

9 S. Thernstrom and A. Thernstrom, *America in Black and White: One Nation, Indivisible* (1997).
10 M. Enchautegui et al., *Do Minority-Owned Businesses Get a Fair Share of Government Contracts?* (1997).

162

employment, and contracting. The most definitive case regarding MBE programmes, and arguably the most significant Supreme Court opinion regarding race since the time of *Regents of California* v. *Bakke*[11] was decided in 1989. In *City of Richmond* v. *Croson*, Justice O'Connor began the opinion recognizing 'the tension between the Fourteenth Amendment's guarantee of equal treatment to all citizens, and the use of race-based measures to ameliorate the effect of past discrimination on the opportunities enjoyed by members of minority groups in our society.'[12] The question of how to balance the competing goals of equality – process and outcome – had come to the judiciary. The specific issue before the Court was whether the MBE programme promulgated by the City of Richmond violated the Fourteenth Amendment's Equal Protection Clause.

The relevant components of the Fourteenth Amendment provide that '[n]o State shall ... deny to any person within its jurisdiction the equal protection of the laws.' Yet since nearly all conceivable legislation distinguishes between individuals (for example, drunk driving statutes affect drunk drivers and sober drivers differently), courts employ varying degrees of scrutiny in determining whether challenged legislation violates the constitutional guarantee of equal treatment. Courts employ one of three standards of review in analysing the constitutionality of disputed legislation: rational basis review, intermediate scrutiny, and strict scrutiny.[13]

For a time, the Supreme Court held that affirmative action programmes, or benevolent race-based ameliorative efforts, enjoyed a more relaxed level of judicial scrutiny than other race-based legislation.[14] Under *Fullilove* v. *Klutznick*[15] the Court held that if a legislature passed legislation that differentiated on the basis of race and if the intention was to benefit racial minorities, it would be subjected only to intermediate scrutiny. Courts using this standard of review for benevolent differentiating legislation made it more likely that such statutes would be upheld as constitutional, while invidious racially discriminatory legislation that burdened racial minorities would certainly violate the Constitution's equal protection guarantees.

In *Croson*, a full majority of the Court held for the first time that race-based legislation, whether benevolent or malevolent, is subject to the rigours of strict scrutiny. Finding neither a 'compelling state interest' nor legislation 'narrowly tailored' to that interest, Richmond's programme failed both prongs of the strict scrutiny test and was ruled unconstitutional.[16] In a later

---

11 *Regents of California* v. *Bakke*, 438 US 265 (1978).
12 *City of Richmond* v. *Croson*, 488 US 494 (1989).
13 L. Tribe, *American Constitutional Law* (1988).
14 *Fullilove* v. *Klutznick*, 448 US 448 (1980); compare *Wygant* v. *Jackson Board of Education*, 476 US 267 (1986); *Bakke*, op. cit., n. 11; see, also, R. Dworkin, 'Affirming Affirmative Action' (1998) 45(16) *New York Rev. of Books* 91.
15 *Klutznick*, id.
16 Failure on either one of the two components of strict scrutiny would have been sufficient to declare the statute unconstitutional.

case extending the *Croson* ruling to restrict *federal* affirmative action efforts, the Court held that:

> [a]ny person, of whatever race, has the right to demand that any governmental actor subject to the Constitution justify any racial classification subjecting that person to unequal treatment under the strictest of judicial scrutiny.[17]

In 2003, the United States Supreme Court handed down two companion decisions ruling on affirmative action programmes at the University of Michigan that have given some minor hope to supporters of affirmative action. In *Grutter* v. *Bollinger*[18] the Court upheld the law school's affirmative action programme using strict scrutiny. The Court found that the University of Michigan Law School had a compelling interest in achieving a diverse student body and that its method of individually assessing each applicant's ability to contribute to that diversity was narrowly tailored to that end. The Court, however, in *Gratz* v. *Bollinger*[19] held that the same university's undergraduate admissions scheme, which had granted categorical benefits for all protected minority applicants (black and Hispanic, but not Asian, applicants) was unconstitutional. The Court found that such across the board preferences were not narrowly tailored to achieve a diverse student body.

While the cases over the last twenty five years have apparently alternated between pro- and anti-affirmative action outcomes, the overall judicial tenor in the United States is quite hostile to affirmative action. In essence, the *Grutter* ruling is a small exception to a largely blanket prohibition against affirmative action. With the expected change in personnel on the United States Supreme Court, there is very little reason to expect the Court to become more amenable to allowing more affirmative action. In fact, it is much more likely that the few positive rulings regarding affirmative action will be overturned. However, despite the unwelcoming reaction to affirmative action from the Supreme Court – as well as from the lower courts – affirmative action continues to be practised in the United States.[20] This is all the more peculiar in that affirmative action appears to accomplish little of its professed intended aims.

POLICY EFFECTIVENESS OF AFFIRMATIVE ACTION

Opponents of affirmative action who argue that the policy is morally wrong may not be overly concerned with its effectiveness, but for nearly all others who are interested in race and economics, the outcomes associated with

17 *Adarand Constructors, Inc.* v. *Peña*, 515 US 200, 224 (1995).
18 *Grutter* v. *Bollinger*, 539 US 982 (2003).
19 *Gratz* v. *Bollinger*, 539 US 244 (2003).
20 See M. Sweet, 'Supreme Policymaking: Coping with the Supreme Court's Affirmative Action Policies' (unpublished PhD dissertation, University of Wisconsin – Madison, 2003).

affirmative action are of enormous concern. For proponents of affirmative action, evidence that such a programme achieves its goals may cause a reinvigoration or reallocation of mobilization resources geared towards the political arena or the courts, respectively. And for the undecided, evidence on the consequences of the affirmative action policy may sway those individuals in a particular direction. Yet despite the enormous importance of the issue, there is comparatively very little research on the subject.

The research presented here focuses on only one limited segment of affirmative action: government contracting, or MBE programmes. Specifically, within government contracting I analyse only the construction industry in three American cities from 1981 to 2000: Philadelphia, Pennsylvania; Portland, Oregon; and Miami, Florida. Yet this somewhat narrow window into affirmative action provides significant leverage into answering the question whether affirmative action works. First, scholars note, and interviews with MBE consultants confirmed, that the major focus of MBE programmes is construction, just as the originating Philadelphia Plan during the Johnson and Nixon Administrations was limited to the construction industry.[21] Construction is the segment of government contracting most likely to assist minority contractors and consequently hurt majority contractors. Because of the transitory nature of the work, low or semi-low skills required, combined with high wages and few barriers to entry – especially in terms of capital – construction is the dominant landscape for affirmative action programmes. Second, the time period at issue encompasses both the rise and decline of affirmative action policy in the United States.[22] Race-conscious programming rarely trickled down to the municipal level until after the 1970s, and in the face of both a hostile judiciary and changing public opinion, affirmative action saw less innovation in the 1990s.

And third, these three cities in particular provide a high-quality collection of cases to analyse affirmative action in action. The study of these cities offers geographic, racial, and governance diversity that can then be extrapolated to a wide array of other American cities and contexts. As can

---

21 Interest Group Interviews, 2001–2002. Philadelphia interviews include representatives from the National Minority Supplier Development, Associated General Contractors, Hispanic Association of Contractors and Enterprises, Ben Franklin Technologies, Philadelphia Minority Business Development Center, Philadelphia Building and Trades Council, AFL-CIO Laborers' Local 332, Temple University Small Business Development Center. Portland interviews include representatives from OAME, Associated General Contractors, and the Housing Development Center. Miami interviews include representatives from Contractors Resource Center, Latin Builders Association, Black Business Association, One Florida, The Miami Herald, Spanish American League Against Discrimination, Miami Partners for Progress, Cuban American National Foundation, Greater Miami Chamber of Commerce, and BBC Research and Consulting.
22 La Noue, op. cit., n. 8; L. Nay and J. Jones, 'Equal Employment and Affirmative Action in Local Governments: A Profile' (1989) 8 *Law and Inequality: J. of Theory and Practice* 103.

Figure 1. Three-City Case Study, Population by Race** and Ethnicity, 2000

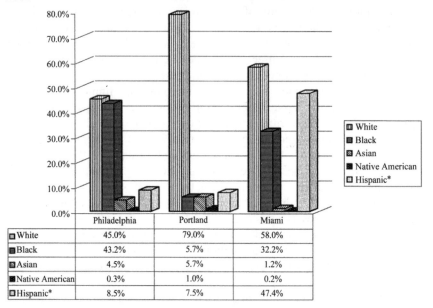

	Philadelphia	Portland	Miami
▥ White	45.0%	79.0%	58.0%
▣ Black	43.2%	5.7%	32.2%
▨ Asian	4.5%	5.7%	1.2%
▪ Native American	0.3%	1.0%	0.2%
☐ Hispanic*	8.5%	7.5%	47.4%

Source: United States Census Bureau: General Population and Housing Characteristics 2000.
* Hispanic designation can be of any race. Thus, totals do not equal 100 per cent.
** Excludes 'more than one race' designation.

be seen in Figure 1, these cities provide sharp differences in their racial and ethnic populations. To generalize, Philadelphia represents a mixed black and white, eastern, unionized, strong-mayor industrialized city of the past. The Philadelphia experience can speak to Baltimore, Boston, Cleveland, and Pittsburgh. Portland is western, overwhelmingly white, commission form of government, new modern city. Portland, speaks to Denver, Minneapolis, San Francisco, and Seattle. And Miami is very different. While it operates with a council-manager form of government and shares a large Hispanic population with both Los Angeles and San Antonio, the Cuban exiles in Miami's population place the city in its own category. Though analysing a completely random sample of cities, or even just a greater number of cities, could enhance the generalizability of this study, the time and resources necessary for such research limit the chances of it occurring.

THE LITERATURE

The literature to date on the effectiveness of affirmative action has suffered from two significant limitations. First, researchers have so far been unable to

166

create a valid and reliable method of adducing the purposes of affirmative action. Those who have studied the impact of MBE programmes empirically rarely explicitly addressed the issue of goals of such programmes, but instead have implicitly attributed goals to them by testing whether they increased sales,[23] increased the number and dollar amounts of contracts,[24] decreased racial disparity in contracting,[25] increased the number of minority owned businesses,[26] or increased rates of entrepreneurship.[27] Taken together, these scholars suggest that effective MBE programmes should: (i) increase the number and size of contracts with MBEs; (ii) increase the ratio of utilized to available MBE; (iii) increase the number of individuals starting MBEs; and/or (iv) prolong the survival of existing MBEs. Although each of these goals seems genuine, none of the researchers tested whether these were in fact the aims of the programmes. This raises the possibility that a form of bias has entered into the evaluations, though the attribution of invalid purposes to these programmes.

Second, most of the existing evaluations treat the mere presence of an MBE programme on paper as the same thing as a fully implemented programme. While public law scholars have long noted the discrepancy between 'official' and 'implemented' law,[28] these MBE aggregate studies nevertheless generally treat laws as dichotomous variables – either 'on' or 'off.'[29] Enacted, but non-implemented programmes could scarcely be expected to result in costs or benefits for contractors that would be revealed in such an aggregate analysis. One way by which to confidently distinguish between 'hollow' and fully implemented programmes is to spend a significant amount of time studying spending and behaviour of agencies charged with administering these MBE programmes. Time and financial resource constraints may, however, limit the number of samples to be included in such a study.

Despite some gaps and insufficiencies in this literature, there are several noteworthy studies that have increased our knowledge of MBE programme impact. A brief survey of their findings provides a frame to shape the expectations for future MBE evaluation studies. These findings can be broken down into four main issues: use, disparity, creation, and capacity.

---

23 Bates and Williams, op. cit., n. 6; T. Bates and D. Williams, 'Preferential Procurement Programmes and Minority-Owned Businesses' (1995) 17 *J. of Urban Affairs* 1; T. Bates and D. Williams 'Racial Politics: Does it Pay?' (1993) 74 *Social Science Q.* 507.
24 S. Myers and T. Chan, 'Who Benefits from Minority Business Set-Asides? The Case of New Jersey' (1996) 15 *J. of Policy Analysis and Management* 202.
25 Enchautegui et al., op. cit., n. 10.
26 T. Boston, *Affirmative Action and Black Entrepreneurship* (1999).
27 K. Chay and R. Fairlie, 'Minority Business Set-Asides and Black Self-Employment' [1998] <*http://econ.ucsc.edu/~fairlie/*>.
28 S. Wasby, *The Impact of the United States Supreme Court: Some Perspectives* (1970).
29 Chay and Fairlie, op. cit., n. 27; Bates and Williams op. cit., n. 6; Bates and Williams, op. cit. (1995), n. 23.

1. *Use*

Myers and Chan measured the change in the average number and size of contracts between the State of New Jersey and firms by race in three periods.[30] They measured these changes from the five-year period before New Jersey instituted its set-aside programme, the four years in which the State operated the programme, and in the two years immediately following the *Croson*-spurred programme dismantling. Myers and Chan found that the extant disparities between black and white-owned firms actually *widened* during the set-aside period. Though the number and size of contracts for MBEs increased during the set-aside period, the even greater changes for white firms during the same period seemed to discount the notion that the MBE programme was the causal mechanism by which the MBE firms increased their contracting with New Jersey. While this research is limited to studying just one particular state, it suggests that affirmative action does not increase the use of minority-owned firms.

2. *Disparity*

The Urban Institute compared contracting disparities in cities with programmes and cities without programmes. The study found that there were smaller disparities in cities with programmes and larger disparities in cities without programmes.[31] Thus to some the study seemed to indicate that these programmes are associated with less discrimination. Yet caution is warranted before leaping to such a conclusion. While MBE programmes may co-vary with disparity in contracting, the causal mechanism here has not been isolated. Because the study did not measure any changes in disparities, the existing differences in disparities may be more indicative of the cities or city cultures, rather than the programmes. As Chay and Fairlie stated:

> it is also possible that the areas in which minority businesses are more viable and competitive with non-minority firms for government contracts are also places in which set-aside programs are politically feasible and attractive to implement.[32]

Without further study in this area, there is again little ability to point to the MBE programme as the causal influence in reducing contracting disparities.

3. *Creation*

Boston compared the growth rate of black owned businesses in cities with MBE programmes to cities without MBE programmes from 1982 to 1987 and from 1987 to 1992.[33] He found that in the 76 cities with MBE programmes,

---

30 Myers and Chan, op. cit., n. 24.
31 Enchautegui et al., op. cit., n. 10.
32 Chay and Fairlie, op. cit., n. 27, p. 5.
33 Boston, op. cit., n. 26, p. 16.

black businesses grew at a slightly higher rate than in twelve cities without. However, these differences were not statistically significant. Bates and Williams made similar comparisons to Boston's study, but instead of using 'programme' and 'non-programme' cities, divided cities according to the presence of a black mayor.[34] Bates and Williams found increased sales for black businesses and a growth in the number of black businesses in cities with black mayors. They argue, in part, that black mayoral support of MBE programmes may account for some of this growth. Chay and Fairlie examined self-employment rates by race and gender in 33 cities from 1979–1989 (the period immediately preceding *Croson*). With significant qualifications, because of the lack of knowledge of programme start dates, Chay and Fairlie 'suggest that city-level set-aside programs may have positively impacted [sic] minority self-employment ... [and] the number of minority-owned construction firms.'[35] These studies, taken together, give only tepid support to the argument that MBE programmes create new MBEs.

4. *Capacity*

Bates and Williams contrasted the survival patterns of MBEs that contracted with the government and MBEs that did not derive the bulk of its work from the government.[36] They found that increasing the percentage of work for the government did not increase the survival chances of MBE. In fact, businesses that derived more than one quarter of their revenues from the government were less likely to survive than firms with more a more diversified clientele. In an earlier study, Bates and Williams analysed the characteristics of successful MBE programmes, as measured by survival rates of MBEs. They found that programmes that comprehensively certified firms for MBE programme participation, made working capital available, waived bonding requirements, and provided assistance to MBEs directly from staff had a positive effect on MBE survival.[37]

Boston collected data in Atlanta, and found that these programmes help income and employment in the most distressed urban areas.[38] His data revealed that firms located in the economically worst-off neighbourhoods had more employees and higher revenues than firms located elsewhere. However, in his qualitative study of Atlanta's set-aside programme, Jacoby painted a much less optimistic picture of MBE programmes in the Atlanta construction industry.[39] He found that the Atlanta programme was rife with abuses, especially through the use of 'fronts.' Fronts are non-minority-owned

---

34 Bates and Williams, op. cit. (1993), n. 23.
35 Chay and Fairlie, op. cit., n 27, p. 16.
36 Bates and Williams, op. cit., n. 6.
37 Bates and Williams, op. cit. (1995), n. 23.
38 Boston, op. cit., n. 26.
39 Jacoby, op. cit., n. 2.

169

businesses that use qualified minorities as either pass-through organizations or businesses that sign over control to a minority owner in name only.

Whether these MBE programmes prolong the survival of existing MBEs is still an open question. While the Bates and Williams work seems to indicate that they do not, the Boston study – even in the face of Jacoby's work – provides some evidence that at least marginal differences in specific areas can be attributed to the presence of MBE programmes.

METHODS

In my study, I spent between two and three weeks in 2000 and 2001 interviewing a wide range of MBE stakeholders in each of three case-study cities. I interviewed approximately 60 individuals, including those who personally created the legislation or programmes, legislators who currently fund such programmes, bureaucrats who administer or utilize MBE programmes, contractors who either use or do not use such programmes, and interest groups involved in the government contracting process. In each interview I asked each respondent, among other things, about the MBE programme used in each city, the purpose of MBE programmes, compliance with the programme mandates, and any perceived outcomes of the programmes.

While the realm of adducing causation in social science is nearly always fraught with difficulties, awareness of implementation and goal identification are two improvements upon earlier affirmative action evaluations. These principles taken alone will not fully isolate the independent and dependent variables involved in this impact evaluation. First, other causal possibilities exist as an explanation for the outcomes observed from each of the cities. And second, expecting a uniform result across jurisdictions is somewhat suspect, given the varying budgets between jurisdictions, the variance in amount of resources allocated for contracting, different levels of political support for programming, and sometimes overlapping programmes between jurisdictions. These concerns, however, can be minimized by combining the knowledge gained from the qualitative evaluations in this study and using a series of quantitative tests, including regression analysis. In all cases, however, the methods of programme evaluation used below have been utilized in other empirical MBE impact evaluations.

RESULTS: MBE PROGRAMME EFFECTIVENESS AND MINORITY UNEMPLOYMENT

1. The goals of affirmative action

The case studies of the three cities, and in particular the interviews I conducted, revealed multiple goals for MBE programmes. These include

170

wealth redistribution, increasing the capacity of minority-owned firms, increasing the number of minority business owners, decreasing minority unemployment, City benefits, electoral benefits, and compliance. The three dominant rationales, as defined by achieving consistency among policy stakeholder typologies and across cities, were to (i) increase the number of minority business owners, (ii) increase the capacity of existing minority-owned firms, and (iii) decrease minority unemployment.

First among these goals, MBE programmes should create new minority-owned businesses. As the government has created a financial incentive for the creation of minority entrepreneurs, new MBE programmes should be associated with new minority-owned firms. Researchers who have tested whether MBE programmes increase minority-owned businesses have found only highly qualified evidence of success. According to the second goal, MBE programmes should assist existing MBE firms in flourishing to the extent of majority-owned firms. These programmes are designed to level the playing field, and as such should result in similar experiences for minority-owned firms as majority-owned firms. Similar to the first goal, researchers testing whether MBE programmes increase the capacity of existing firms either found discouraging or highly qualified evidence of success.

The third goal specified by policy stakeholders was that MBE programmes should increase minority employment through a spillover effect. This could be created by minority tradesmen and women who want to gain experience before becoming an entrepreneur, or simply by assuming that minority-owned businesses will employ minority tradesmen and women. This goal has not yet been tested by researchers, and is the subject of this empirical investigation.

While some may believe that measuring minority employment is simply a secondary or tertiary goal of the programme, it should be noted that such spillover goals are at the heart of most redistributive policies. Rather than creating programmes that simply change government spending, redistributive policies are designed to foster long-term changes in behaviour that will eventually obviate the need for the government programme. The creation of minority employment, or reduction in minority unemployment, is precisely that type of behaviour expected in fulfilment of redistributive policies.

2. Programme coverage dates

One of the most startling findings in this area of research is how little of the most basic information is known about MBE programmes across the country. For example, two major studies documenting the growth of affirmative action dispute which time period saw the creation of the majority of MBE programmes. Nay and Jones find that local governments created the vast majority of MBE programmes in the 1970s,[40] whereas the Minority

---

40 Nay and Jones, op. cit., n 22.

Business Enterprise Legal Defense and Education Fund (MBELDEF) survey data show that most programmes were created in the early to mid-1980s.[41] Similarly, two major studies of MBE programmes in major metropolitan areas dispute the start date and coverage dates for significant portions of their studies. When one compares the MBELDEF study with a similar study conducted by the Joint Center for Political and Economic Studies (JCPES), one sees massive inconsistencies with each other,[42] and as I determined during the course of this research, the JCPES study in the case of the City of Miami is wrong in all respects. These discrepancies and mistakes plague this entire line of research.

There is little hope of creating a comprehensive list of MBE programmes. They can take place at any level of government, from housing authorities to municipalities to counties to metropolitan commissions to states to the federal government. The Census Bureau's 1997 Census of Governments reveals that there are over 80,000 separate state and local governments nationwide.[43] While online legal research can retrieve some information about federal and state programmes, and surveys can approximate the total number of MBE programmes, discussions with experts in this area suggest that, because of high turnover and poor record keeping in local government agencies, accurately documenting all such programmes could be impossible or at least take years. Absent such a comprehensive list, the prospect of obtaining valid nationwide results for the impact of local MBE programmes is dim.

Yet by conducting intensive work within the three case study cities, I was able to confidently assess the presence of an implemented programme. Philadelphia began its programme in 1982 and dismantled it under a federal court order in 1996. Portland also began its programme in 1982, dismantled it in the face of *Croson* in 1989, but resurrected it in 1998, albeit with some significant limitations. Miami, however, proved to be somewhat con-founding. Like Portland, it maintains a MBE programme on paper. But the City of Miami has cut the size of the office staff, moved the MBE bureaucracy under the power of one of the historically worst offending City agencies, placed individuals in charge of the programme who were not committed to the programme's goals, and has never given more than 6 per cent of its contracting business to black-owned firms – despite a spending goal of 17 per cent of all contract dollars. Thus, after conducting my research in Miami, I was initially tempted to categorize Miami as a non-MBE locale due to the non-implementation of its programme by the *City* of Miami. But further investigation revealed that Miami-Dade *County*'s programme had not

---

41 Chay and Fairlie, op. cit., n. 27.
42 Minority Business Development Agency, *Assessment of Minority Business Development Programmes: Report to the US Department of Commerce* (1994).
43 US Dept. of Commerce, Bureau of the Census, 'Government Organization' *1997 Census of Governments Vol I* (1999).

172

only been implemented (prior to being shut down as a result of litigation), but that its budget exceeded that of the City's programme tenfold. In Florida, counties spend the bulk of construction dollars, whereas in Pennsylvania and Oregon, municipalities are the driving force behind local government construction. Thus by substituting Miami-Dade County's MBE programme data for the City's MBE programme, I was able to include Miami as a MBE locale for some years.

For my dependent variable of minority employment I rely upon data derived from the Current Population Survey (CPS). I gathered data from the Bureau of Labor Statistics' (BLS) annual publication, *Geographic Profile of Employment and Unemployment*, from 1981 to 2000. In Figures 2, 3, and 4 below, I present graphically the annual percentage of three racial/ethnic groups employed in construction in the three cities during the time period at issue.

To account for other factors related to minority employment, I located population and other control variables in the US Bureau of Economic Analysis's Regional Economic Information Service (REIS). The REIS provided annual information from 1981 to 2000 on the metropolitan statistical area (MSA) population, average construction wages by MSA, and the number of state and local government employees by MSA. Finally, I collected annual data on the 'value of construction put in place for nonresidential building projects' from the US Census Bureau's Construction and Minerals Branch. This measure, however, is only provided at the national and census sub-regional level (that is, Middle Atlantic, South Atlantic, and Pacific). Taken together, these variables allow for elastic and inelastic, and local and regional, measures of the strength of the construction industry. Further the number of government employees provides for some

Figure 2. Percentage of race/ethnicity employed labour force in construction in Philadelphia, 1981–2000

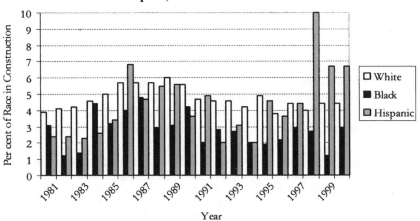

173

Figure 3. Percentage of race/ethnicity employed labour force in construction in Portland, 1981–2000

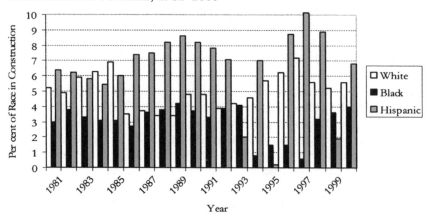

Figure 4. Percentage of race/ethnicity employed labour force in construction in Miami, 1981–2000

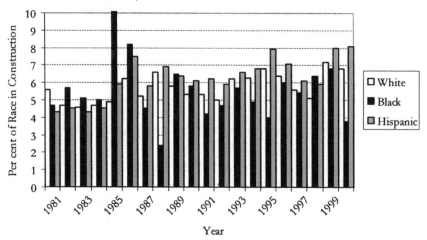

leverage on grappling with whether the size of government – and hence its ability to affect employment – varies over time.

Each of the three groups (white,[44] black, and Hispanic) enter the construction industry in different rates. Differences around the country also

44 'White' is more accurately 'non-Hispanic, and non-black' or 'Total MSA Population – Black MSA Population – Hispanic MSA Population.' Hispanic is an ethnic categorization: one can be Hispanic and be of any race. Eligibility for MBE programmes, however, in some locales (for example, Miami) requires a distinct choice on behalf of a prospective contractor – either black, Hispanic, or female. The Miami programme does not include programming for Asian or Native American contractors.

174

appear to affect the rates at which racial and ethnic groups enter the construction industry. For example, in 1992 in the Midwest approximately 5.4 per cent of whites were employed in construction, 3.0 per cent of Hispanics, and only 1.7 per cent of blacks. These rates vary more substantially when comparing sub-regions, states, and MSAs. MBE programmes, however, theoretically should have an approximately equal (albeit perhaps opposite in the case of included and excluded groups) effect on these groups. All other things being equal, more contract dollars for black contractors means fewer for white contractors. Philadelphia operated its MBE programme from 1983 to 1996. Portland began its first MBE programme in the 1970s and ran a twice-amended version of that programme until early 1989. Almost ten years later, Portland reintroduced its MBE programme. Miami-Dade County operated a black-only MBE programme from 1982 to 1993. From 1993 until 1996, Miami-Dade County expanded its programme to include Hispanics. In 1996 the programme was ruled unconstitutional and terminated.

3. Modelling MBE impact

To test the impact of MBE programmes on the percentage of each group's participation in the construction industry, I estimate the following model:

$$RCON = \alpha_0 + \beta_1 MBE + \beta_2 CONWAGE + \beta_3 CONVL + \beta_4 GOVEE + \mu$$

The model is estimated using OLS regression with Huber-White sandwich errors to account for correlation issues.[45] *RCON* represents three different variables: WCON, BCON, and HCON, the percentage of whites, blacks, and Hispanics, respectively employed in the local construction industry. In addition to the localized economic incentive associated with MBE programmes to enter or leave the construction field, there must also be some accounting of other economic conditions in the private and public sectors. *CONWAGE* is the log of the average annual construction wages in each MSA, adjusted with that locality's MSA Consumer Price Index (CPI) in constant year 2000 dollars. *CONVL* is the log of the annual value of construction put in place for private non-residential building projects from the sub-region, also corrected for inflation and put in constant year 2000 dollars. To control for the growth or contraction of the government and its influence of government contracting, I use government employees as a proxy for government size. *GOVEE* is the number of state and local government employees in each MSA, in thousands. Table 1 below presents the results of this regression.

In this model, the MBE programme is not significantly related to the percentage of any group in the construction industry. Despite the broad

45 Regression results using standard non-robust error estimates provided nearly identical results.

175

Table 1. MBE Programmes and Construction Employment

Dependent Variable: Percentage of race/ethnicity employed labour force in construction, Philadelphia, Portland, and Miami, 1981–2000.

Ordinary least squares regression results:

	Whites	Blacks	Hispanics
MBE Programme	0.21	0.61	−0.58
	(0.24)	(0.37)	(0.71)
Construction Wages	−0.84	−5.60***	2.33
	(1.13)	(1.13)	(3.09)
Non-Residential Construction Value	3.87***	7.72***	11.98***
	(1.18)	(2.63)	(2.95)
Government Employees	5.14E-03	0.023***	-3.37E-03
	(0.005)	(0.006)	(0.015)
Constant	−7.38	2.40	−62.05***
	(8.73)	(12.83)	(22.96)
R Squared	0.191	0.418	0.271
N	60	60	60

Robust standard errors computed using Huber/White/sandwich estimator and appear in parentheses.
* significant at the 0.1 level; ** significant at the 0.05 level; *** significant at the 0.01 level.

geographic coverage of the regional non-residential construction value variable (note this number would be the exact same for pairs Miami and Atlanta, Philadelphia and Washington, DC, and Portland and Los Angeles), the condition of the broader construction market seems to be the single best indicator of the percentage of each group in construction. If one wants to increase the number of minorities in construction, the best option seems to be simply to build more and more projects. Localized construction wages, which are a more geographically precise – but probably more inelastic measure of the growth of the construction industry – are only significantly related to the percentage of blacks employed in construction. It should be noted, however, that this relationship is negative. As wages for all construction workers increase, there are fewer blacks employed in construction. This is at least suggestive that black construction workers are probably the first to be let go during weak economic conditions.

The number of government employees is also significantly related to the percentage of blacks in construction. As the government grows in terms of employment, it is also likely that the governments are financially flush enough to engage in business with contractors. If there is more contracting business done by the government, the more opportunities there are for black construction employment. Thus, one would expect that, as the number of government employees increases, the percentage of each group in construction should also fluctuate. While this is true for blacks, no such systematic relationship exists with Hispanics or whites.

The model above, however, hypothesizes that the effect of MBE programmes is constant across the cities in this study and unrelated to annual 'secular' changes, such as time and effects of particular cities. Table 2 below

Table 2. MBE programmes and construction employment, expanded model

Dependent Variable: Percentage of race employed in construction, Philadelphia, Portland, and Miami, 1981–2000.

Ordinary least squares regression results:

	Whites	Blacks	Hispanics
MBE Programme	1.50***	−0.16	1.17
	(0.50)	(0.95)	(1.33)
Portland	17.77***	−9.66	−25.48*
	(5.01)	(8.14)	(14.29)
Miami	15.65***	−5.95	−20.25*
	(4.24)	(6.81)	(11.87)
Portland* MBE Programme	−1.14**	0.072	0.85
	(0.54)	(0.71)	(1.52)
Miami* MBE Programme	−0.94*	−0.059	3.67**
	(0.51)	(0.95)	(1.40)
Construction Wages	0.40	−0.50	6.58
	(1.57)	(1.68)	(4.71)
Non-residential Construction Value	2.36	5.96**	9.54***
	(1.46)	(2.61)	(3.48)
Government Employees	0.14***	−0.073	−0.23*
	(.040)	(.067)	(.13)
Year	−0.20***	0.081	0.60**
	(0.07)	(0.12)	(0.25)
Year* MBE Programme	−0.054	0.057	−0.16
	(0.040)	(0.06)	(0.12)
Constant	−32.99***	−7.11	−44.03
	(10.38)	(15.41)	(26.64)
R Squared	0.460	0.575	0.505
N	60	60	60

Robust standard errors computed using Huber/White/sandwich estimator and appear in parentheses.
* significant at the 0.1 level; ** significant at the 0.05 level; *** significant at the 0.01 level.

presents the results from this modified model, adding dummy variables for Portland and Miami (with Philadelphia as the baseline) and interaction terms between Portland and Miami and the MBE programmes. Table 2 also uses a variable for the year and interactions terms between the year and the relevant MBE programme.

As can be seen in Table 2, by adding variables for the City and year effects, and interaction terms, a nearly identical picture for minorities is present. For whites, however, the picture is slightly different from Table 1. The regional construction market is still the best indicator for predicting the percentage of minorities in the construction industry. But for whites, both the MBE programme and the City variables are significant. But rather than the negative relation expected between the MBE programme and the percentage of whites in construction, the relationship is positive. That is to say, the percentage of whites employed in construction systematically varies according to the presence of an MBE programme. Probably the best explanation of this phenomenon is that, rather than MBE programmes causing whites to change their industry into construction, the causal arrow points in the other direction. Cities probably use the information of a high percentage of whites in the construction industry as a cue to trigger implementation of MBE programmes.

The dependent variable of percentage of group employed in construction is a measure of the varying incentives to enter or leave construction for racial and ethnic groups in the face of an MBE programme. Beyond creating incentives for minorities to enter construction, MBE programmes are also designed to reduce extant disparities in the local construction employment markets. In Table 3 below, I present the results from changing the dependent variable from 'Percentage of Group Employed in Construction' to an 'Employment Disparity Ratio' (EDR). The EDR is the quotient of the percentage of the construction industry that is white, black, or Hispanic, divided by the percentage of the employed labour force that is correspondingly white, black, or Hispanic.

In the case of Employment Disparity Ratios, the MBE variable was not significantly related to the EDR for any of the groups. In fact, no single variable was significantly related to the EDR measure for more than any one group. Attacking racial disparities in construction employment seems to be a much more difficult task than merely increasing the percentage of a group in construction. The lack of a relationship between these programmes and minority employment persisted across minority groups, and across other versions of my model not reported here. Whether I included a 'period' variable (pre-*Croson*) or used different control variables for the private and public sectors, MBE programmes were never significantly related to minority employment.

Whether one is attempting to increase minority representation in construction, or more systematically to attack racial disparities in employment construction, MBE programmes in their current form are

Table 3. MBE Programmes and Construction Employment Disparity

Dependent Variable: Construction employment disparity ratios, Philadelphia, Portland, and Miami, 1981–2000.

Ordinary least squares regression results:

	Whites	Black	Hispanic
MBE Programme	−0.015	−0.14	−0.365
	(0.041)	(0.19)	(0.28)
Portland	0.075	−3.27**	−3.85
	(0.31)	(1.28)	(2.76)
Miami	0.068	−2.32**	−3.48
	(0.26)	(1.09)	(2.30)
Portland* MBE Programme	0.0040	0.11	0.61
	(0.030)	(0.15)	(0.38)
Miami* MBE Programme	−0.056	−0.038	0.87***
	(0.044)	(0.16)	(0.28)
Construction Wages	0.067	0.15	0.36
	(0.071)	(0.35)	(0.93)
Non-Residential Construction Value	−0.27**	0.42	1.16
	(0.11)	(0.50)	(0.77)
Government Employees	0.0010	−0.027**	−0.032
	(0.003)	(0.011)	(0.024)
Year	−0.0051	0.033	0.073
	(0.005)	(0.020)	(0.049)
Year* MBE Programme	0.0027	0.012	0.018
	(0.002)	(0.012)	(0.025)
Constant	1.68***	2.99	−1.01
	(0.54)	(3.03)	(4.83)
R Squared	0.700	0.468	0.376
N	60	60	60

Robust standard errors computed using Huber/White/sandwich estimator and appear in parentheses.
* significant at the 0.1 level; ** significant at the 0.05 level; *** significant at the 0.01 level.

not achieving these goals. This is not to say that these programmes cannot achieve this goal – especially if the funding of these programmes were to be increased dramatically – but given the status of affirmative action in this country, both legally and politically, advocates for economic change in minority communities would be wise to create an alternative avenue for reform.

CONCLUSION

In the present cases, prior MBE programmes had been implemented in the City of Philadelphia, the City of Portland, and Miami-Dade County – though not the City of Miami. In each jurisdiction, increasing minority employment was a central goal of the respective MBE programmes. Yet it appears that in none of the three jurisdictions was this goal actually accomplished. As a result of the MBE programmes in these three cities, minority employment did *not* significantly increase and extant racial disparities in employment did *not* significantly decrease.

While in Portland, Oregon, there was an increase in black and Hispanic employment in construction during the time of the MBE programmes, it has been shown that economic factors unrelated to the MBE programme were more systematically associated with these increases. Instead of MBE programmes driving how different groups enter and leave the construction industry, or are represented in the construction industry in comparison to the employed labour force, other factors appear responsible for this particular incentive creation. These factors, however, are not even consistent across cities. In some instances, the broader regional construction industry seems to be the primary factor in explaining entry into and exit from the construction industry. At other times, the size of the government seems to be the key feature in addressing employment disparities.

Although the empirical literature to date has mostly been replete with the limited prospects for MBE programmes,[46] some studies have at least tentatively found a positive relationship between MBE programmes and the creation of minority business owners.[47] And while this may offer a glimmer of hope for proponents of affirmative action in creating a new class of minority entrepreneurs, the payoffs for the other commonly perceived goals of MBE programmes are apparently minimal. Given such meagre returns on the political investment necessary to create and sustain such programming, it would seem that those who are concerned about a substantial transformation of minority economic conditions may be forced to direct their efforts elsewhere.

46 Boston, op. cit., n. 26; Myers and Chan, op. cit., n. 24; Bates and Williams, op. cit., n. 6.
47 Chay and Fairlie, op. cit., n. 27.

180

JOURNAL OF LAW AND SOCIETY
VOLUME 33, NUMBER 1, MARCH 2006
ISSN: 0263-323X, pp. 181–98

Is There a Duty to Legislate for Linguistic Minorities?

ROBERT DUNBAR*

In April 2005, the Scottish Parliament passed the Gaelic Language (Scotland) Act 2005, requiring certain public bodies in Scotland to provide some services through the medium of Gaelic. This Act was modelled to a certain degree on similar legislation for Welsh, the Welsh Language Act 1993. Both Welsh and Gaelic, and to a lesser extent Irish in Northern Ireland, benefit from a range of other measures of legislative support. Many other languages are, however, spoken in the United Kingdom, and their speakers have needs and expectations. In this article, the extent to which a state is obliged to legislate for these is assessed. Fundamental principles such as the right to freedom from discrimination, equal protection of the law, substantive equality, and the protection and promotion of cultural and linguistic diversity may argue for legislative intervention and support, and the provision of such support to linguistic minorities must itself be non-discriminatory.

INTRODUCTION

The question whether there is a duty to legislate for linguistic minorities seemed to be answered in the affirmative – at least in respect of one of Scotland's linguistic minorities – by the Scottish Parliament in April 2005, when it passed the Gaelic Language (Scotland) Act 2005 (the 'Gaelic Act') without a single dissenting vote. The Gaelic Act created a statutory body, *Bòrd na Gàidhlig*, to develop a national plan for the language, and will require selected public bodies to prepare and implement Gaelic language plans in which they specify the services that they will provide to the public

* School of Law, University of Aberdeen, Taylor Building, Old Aberdeen AB24 3UB, Scotland
cel052@abdn.ac.uk

The author is a member of the board of *Bòrd na Gàidhlig* and of *Seirbhis nam Meadhanan Gàidhlig* (the Gaelic Media Service), but this article expresses his views alone.

through the medium of Gaelic. The Gaelic Act is not, however, the first piece of legislation to make provision for Gaelic,[1] and a significant range of legislative measures have also been taken with respect to the Welsh language.[2] Indeed, the Gaelic Act is largely modelled on the Welsh Language Act 1993 (the 'Welsh Act'), which also creates a language development body and requires certain public bodies to prepare and implement language schemes under which they will treat Welsh and English equally.

Notwithstanding the overwhelming dominance of English, Britain is a country of considerable linguistic diversity, and one in which speakers of minority languages have a complex array of linguistic needs and desires. From this perspective, existing legislative provision, largely for the benefit of Welsh and Gaelic only, raises a number of questions, some of which I shall explore in this article.

I shall not discuss the detailed content of the Gaelic Act[3] or the wider legislative framework in support of Gaelic or Welsh. Rather, I shall consider the bases on which legislative provision for minority languages could be justified and the principles upon which such provision should be based. In doing so, I shall consider both the United Kingdom's international legal obligations and relevant normative principles. I shall give particular consideration to the broader equality issues that are implicated in any discussion of language, and in particular, of minority languages. I shall argue that legislative measures can be justified on a number of grounds, such as protection against discrimination, promotion of equality of access, promotion of substantive equality, and promotion of cultural diversity. However, the application of these principles has different implications for the sort of legislative measures which should be taken, depending on the circumstances of the speakers of the minority language in question. Moreover, the differential treatment of various minority languages used in Britain itself raises equality considerations. To illuminate the discussion of these various issues, I begin with a brief consideration of the complex linguistic picture which actually exists in Britain.[4]

MINORITY LANGUAGES IN BRITAIN

Several languages other than English have been spoken in Britain for many centuries and could be said to be 'indigenous' or 'autochthonous' languages. These are Celtic languages such as Welsh and Gaelic, as well as Irish,

---

1 See R. Dunbar, 'Language Legislation and Language Rights in the United Kingdom' (2004) 2 *European Yearbook of Minority Issues* 95.
2 id.
3 See R. Dunbar, 'The Gaelic Language (Scotland) Act' (2005) 9 *Edinburgh Law Rev.* 466.
4 See, further, G. Price (ed.), *Languages in Britain and Ireland* (2000).

Cornish and Manx, and Scots and its Northern Irish variant, Ulster-Scots, both of which are Germanic languages fairly closely related to English. There is also a much larger number of languages which have been brought to the United Kingdom by more recent mass immigration: these so-called 'community languages' include, Urdu, Turkish, Arabic, Cantonese, Yoruba, and so forth. Finally, there are various forms of sign language used by the hearing impaired.

One difficulty in discussing minority languages in the United Kingdom is a lack of reliable data. Successive censuses have contained questions relating to ability to use Welsh in Wales, Gaelic in Scotland, and Irish in Northern Ireland, but nothing in respect of any other languages. This, in itself, is revealing. One of the main purposes of the census is to produce data that will guide the development and implementation of public policy. The non-collection of data regarding language ability – including the ability to speak English – arguably implies an assumption that, aside from Welsh, Gaelic and Irish, language raises no particularly important public policy issues. As I shall argue, this is an unfortunate and mistaken assumption.

With regard to the languages about which information is solicited, the 2001 Census indicated that Welsh was spoken by 575,640 people in Wales (20.52 per cent of the Welsh population),[5] that 167,490 people (9.98 per cent of the Northern Irish population) reported themselves as having an ability to speak Irish,[6] and that there were 58,562 Gaelic-speakers in Scotland (1.21 per cent of the Scottish population).[7] Unlike Welsh and Gaelic, Irish is spoken by a significant number of people in another state, the Republic of Ireland, where it has the status of being the 'national and first official' language under the Constitution and where it benefits from a range of supporting measures.

All the Celtic languages have suffered considerable long-term decline in numbers of speakers,[8] although the 1991 census showed that this had stopped for Welsh and the 2001 census indicated some growth in numbers of Welsh and Irish speakers. There are now no monolingual speakers of the Celtic languages, and even native speakers are usually perfectly fluent in

5 See Office for National Statistics (ONS), *Census 2001: Report on the Welsh Language* (2004).

6 See <http://www.nisra.gov.uk/Census/pdf/standard_tables_section5.pdf>. Unlike Welsh and Scottish Gaelic, a very small percentage are native speakers, and only a small minority speak the language fluently or use it regularly.

7 See General Register Office for Scotland, *Scotland's Census 2001: Gaelic Report* (2005).

8 For example, in 1891, 54.4 per cent of the Welsh population were Welsh speakers (J. Davies, 'Welsh' in Price (ed.), op. cit., n. 4, p. 89), and 6.75 per cent of the Scottish population were Gaelic speakers (General Register Office for Scotland, *1991 Census: Gaelic Language/Cunntas-sluaigh 1991: A' Ghàidhlig* (1994) 24–5). Cornish and Manx ceased to be spoken altogether in the eighteenth and twentieth centuries, respectively, though there are now small numbers of speakers of both, due to language revival movements.

English. All three Celtic languages are, however, threatened minority languages, Gaelic particularly so, and Welsh and Gaelic are only spoken as community languages – and will therefore only survive – in the United Kingdom.[9] These demographic and sociolinguistic facts are a product, to a very significant degree, of state language policy, which until fairly recently has been directed at promoting the acquisition of English, with little or no regard to the impact of this policy on minority languages. On the one hand, such policies can, as we shall see, be justified on equality grounds; by equipping non-speakers with fluency in the state's dominant language, they ensure fuller integration and a greater range of economic, social, political, and other opportunities. On the other hand, where such policies are not accompanied by respect for minority languages and identities, they can lead to assimilation, rather than integration. Frequently, minority languages such as the Celtic languages have been viewed by the majority as not merely 'less widely spoken', but also as 'inferior', 'backward', 'parochial', and these value judgments have too often coloured attitudes to the speakers of such languages.[10] When such attitudes guide the implementation of an integrationist policy, the effect changes from one of equipping the minority with skills in the majority language to one of removing the minority language and identity altogether.

Such attitudes have undoubtedly coloured state policy in Britain. Take, for example, the introduction of universal state-supported education in the 1870s. No provision was made for the teaching of the minority language to Welsh-speaking and Gaelic-speaking children. Consequently, generations of such students, who came to school with little or no English, were educated wholly in an English-speaking environment, where their mother tongue was discouraged, often by corporal punishment.[11]

Despite recent policy developments in Wales and Scotland, negative attitudes towards the autochthonous languages remain, as is evident in the crude stereotyping which often appears in the British media when issues relating to languages such as Gaelic and Welsh are raised. Such attitudes, and the policies they engender, have almost certainly also had a negative impact on the demographic and social situation of Scots and Ulster Scots; again, although no census data exists about how many people speak these languages, they still enjoy almost no place in the education system and receive little institutional recognition.

With regard to 'community languages' and sign languages, definitive statements are hard to make because of a lack of demographic and socio-

---

9 There are still Welsh-speakers in Patagonia, Argentina, and Gaelic-speakers in Cape Breton, Canada, but both language communities are very small and vulnerable.
10 See, for example, K. Fenyo, *Contempt, Sympathy and Romance: Lowland Perceptions of the Highlands and Clearances During the Famine Years, 1845–1855* (1997).
11 See K. MacKinnon, *Gaelic: A Past and Future Prospect* (1991) ch. 5; J. Davies, *The Welsh Language* (1993).

linguistic information. The Census does solicit information on ethnicity, and in 2001 revealed that 7.9 per cent of the population of the United Kingdom belonged to ethnic minorities;[12] however, not all persons who identify themselves in this way necessarily speak their community language, and 'ethnic' affiliation identified on the census (Indian, Black African, and so on) can itself hide a considerable range of linguistic affiliations. Recent research in London, however, reveals its huge linguistic diversity, and this pattern will be replicated, at least to some degree, in other major British cities.[13] Though many speakers of community languages will also speak English, almost certainly some, particularly adult immigrants, speak little or no English.[14] Thus, unlike speakers of autochthonous languages, many speakers of community languages face linguistic barriers to full integration in British society and full access to public services, where such are not provided in languages other than English. The hearing impaired face similar barriers. However, unlike the autochthonous minority languages (except Irish), community languages are generally not threatened minority languages, as they are generally spoken by significant numbers of people in other states, and some are official languages of other states, with a commensurate status and prestige.

NON-DISCRIMINATION

There is a strong argument in favour of legislative intervention where speakers of minority languages suffer discrimination based on their language, or, where their language is closely associated with ethnicity or national origins, discrimination based on ethnicity or national origins. As a practical matter, though, the extent to which speakers of minority languages in Britain do suffer discrimination based on language is not clear. While there is evidence that prejudice towards Gaelic and the other autochthonous languages of the United Kingdom still exists, there is little evidence that this leads to significant or widespread acts of discrimination.[15] Speakers of community languages may suffer discrimination, but it is not clear to what extent this is based on language, rather than more obvious markers of difference, such as colour.

12 <http://www.statistics.gov.uk/CCI/nugget.asp?ID=764&Pos=1&ColRank=1&Rank=176>.
13 See V. Edwards, 'Community Languages in the United Kingdom' in *The Other Languages of Europe: Demographic, Sociolinguistic and Educational Perspectives*, eds. G. Extra and D. Gorter (2001) 243–7.
14 Child immigrants and children born in the United Kingdom to non-English speaking immigrants, will generally acquire fluency in English at school and in the community.
15 The situation in Northern Ireland is, however, complex, as the Irish language tends to be associated with Irish nationalism and Catholicism; space does not permit an analysis of the special legislative responses taken there.

To the extent that language-based discrimination does exist, though, Britain already has a fairly rigorous framework for dealing with it, and it is doubtful that further specific legislation would be necessary. The United Kingdom has, for example, been a party to the European Convention on Human Rights (ECHR) for over fifty years, and Article 14 provides that the enjoyment of the various Convention rights and freedoms shall be secured without discrimination on any ground, including language.[16] This guarantee is now enforceable in domestic law against public authorities under the Human Rights Act 1998 (HRA).

With regard to discrimination in the private and voluntary sectors, the Race Relations Act 1976 (RRA) provides that discrimination, both direct and indirect, on 'racial grounds' is unlawful in employment, education, training, and related matters, the provision of goods, facilities, services, and premises, and the disposal of premises. For these purposes, 'racial grounds' is defined to mean colour, race, nationality or ethnic or national origins,[17] but does not explicitly refer to language. Thus, discrimination based on language alone is not prohibited by the RRA, and so a claim would have to be framed in terms of discrimination on one of the other listed grounds, most likely ethnicity. In the leading case of *Mandla* v. *Dowell Lee*,[18] the House of Lords set out a number of factors to be considered in determining whether an 'ethnic group' within the meaning of section 3(1) of the RRA exists, one of the 'relevant characteristics' (though not an 'essential' characteristic) of which is a common language.[19]

While speakers of minority languages in the United Kingdom will generally be members of ethnic groups within the meaning of the RRA, this is not necessarily the case. As a result of the Employment Appeal Tribunal's (EAT) decision in *Gwynedd County Council* v. *Jones*,[20] speakers of autochthonous minority languages, in particular, cannot assume that they will benefit from the RRA's protection. The appellants were refused employment because they did not speak Welsh, and hence claimed to have suffered discrimination. However, the EAT ruled against them on the basis that, although the Welsh may have constituted a 'racial group' based on nationality, English- and Welsh-speaking Welsh people were not separate ethnic groups, and therefore not separate racial groups, because differences in language alone were not sufficient to create separate ethnic groups within the meaning of the RRA. This conclusion is correct, at least in terms of a strict reading of the criteria laid down in *Mandla*. However, it could still be

16 The United Kingdom is also party to the United Nations International Covenant on Civil and Political Rights (ICCPR), Art. 2(1) of which is similar to Art. 14 ECHR. The ICCPR goes beyond the ECHR in that it contains a 'stand-alone' non-discrimination and 'equal protection' provision (Art. 26).
17 RRA 1976, s. 3(1).
18 [1983] AC 548.
19 id., p. 562.
20 [1986] 1 ICR 833.

186

criticized on the basis that differences between Welsh- and non-Welsh-speakers go well beyond differences in language, and that many of the other markers of ethnicity identified in *Mandla* are also present.[21] It is, nevertheless, strange, and indeed discriminatory, that certain linguistic minorities may not enjoy the RRA's full protection because their linguistic difference might not, based on a strict reading of *Mandla*, be sufficient for them to be considered to be members of a protected racial group. The RRA should provide protection from discrimination on the same grounds as the ECHR/HRA, and should be amended accordingly to ensure that all speakers of minority languages are protected from discrimination based on their language.

In general, though, the ECHR/HRA and the RRA provide significant (albeit potentially incomplete) protection to speakers of minority languages against linguistic discrimination. There does not, therefore, seem to be an urgent need for specific additional legislation in support of linguistic minorities on this ground.

ACCESS

In many states, there are significant numbers of people who have no or only a limited command of the language or languages of wider communication of the state. This typically excludes them from full participation in economic, political, and social life. Thus, state language policy can have an impact on equality of opportunity and access to services. However, international law is not particularly clear about states' obligations in this regard, and there are few relevant provisions in United Kingdom domestic law.

With regard to the United Kingdom's international commitments, recent minority-specific treaties do impose an obligation to foster participation of minorities in the life of the country. A good example is the Council of Europe's Framework Convention for the Protection of National Minorities (the 'Framework Convention'),[22] Article 15 of which provides that states shall create conditions necessary for the effective participation of persons belonging to national minorities in cultural, social, and economic life, and in public affairs, particularly those concerning them. Neither the treaty nor its explanatory report provides guidance as to how this is to be accomplished, but equipping members of such minorities with a competence in the state's official language could certainly be one way of doing so. Article 14, which provides for the teaching of, or instruction through the medium of, minority languages, also makes clear that such teaching or instruction shall be implemented

---

21 See R. Dunbar, 'Legislating for Diversity: Minorities in the New Scotland' in *The State of Scots Law: Law and Government after the Devolution Settlement*, eds. L. Farmer and S. Veitch (2001) 49–50.

22 Ratified by the United Kingdom 15 January 1998; in force 1 May 1998.

'without prejudice to the learning of the official language or the teaching in this language',[23] and the explanatory report notes that knowledge of the official language is a factor in promoting social cohesion and integration of minorities,[24] both of which are goals of the Framework Convention.

As noted above, British language policy has traditionally been directed at integration of linguistic minorities through promoting the acquisition of English through the education system. Like many jurisdictions, the United Kingdom seeks to equip immigrants, or at least school-age children of immigrants, with requisite skills in English. This is not undertaken, however, under any particular statutory obligation, but administratively, as a matter of education policy, through English-as-Second-Language ('ESL') programmes in primary and secondary schools, for example.

The acquisition of full fluency in English certainly promotes equality of opportunity and access in a society such as the United Kingdom, in which English is the de facto official language and the socially dominant language. As noted earlier, though, such a policy can promote assimilation and threaten the existence of linguistic minorities. Furthermore, increasing amounts of research indicates that dominant-language medium education for children without a sufficient command of that language does not always succeed, and can leave them less than fully fluent in both their mother tongue and the dominant language, and prone to underachievement in the classroom.[25] Therefore, the mode by which fluency in English is acquired is crucial; mother-tongue education, especially in the early primary school years, would be justified in order to overcome these limitations.

However, it is often not possible to ensure that every non-speaker of the state language acquires that language, as many non-speakers are not in formal education, the locus of most language acquisition efforts. What obligations do states have to members of linguistic minorities in these circumstances? In the United Kingdom, there is a growing awareness that the provision of translation services to speakers of minority languages who have insufficient command of English is important. This is particularly true of public authorities operating in areas with significant ethnic minority populations, and is reflected in language policies that those authorities are developing. There are, however, no clear legal obligations in this regard, and little evidence of a coherent and comprehensive policy.

As regards the criminal justice system, some provision is made in the major international human rights treaties such as the ECHR and the ICCPR to allow for the use of translators where persons in detention or facing criminal trial do not speak the language of the legal system.[26] These are,

23 Art. 14(3).
24 Para. 78 of the explanatory report.
25 See C. Baker, *Foundations of Bilingual Education and Bilingualism* (2001, 3rd edn.) ch. 14.
26 Art. 5(2) and Art. 6(3)(a) and (e) of the ECHR, and Art. 14(3) of the ICCPR.

however, very limited rights, aimed at procedural justice. Beyond these provisions, the major human rights treaties have little to say about ensuring access to other important services by speakers of minority languages who have insufficient command of the official language.

Relatively recent developments in the jurisprudence of certain international treaty bodies may point the way to broader state obligations with respect to ensuring effective access for non-speakers of the official language by providing a greater range of services through minority languages. An example is *Diergaardt* v. *Namibia*.[27] Under the constitution, English was the only official language. Staff members in local public offices were instructed by the government not to communicate with the public in any language other than English, notwithstanding that public servants could speak the minority language in question – a form of Afrikaans – and that at least some members of the community allegedly could not speak English. The United Nations Human Rights Committee (UNHRC) found this to be a violation of Article 26 of the ICCPR. As the grounds for this conclusion were not spelled out, its basis is not clear. However, a strong but plausible reading of the case would be that the denial of minority-language public services to members of a linguistic minority who cannot speak the language of the state constitutes a violation of the right to the equal protection of the law.

Recent European Court of Human Rights jurisprudence in respect of the right to education (Article 2 of Protocol One ECHR) may also have longer-term implications for the education of children from linguistic minorities. The ECHR provides that no person shall be denied the right to education, and that the state must respect the right of parents to ensure that such education is in conformity with their own religious and philosophical principles. In the famous *Belgian Linguistics* case,[28] the Court ruled that this did not include a right to be taught in the language of parents' choice. However, the recent decision in *Cyprus* v. *Turkey*[29] must now be considered. One of the complaints brought against Turkey involved the closure of the only secondary school in Turkish-controlled Cyprus which offered education through the medium of Greek. The Court found that the discontinuance of Greek-medium education at the secondary level in these circumstances amounted to a denial of the substance of the right to education, as it was unrealistic to expect Greek-speaking students from Greek-medium primary schools to be able to switch to Turkish- or English-medium secondary schools.[30] Clearly, the decision does not imply anything like a generalizable right to minority-language education. However, the underlying principle could potentially be applied to cases in which children from a linguistic minority who do not speak the language of the school are forced into

---

27 Communication No. 760/1997, CCPR/C/69/D/760/1997, 25 July 2000.
28 Judgment of 23 July 1968, Series A, no. 6.
29 Judgment of 10 May 2001, application no. 25781/94.
30 See paras. 277 and 278.

majority-language education. Given what the research referred to above shows about the adverse effects of such a policy, the denial of minority-language education could now arguably constitute a violation of Article 2 of Protocol One in those circumstances.

Thus, while there are few formal guarantees under United Kingdom law in respect of the provision of effective access to public services for speakers of minority languages who have an insufficient command of English, there are some important developments under various international treaties to which the United Kingdom is a party. While these rights are not clearly articulated outside of fairly explicit guarantees with respect to detention and criminal trials, the requirement to facilitate effective participation of minorities, including linguistic minorities, set out in the Framework Convention, developments with respect to the right to non-discrimination and equal protection of the law, and developments with respect to the right to education all suggest that United Kingdom law and practice may need to be more comprehensively considered. In particular, language legislation for speakers of minority languages may be necessary and desirable, both to implement the existing and emergent guarantees in the international instruments to which the United Kingdom is party, and to bring coherence and equity with respect to provision at local level (as noted, the provision of minority-language services to non-speakers of English is generally wholly left to the discretion of public bodies and local authorities themselves). The argument for such legislation is, however, most compelling in respect of speakers of minority languages who lack a sufficient command of English. As all speakers of United Kingdom's autochthonous languages are fully fluent in English, the question of access provides a less compelling basis for legislation in support of such languages. At present, though, both the Gaelic Act and the Welsh Act anticipate the provision of a range of services through Gaelic and Welsh. Hence we must generally look elsewhere for a justification for such legislation.

SUBSTANTIVE EQUALITY

Over the last several years, even liberal theorists, traditionally highly suspicious of group identity-based claims, have been seriously addressing the implications of minority identity in the context of rights and obligations. Consequently there is a growing acceptance of the legitimacy of positive measures of support to ensure the continuity of and respect for aspects of minority identity, particularly language.[31] Building on the recognition that people are embedded to some significant degree in their own cultural – and linguistic – identities, it is argued that these identities affect how we perceive

31 See, especially, W. Kymlicka, *Multicultural Citizenship* (1995); *Politics in the Vernacular: Nationalism, Multiculturalism, and Citizenship* (2001).

190

the available choices and possibilities of life. Members of linguistic majorities, supported by a familiar and dominant linguistic environment, are better equipped to approach the liberal ideal of an autonomous and self-determined life than members of minorities who, by definition, live immersed in a different and dominant linguistic environment which tends not to value, and is often hostile or at least indifferent to their identities.[32]

As a practical matter, many minorities, while aspiring to fuller integration in the societies to which they belong, do not want to lose completely their cultural and linguistic identity as the price of full admission. While certain core civil and political rights, such as the right to freedom of expression, freedom of association, and freedom of religion, help to create the social space necessary for the expression and transmission of many aspects of minority identity, the reality of a monolingual and monocultural society – majority-language education, majority-language services, and majority-language mass-media – necessarily impairs the ability to maintain crucial aspects of minority identity. True substantive equality for members of linguistic and cultural minorities requires special support for aspects of such identity, a principle which was recognized in international law as early as the decision of the Permanent Court of International Justice in 1935 in the *Minority Schools in Albania*[33] case. As discussed above, generations of Welsh and Gaelic speakers have effectively had to give up their native language as the price of admission into British society. The efforts of members of such communities to win legislative support for minority-language services, broadcasting, and education have been based on a desire to participate in British society, without having to sacrifice completely their linguistic and cultural identity. Legislative measures such as the Gaelic Act, to the extent that they promote the respect for and the means of maintaining such identities, are consistent with the promotion of this difference-aware equality.

While legislative support for speakers of minority languages could be seen as a form of affirmative action, it is important to recognize that there are subtle differences between such measures and affirmative action policies, as those are commonly understood. The latter are generally aimed at redressing historical barriers to full participation in society that have resulted from persistent and long-term discrimination, usually based on immutable characteristics such as colour and gender. Their goal is a fuller integration of members of affected groups and the promotion of full equality of opportunity. Members of cultural and linguistic minorities who wish to preserve their identities are not necessarily concerned with redressing historical barriers in quite the same way. The acquisition of the dominant language

---

32 See, for example, P. Keller, 'Rethinking Ethnic and Cultural Rights in Europe' (1998) 18 *Oxford J. of Legal Studies* 29; S. May, *Language and Minority Rights: Ethnicity, Nationalism and the Politics of Identity* (2001) especially ch. 3.

33 Advisory Opinion, PCIJ Series A/B, no. 64, 1935.

191

has, in a sense, acted as an affirmative action programme for non-speakers of that language, as it has opened up the possibility of wider participation in the society of the dominant linguistic group. Their immediate concern, therefore, is not necessarily fuller integration into society, but the fact that such integration has historically tended towards the loss of their identities as members of linguistic and cultural minorities. The challenge is the achievement of full participation without the loss of linguistic and cultural identities.

While the passage of legislation such as the Gaelic and Welsh Acts is consistent with the promotion of substantive, difference-aware equality for speakers of such languages, the tendency to limit such support to certain linguistic minorities, generally, autochthonous linguistic minorities such as Gaels and Welsh-speakers, raises further problems, because it is difficult to see why the same principles should not be applied in respect of members of other linguistic minorities. The limitation of positive measures of support to members of autochthonous minority linguistic groups has been justified on the basis that many speakers of community languages are immigrants, and that by choosing to move from a supportive linguistic environment, they have somehow sacrificed their claim to the autonomy and self-determination that comes with such an environment. However, this is not a particularly satisfying justification. First, it is not always the case that speakers of community languages enjoyed such a supportive linguistic environment in their state of origin. Second, many speakers of community languages are not immigrants, but were born and raised in minority communities in the United Kingdom. Third, and more fundamentally, it is difficult to see why society should extract the right to autonomy and self-determination as the price of admission if it is possible to accommodate difference.

CULTURAL DIVERSITY

In recent years, there has been growing awareness of the world's linguistic and cultural diversity and growing concern about the perceived threat to that diversity. It has been estimated that between 50 and 90 per cent of the world's 5,000–6,000 languages could disappear before the end of this century, and that in order to avoid this, states must take special measures to support threatened languages.[34] The protection and promotion of cultural diversity is an increasingly important value in many of the international obligations which the United Kingdom has undertaken, and it was also an important – perhaps the most important – rationale behind legislation such as the Gaelic Act.[35]

---

34 See, for example, D. Nettle and S. Romaine, *Vanishing Voices: The Extinction of the World's Languages* (2000), and M. Abley, *Spoken Here: Travels Among Threatened Languages* (2003).
35 See Scottish Executive, *The Gaelic Language Bill: Consultation Draft* (2003) 5–6.

192

The cultural diversity rationale is one of the main bases for the development of the most important international instruments on the protection of minorities to which the United Kingdom is a party,[36] such as the Framework Convention and the European Charter for Regional and Minority Languages (the 'Languages Charter').[37] For example, the preamble to the Framework Convention recognizes pluralism and cultural diversity as important values. The preamble to the Languages Charter also places considerable emphasis on cultural diversity as a positive value in and of itself; it makes clear that the protection of 'the historical regional or minority languages of Europe' 'contributes to the maintenance and development of Europe's *cultural wealth and traditions*' and that the protection and promotion of such languages represents 'an important contribution to the building of a Europe based on the principles of democracy and *cultural diversity*'.[38] Thus, as paragraph 11 of the explanatory report explains, '[t]he charter sets out to protect and promote regional or minority languages, not linguistic minorities', and for this reason, 'emphasis is placed on the cultural dimension and the use of a regional or minority language in all the aspects of the life of its speakers'. The substantive commitments of the Languages Charter are set out in two parts, Part II and Part III. Part II contains the general principles which should guide states' policies, legislation, and practices in respect of all of their 'regional or minority languages'. Part III contains a number of more detailed articles that apply only in respect of those regional or minority languages that the states themselves identify. In its instrument of ratification, the United Kingdom has designated Gaelic in Scotland, Welsh in Wales, and Irish in Northern Ireland, for these purposes. The Part III articles deal with the use of the specified minority languages in education, the legal system, the media, cultural activities, economic and social life, and by administrative authorities and public services.[39]

The general question of the concept of cultural diversity in international law is a large one, which cannot be fully discussed here. It is, however, a value that is gaining increasing prominence. It can, for example, be seen in the recently concluded UNESCO *Convention for the Safeguarding of the Intangible Cultural Heritage*,[40] as well as in ongoing efforts in various fora, including UNESCO, the Council of Europe, and through Canadian government-sponsored initiatives on the drafting of an International Convention on

---

36 See A.S. Åkermark, *Justifications of Minority Protection in International Law* (1997).
37 Ratified by the United Kingdom 27 March 2001; in force 1 July 2001.
38 Emphasis added.
39 For fuller discussion, see R. Dunbar, 'The Ratification by the United Kingdom of the European Charter for Regional or Minority Languages', Mercator linguistic rights and legislation, working paper no. 10 (2003), available at <http://www.ciemen.org/mercator/index-gb.htm>.
40 The United Kingdom has not ratified this treaty, although 22 states have. It is available at: <http://unesdoc.unesco.org/images/0013/001325/132540e.pdf>.

Cultural Diversity.[41] It is also an emerging value in European Union law. For example, Article I-3(3) of the Draft Constitution provides that the EU shall respect Europe's 'rich cultural and linguistic diversity' and shall ensure that Europe's cultural heritage is 'safeguarded and enhanced'. The first of these obligations is repeated in Article II-82, in the Draft Constitution's Charter of Fundamental Rights.

Neither the Languages Charter nor other international obligations explicitly require that states enact legislation such as the Gaelic or Welsh Acts. They do, however, require states to take positive measures of support by providing certain minority language services to speakers of such languages. There is no doubt that United Kingdom legislation in support of Gaelic and Welsh is consistent with and promotes the achievement of these treaty obligations, and is also consistent with the promotion of cultural diversity.

DIFFERENTIAL TREATMENT OF LINGUISTIC MINORITIES

An interesting, and controversial, aspect of the Languages Charter is that it does not require measures to be taken in respect of all minority languages. This is because of its definition of what constitutes a 'regional or minority language'. Under Article 1, these are languages that are traditionally used within a given territory of a state by nationals who form a group numerically smaller than the rest of the state's population and that are different from the official language(s) of the state. The definition goes on to exclude both dialects of the official language(s) and the languages of migrants. Thus, in the United Kingdom, only the Celtic languages, Scots, and Ulster-Scots are 'regional or minority languages'; the Languages Charter imposes no obligations on the United Kingdom in respect of other languages, including the large number of community languages spoken by United Kingdom residents. In this respect, the Languages Charter may differ from the Framework Convention. The latter does not define the term 'national minorities', and given the wide approach that the United Kingdom has taken to the application of the term, employing the concept of 'racial group' as defined in the RRA,[42] the treaty's protection need not be limited to autochthonous languages. In practice, however, the United Kingdom, like most states which take legislative measures in support of minority languages, does, in fact, limit such support to autochthonous languages, and generally to

---

41 See: <http://portal.unesco.org/culture/en/ev.php-URL_ID=11281&URL_DO= DO_TOPIC&URL_SECTION=201.html>.

42 *Report Submitted by the United Kingdom Pursuant to Article 25, Paragraph 1 of the Framework Convention for the Protection of National Minorities* 26 July 1999, ACFC/SR(1999)013, para. 2.

194

only a few of them; only Gaelic and Welsh have benefited from significant legislative support to date.[43]

It is, however, not clear why measures of support should not extend to other languages, including community languages. The fact that the Languages Charter does not require such support is not a convincing answer. It is true that the protection of autochthonous languages such as Gaelic, which are very small, threatened with extinction, and are not generally found elsewhere, may, from the perspective of the preservation and promotion of cultural diversity, have a special urgency. However, community languages also contribute to cultural diversity, particularly that of the states to which the speakers of such languages come. If the legislative protection of minority languages is also consistent with and arguably required by the notion of substantive, difference-aware equality, it is unclear why speakers of community languages should not also benefit.

Furthermore, if special support is provided to speakers of certain minority languages, does the principle of non-discrimination based on language not also require similar measures of legislative support for speakers of other minority languages? The views of the UNHRC in *Waldman* v. *Canada*[44] provide an illustration of the difficulties that the provision of special measures of support to one group but not others can raise. The case involved a law which provided public funding for Roman Catholic schools in Ontario but not schools of other religious denominations. A parent of a child in a Jewish school claimed that the preferential treatment of Catholic schools violated Article 26 of the ICCPR, a stand-alone guarantee of non-discrimination and equal protection of the law, and that similar measures of state support therefore had to be provided to the schools of other religious groups.

The HRC noted that if a state chooses to provide public funding to religious schools, it should make the funding available without discrimination. This does not mean that the state must provide the same treatment to schools of every religious denomination, but that any difference of treatment must be based on 'reasonable and objective criteria'.[45] The HRC concluded that the provision of public funding to Roman Catholic and not Jewish schools was not based on 'reasonable and objective' criteria. In his concurring view, Martin Scheinin noted that these same principles would apply in respect of minority language education; the provision of such education for one minority language alone would not, as such, amount to discrimination, but 'care must of course be taken that possible distinctions between different minority languages are based on objective and reasonable

---

43 Irish has benefited from some state support, although generally not through legislative means: see Dunbar, op. cit., n. 1.
44 Communication No 694/1996, CCPR/C/67/D/694/1996, 3 November 1999.
45 id., para. 6.10.

grounds'.[46] Scheinin suggested that 'constant demand' for minority language education and the question of 'whether there is a sufficient number of children to attend [the minority school] so that it could operate as a viable part in the overall system of education' were relevant considerations.[47] Indeed, it is difficult to see why this principle should only apply in respect of minority language education; it would likely extend to any minority language service provided to speakers of one minority language but not others.

This issue was raised by the Scottish office of the Commission for Racial Equality (CRE) during the consideration of a Gaelic Language (Scotland) Bill which came before the Scottish Parliament in late 2002 and early 2003.[48] The CRE objected to the Bill, partly because of its resource implications, arguing that allocation of resources for translation and interpretation 'should be made on the basis of meeting needs in an equal way', and that 'the development of Gaelic services should not be prioritised over other minority language needs'. Significantly, the CRE concluded that, as Gaelic speakers are generally bilingual, whereas many immigrants are not, priority should be given to languages spoken by such immigrants, to ensure that they are not excluded from participation in society. Even more significantly, the CRE felt that, 'to promote one language and its associated culture above others to the degree that this Bill proposes' could actually be harmful to race relations in Scotland.[49]

The concern with access to services for non-English speakers is wholly appropriate, for the reasons considered above. However, the CRE seemed to be arguing that, as the Bill was not providing positive measures of support for speakers of all minority languages in Scotland, the state should therefore not be taking action which would benefit the speakers of any such language. In doing so, it has taken a position that is inconsistent with the positive value attached to cultural diversity, and to the concept of difference-aware equality, from which speakers of minority languages should benefit regardless of their command of the predominant or official State language. Interestingly, the CRE in Wales took a different approach to the question of the promotion of the Welsh language, and is supportive of existing legislation such as the Welsh Act, although the same objections could be made to it.[50]

46 id., appendix, para. 5.
47 id.
48 This was a Scottish National Party-sponsored Member's Bill, which differed in important respects from the Gaelic Act. It died on the order paper when the Parliament rose in April 2003.
49 Education, Culture and Sport Committee, 4th Report, *Stage 1 Report on the Gaelic Language (Scotland) Bill*, Vol. 2, Evidence, SP Paper 785, Session 1 (2003).
50 See 'Together Towards Equality', an accord between the CRE and the Welsh Language Board of 25 July 1996. Significantly, the CRE in Scotland has, in its submission to the Scottish Parliament in respect of the Gaelic Act, changed its position somewhat; it continued to highlight the need for certain measures of support for other linguistic minorities, but did not oppose the Gaelic Act.

196

It is suggested that the proper starting place for a discussion of the application of the principle of non-discrimination as between minority languages is one which accepts that the taking of positive measures of support, through legislation and otherwise, is consistent with both the United Kingdom's international treaty obligations and the principles of the protection and promotion of cultural diversity, and the promotion of difference-aware equality. The appropriate response to the provision of such measures of support to one linguistic group should not be one of opposition – it is difficult to see how the proper treatment of other linguistic minorities is advanced by the denial of legitimate support to another linguistic minority. Rather, the appropriate response should be to consider whether, based on the principle of non-discrimination, similar measures should also be taken in respect of those other linguistic minorities.

In this regard, it must be recognized that the principle of non-discrimination does not require completely identical treatment for all linguistic minorities. As the HRC pointed out in *Waldman*, differential treatment is permissible, so long as it is based on objective and reasonable grounds. Indeed, differential treatment may be appropriate in respect of speakers of the same minority language, when those speakers find themselves in differing circumstances. Pursuant to the language schemes or plans created under the Welsh Act and the Gaelic Act, speakers of Welsh or Gaelic who live in parts of Wales or Scotland where there are relatively few other speakers will generally not benefit from the same level of minority-language services as those living in areas with relatively more speakers.

There may be both 'objective' and 'reasonable' grounds which justify the special support for Gaelic and Welsh provided by the Gaelic and Welsh Acts respectively. Indeed, the Scottish Executive seemed to anticipate this very issue in its October 2003 consultation draft on the Gaelic Language Bill, which ultimately became, in significantly revised form, the Gaelic Act. It made the point that there are many languages spoken in Scotland 'but the situation facing Gaelic is unique', noting that '[o]nly Gaelic is in such a fragile condition and depends almost entirely on Scottish institutions and Scottish communities for its continued existence'.[51] Unlike most other languages spoken in Scotland, and, indeed, in the United Kingdom, Gaelic is a seriously threatened language, is unique to Scotland, and given its long history here, often characterized by marginalization and even persecution, it has a special claim to support. As already discussed, the United Kingdom's international commitments, and in particular, the Languages Charter, also require special treatment for Gaelic. Although we do not know precisely how many people speak other minority languages in Scotland, it is almost certain that Gaelic is the most widespread. It is still a community language in large parts of the Hebrides. And, crucially, despite the evidence of the CRE in response to the earlier Gaelic Bill, there is little evidence that speakers of

51 Scottish Executive, op. cit., n. 35, p. 5.

other minority languages in Scotland objected to legislation in support of Gaelic or that they aspire to such legislative support themselves. These, then, are at least some of the considerations upon which differential treatment could objectively and reasonably be based.

CONCLUSION

We have seen that the United Kingdom provides legislative support for the benefit of speakers of a few minority languages, most notably Welsh and Gaelic. We have also seen that such measures are both consistent with the United Kingdom's international commitments and justified by considerations such as the promotion of substantive equality and cultural diversity.

However, there is little if any legislative support for other linguistic minorities in the United Kingdom, and this lacuna is difficult to justify. In many cases, many speakers of community languages have an insufficient command of English, and therefore have greater difficulties in more fully participating in society and, in particular, in accessing key public services. While promoting acquisition of English is an important means of guaranteeing such access and fuller participation, many non-speakers of English will not, practically speaking, be able to benefit from such policies. Some, such as the hearing impaired, will by definition be permanently dependent on communicative skills in sign languages. While there is an increasing tendency for some public bodies in the United Kingdom to offer minority-language and other interpretative services to such persons, there is, at present, no legal framework which guarantees this, with the result that the linguistic needs of persons having an inadequate command of English and users of sign languages are simply not being met in a comprehensive and equitable manner. Furthermore, many of the arguments in support of legislative provision for the autochthonous minority languages, such as the provision of substantive equality and the promotion of cultural diversity, are relevant to the question of support for speakers of community languages and users of sign languages. So, while the United Kingdom has taken positive steps with regard to Gaelic and Welsh, there is a clear argument for a much more comprehensive approach to minority-language communities more generally.